PREHISTORIC BRITAIN

ΨB

- The Stonehenge Enigma

Robert John Langdon

Third Edition

Published by ABC Publishing Group
Brynglas
Llanon
SY23 5HT

www.abc-publishing-group.co.uk

Third Edition v3.1

Copyright © ABC Publishing Group 2020

The moral right of the author has been asserted.
All rights reserved. Without limiting the rights under copyright reserved above, no part of this publication may be reproduced, stored or introduced into a retrieval system, or transmitted, in any form or by any means (electronic, mechanical, photocopying, recording or otherwise), without the prior written permission of both the copyright owner and the publisher of the book.

Dedicated to the three 'R's
Alexandra, Jack and James, whose 'encouragement'
Lead to the discovery of Stonehenge's true construction date
and purpose in the summer of 2009

Edited by Bob Davis

Prehistoric Britain – The Stonehenge Enigma

Contents

Preface to THIRD EDITION	08
Prologue	09
Introduction	17

Section One: THE GEOLOGICAL EVIDENCE

Chapter 1 Post-Glacial Flooding Hypothesis — 22
- Case Study – River Avon — 32

Section Two: THE ARCHAEOLOGICAL EVIDENCE

Chapter 2 Stonehenge Phase I — 40
- The Ditch/Moat — 43
- Health Spa & Bluestone — 53
- Aubrey Holes — 58
- Bluestones — 62
- North West Entrance — 65
- Palisade — 67
- An Inconvenient Truth (Craig Rhos-Y-Felin) — 70

Chapter 3 Stonehenge Phase II
- The Avenue — 83
- Sarsen Stone — 90
- Station Stones — 94
- Monument to the dead — 96
- Slaughter Stone — 99
- Snails — 104
- Construction phases with dates — 110

Chapter 4 - Durrington Walls (Woodhenge) — 124
- Case study Woodhenge — 135

Chapter 5 - Old Sarum — 143

Chapter 6 - Avebury   149
- Avebury Construction Sequence   155
- Silbury Avenue   156
- Windmill Hill   161
- Silbury Hill   162
- The Harbour   168

Section Three: THE LANDSCAPE EVIDENCE
Chapter 7 - Antler Picks that built ancient Monuments   177

Chapter 8 - Barrows   185
- Barrow Altitude   187
- Long Barrows   188
- Round Barrows   192
- Case Study – Winterbourne Crossroads   195
- Case Study - The Cursus   198

Chapter 9 – Dykes, Ditches and Earthworks   201
- Case Study – Wansdyke   203

Epilogue   213

Appendices
- References   214
- Proofs of Hypothesis   217

Author's Biography   222

Illustrations

FIGURE 1- HISTORICAL SEA LEVEL CHANGE	23
FIGURE 2 - DISCHARGES RATES FROM THE WADDEN SEA	25
FIGURE 3- PEAT GROWTH - REFLECTING THE POST-GLACIAL FLOODING OF BRITAIN (BLUE MAP)	29
FIGURE 4 - CARBON DATED PEAT SAMPLES SHOWING WHEN THESE PEAT FORMATIONS WERE FORMED	30
FIGURE 5 - OSL RESULTS AVON RIVER	33
FIGURE 6- AVON RIVER TERRACE LEVELS	34
FIGURE 7- FLOOD EVENTS OVER THE LAST TEN THOUSAND YEARS ACCORDING TO LEWIS & MACKLIN 2003.	37
FIGURE 8- ANGLO- SAXON MAP SHOWING THE EXTENT OF THE FLOODING EVEN IN RECENT YEARS	38
FIGURE 9 - PROFILE OF STONEHENGE (EAST TO WEST) AND THE PALAEOCHANNEL THAT IT SITS BESIDE.	40
FIGURE 10 - STONEHENGE WITH THE RIVER AVON AS IT WOULD HAVE LOOKED IN 8000BCE.	41
FIGURE 11- PROFILES OF STONEHENGE SHOWING THE RIVER AVON AROUND THE STONEHENGE PENINSULA	42
FIGURE 12 - TYPICAL DEW POND AS FOUND IN WILTSHIRE	44
FIGURE 13- PROFILE OF A TYPICAL DEW POUND CONSTRUCTION	45
FIGURE 14- HAWLEY'S DITCH EXCAVATION AND THE 'DARK MATTER'	47
FIGURE 15- THE DITCH IS BUILT OF INDIVIDUAL PITS – HAWLEY 1922.	52
FIGURE 16- STONEHENGE LAYER SHOWING DISPROPORTIONATE NUMBER OF CHIPPINGS	56
FIGURE 17- MOON CALENDAR	59
FIGURE 18- STONEHENGE OLD CAR PARK ONE METRE POST HOLES	62
FIGURE 19- 'TOTEM POLES' - PLACE AT THE BOTTOM OF THE DRY RIVER VALLEY	64
FIGURE 20- A 'LIFTING DEVICE' THAT COULD RAISE BLUESTONES OUT OF THE BOATS ON TO SLEDGES	65
FIGURE 21- NW PASSAGE WITH Q & R DOLMAN HOLES FOR EXCARNATIONS	66
FIGURE 22- PATH (ORANGE) OF THE WOODEN PALISADE TO CUT OF THE ISLAND FROM LAND ANIMALS	68
FIGURE 23 - HOW THE PALISADE WOULD HAVE LOOKED	69
FIGURE 24 - CRAIG RHOS-Y-FELIN QUARRY	70
FIGURE 25- OLD CAR PARK EXCAVATION IN 1966	72
FIGURE 26- WA 9580 EXCAVATED IN 1988 .	74
FIGURE 27- TIM DAW'S UNPUBLISHED PHOTO OF ANOTHER POST IN THE OLD VISITOR'S CAR PARK.	75
FIGURE 28- NEWLY DISCOVERED POST HOLE D	76
FIGURE 29- CRAIG RHOS-Y-FELIN AS IT WOULD HAVE LOOKED IN THE MESOLITHIC PERIOD	78
FIGURE 30- CRAIG RHOS-Y-FELIN EXCAVATION SHOWING MESOLITHIC HUMAN HEARTHS IN RED	79
FIGURE 31- NORTH AND SOUTH AVENUE DITCH COMPARISON	84
FIGURE 32- THE AVENUE SHOWING ITS TERMINATION AND THE WOODEN POST HOLES	87
FIGURE 33- THE AVENUE TERMINATING AT STONEHENGE BOTTOM SHOWING THE DITCHES ON EACH SIDE	89
FIGURE 34- THE AVENUE SHOWING THE SUMMER SOLSTICE SUNRISE AT THE TIME OF CONSTRUCTION	93
FIGURE 35- ANTLER BONE FOUND IN STONE 27 FILLING DATED 4191 BCE.	94
FIGURE 36- STONEHENGE WAS 'CRESCENT' SHAPED NOT ROUND	97
FIGURE 37 - STONEHENGE HEXAGONAL DESIGN	98
FIGURE 38- SLAUGHTER STONE WAS DELIBERATELY BURIED BELOW THE CHALK SURFACE.	100
FIGURE 39 - SEA LEVEL CHANGES SUNK DOGGERLAND	102
FIGURE 40 - SLAUGHTER STONE ALIGNMENT IS WITH DOGGERLAND	103
FIGURE 41- CONEYBURY HENGE PROFILE	106
FIGURE 42 - THE STONEHENGE AREA IN THE MESOLITHIC WITH THE RAISED RIVER LEVEL OF THE AVON	109
FIGURE 43- ANTLERS FOUND NOT QUITE THE BOTTOM OF THE DITCH AS CLAIMED	112
FIGURE 44- ATKINSON SHOWING THAT FOUR SMALL BOYS	114
FIGURE 45- EXCARNATION PLATFORM	115
FIGURE 46- TYPICAL LAYOUT OF A LONG BARROW SHOWING THE DISTINCTIVE BOAT SHAPE.	116
FIGURE 47- SOUTHERN STATION STONE DITCH	118
FIGURE 48- STONEHENGE MOATS - INCLUDING THE NORTH, SOUTH AND HEEL STONES AND MOATS	119
FIGURE 49 - PALISADE Y & Z HOLES SURROUNDING THE EXCARNATION HOLES Q & R	120
FIGURE 50- DURRINGTON WALLS SHOWING THE POST HOLES SURROUNDING THE DITCHES.	125
FIGURE 51- 2004 MAGNETOMETER SURVEY BY PAYNE AND MARTIN.	128
FIGURE 52- DURRINGTON WALLS BUILT IN A BOWL.	129
FIGURE 53- DURRINGTON WALLS IN THE MESOLITHIC	129
FIGURE 54- DURRINGTON WALLS NEOLITHIC SHORELINE POST HOLES - MOORINGS	130

FIGURE 55- MPP'S MODEL OF DURRINGTON WALLS SHOWING THE INTERNAL DITCHES AND SPRINGS WITHIN ... 132
FIGURE 56- CRANNOGS HAVE THE SAME POST HOLE OUTLINE AS ROUND HOUSES 132
FIGURE 57 - NEOLITHIC DITCHES NORTH SECTION - PART OF A PALAEOCHANNEL DYKE 133
FIGURE 58- DYKE THAT IS THE WESTERN DITCH OF DURRINGTON WALLS **134**
FIGURE 59- CUNNINGTON EXCAVATION PLAN 1929 136
FIGURE 60 - WOODHENGE POST HOLES MUCH LARGER THAN THE CONCRETE POSTS ON THE SITE! 137
FIGURE 61- BROCH WHICH WAS A LATER VERSION OF WOODHENGE - MADE OF STONE 139
FIGURE 62- THE 'CUCUMBER' 25-METRE WOODEN TOWER USING SIMILAR FRAMEWORK 140
FIGURE 63- THE ISLAND OF OLD SARUM IN THE MESOLITHIC PERIOD 143
FIGURE 64- LIDAR MAGNETOMETRY SURVEY SHOWING TWO DYKES 144
FIGURE 65 - NEOLITHIC LOADING POSITION WITH A PATHWAY CUT OVER THE OUTER MOAT TO THE INTERIOR .. 147
FIGURE 66 - PLAN OF OLD SARUM - WITH 'IMPOSSIBLE' ROMAN ROAD TO BATH WITH A 1:1 VERTICAL DROP 148
FIGURE 67- LONG BARROWS AROUND AVEBURY USED AS BEACONS FOR DIRECTION HENCE ORIENTATION 149
FIGURE 68- BRITISH GEOLOGICAL SOCIETY MAP OF AVEBURY SHOWING 'SUPERFICIAL DEPOSITS' 151
FIGURE 69- HAROLD ST. GEORGE GREY, WITH HIS SKETCH OF THE EXCAVATION 153
FIGURE 70- THE 'SMOKING GUN' WATER FOUND AT THE BOTTOM OF THE DITCH - EVEN TODAY 153
FIGURE 71- WINDMILL HILL IS A 'CAUSEWAYED ENCLOSURE' 155
FIGURE 72- WADEN HILL SHOWING THE PATCH MARKS OF STONE HOLES UNDER THE SOIL 156
FIGURE 73 - WADEN HILL IN CONTRAST WITH STONE MARKERS ADDED 156
FIGURE 74 - THE 'ZIG ZAG' AVENUE CURRENTLY SEEN IS SIMPLY EXPLAINED 156
FIGURE 75- WADEN HILL SHOWING THE PATHWAY STONES AND THE ROUND BARROWS AT THE APEX 156
FIGURE 76 - WINDMILL HILL 156
FIGURE 77 - SILBURY HILL MADE LIKE A 'LAYER CAKE' 156
FIGURE 78 - MARLBOROUGH MOUNT - BUILT LIKE SILBURY HILL 156
FIGURE 79 - LEWES CASTLE WITH A 'SECOND MOUNT' - WHICH PREDATES THE NORMAN FORTIFICATIONS 156
FIGURE 80- LEWES TUMP - USED BY THE 'CLUNY' MONKS TO ATTRACT SHIPS FROM THE ENGLISH CHANNEL ... 156
FIGURE 81- SILBURY AVENUE - AT THE START OF THE TRACKWAY LOOKING UP WADEN HILL FROM AVEBURY ... 156
FIGURE 82- WADEN MOUNT 156
FIGURE 83- WADEN HILL SHOWING THE TWO POSSIBLE PATHWAYS FROM THE APEX OF THE HILL 156
FIGURE 84- WINDMILL HILL WAS A LIGHTHOUSE/FIRE BEACON FOR THE HARBOUR BELOW 156
FIGURE 85- TYPICAL ANTLER 156
FIGURE 86 - ENGLISH HERITAGE DISPLAY OF FINDS FROM STONEHENGE SHOWING ANTLERS 156
FIGURE 87- ANTLER PICK FOUND BY HAWLEY 156
FIGURE 88- USED NEOLITHIC STONE AXES FOUND IN CENTRAL EUROPE 156
FIGURE 89- COPPER AXES ALSO AVAILABLE AT THE TIME OF THESE MONUMENTS' CONSTRUCTION 156
FIGURE 90 - FIFTY ANCIENT SITE LOCATIONS AROUND THE STONEHENGE AREA 156
FIGURE 91- ST. MICHAELS LONG BARROW - CARNAC 156
FIGURE 92- STONEHENGE AREA WITH EIGHT LONG BARROWS ALIGNED TO THE RIVER AVON 156
FIGURE 93- ROUND BARROW PATH FROM STONEHENGE TO QUARLEY HILL 156
FIGURE 94- WINTERBOURNE CROSSROADS - SHOWING THE THREE LONG BARROWS 156
FIGURE 95- THE CURSUS 156
FIGURE 96 - OFF'S DYKE 156
FIGURE 97- MAP COMPARING WANSDYKE (GREEN) TO THE KENNET AND AVON CANAL 156
FIGURE 98- STUKELEY'S MAP OF 1724 SHOWING THE ROMAN ROAD 156
FIGURE 99 - WANSDYKE EAST SECTION 156
FIGURE 100- PITT-RIVERS CROSS SECTION SHOWS DITCH FILL SPREAD ON BOTH SIDES - SO NOT DEFENSIVE . 156
FIGURE 101- WANSDYKE SHOWING IT ROLLS WITH THE CONTOURS OF THE LANDSCAPE 156

Prehistoric Britain – The Stonehenge Enigma

This book is the conclusion to a chain of events,

that started with a course in Archaeology at the

Museum of London in the 1990s

and ended in a thunderstorm at Stonehenge in August 2009.

Prehistoric Britain – The Stonehenge Enigma

Preface to Third Edition

This is the third edition of my second book of the series Prehistoric Britain. I have made substantial changes to the content in respect of removing most of the detail of the Post-Glacial flooding evidence and hydrology, which appeared in the First and Second editions, as we have now published a more comprehensive first book of this series 'The Post-Glacial Flooding Hypothesis', which has been expanded and now contains over one hundred academically peer-reviewed references that support my hypothesis. This rewrite is an attempt to stop critics suggesting (incorrectly) that the evidence is unsubstantiated. Therefore, the theory is a pseudoscience – which it is not, as it analyses primary sources through the scientific method of critical analysis.

This edition will also look in-depth at the new evidence and excavations that have been discovered since the second edition was published some seven years ago, in particular the discovery of the Bluestone quarry in Wales and the original Sarsen stone location in Wiltshire, which as establish new radiocarbon dating that also supports our hypothesis.

The last section on 'Ancient Civilisations 'of the first and second edition has also been removed as it was covered in greater depth in the final book of the trilogy 'Dawn of the Lost Civilisation'. Still, it has a summary in the epilogue of this book. I hope you enjoy the rewrite.

R. J. Langdon

Prologue

I love prehistory; I think it should be called pre-mystery. In my mind, it's the greatest ever 'who done it'. Agatha Christie or even Dan Brown would have been proud of leaving so many tantalising clues and artefacts about what happened so long ago in humanity's ancient past.

So, who am I then - Holmes, Poirot or Indiana Jones?

Well, hopefully, a combination of all three as I love to solve puzzles, and this book answers the most captivating of all questions – who built Stonehenge and why? Just think of the clues on offer: strange stone monuments; relics of a bygone age; scientific evidence that seems to contradict each part of the puzzle as it's discovered and an overwhelming realisation that this is not a game - this is reality!

I want to solve the mysteries from the dawn of our civilisation. If that fails to excite you to the bone, I guess nothing in history ever will.

To understand our ancestry, you must be able to detach your mind from the 21st century. You need to picture the land that archaeologists call the 'stone age period' - the problem is that your mind has already created a mental picture of either hairy fur-covered men dragging their women into the cave for fun or Fred Flintstone and Barney Rubble going for a drive in their stone-mobile. Of course, neither of these images is correct or helpful.

As you read this book, you will journey with me back in history. You will need to remember that for a considerable time, the people you will read about, may have only possessed wood and flint as tools. Yet, they still had the foresight, capability, tenacity and organisational skills to build monuments that would last 10,000 years. I don't think even our best known recently built structures – the O2 Millennium Dome, Wembley Stadium or Canary Wharf Tower - will survive for one-tenth of that time. I would strongly argue that we must give our ancestors the respect they deserve and be proud that our forefathers created such a great civilisation.

The story starts with a car journey, driving home from a family holiday in the summer of 2009. I had previously studied Archaeology at the Museum of London in the early 1990s. During my course, the standard format of materials used was poorly photocopied archaeological texts, slides and illustrations – as the use of an available overhead projector was far too modern for this type of dusty establishment. The examples provided showed that humanity originally moved from Africa to the Middle East and then finally, onwards to Northern Europe and eventually Britain. This was the sacred proven pathway of our civilisation, and if anyone dared to write an essay, even hinting at an alternative suggestion, they were branded a heretic and would be marked down accordingly – as you may begin to imagine, I fell into this category.

I have always found this 'traditional' model of our civilisation's pathway to progress difficult to accept or understand. In my mind, civilisations are incredibly old and complex and need many tens of thousands of years to develop the characteristics we see today - therefore to suggest that the first farmers were migrants from Africa who travelled to the Middle East and who then transferred their knowledge onto Europe over only a few thousand years, seems totally unbelievable, naive and somewhat simplistic because in my view, that's not how civilisations develop. I also found it surprising that the literature and teaching provided, failed to include any references to the even more diverse cultures of the Far East. So, I guess, according to traditional theories provided, the Chinese must have never discovered farming. Therefore, they must still be living in caves today, as the maps only showed Europe and Africa?

The Pathway to Civilisation

| 9500 - 7000 BC |
| 7000 - 6500 BC |
| 6300 - 5800 BC |
| 5800 - 5300 BC |
| 5300 - 4800 BC |
| 4800 - 4300 BC |
| 4300 - 3800 BC |

Nonetheless, it is right to say that the antiquated lesson structures and information to which I was exposed did give me an insight into how Archaeology itself has evolved – via a group of amateur enthusiasts, whose dated 'peer-reviewed' theories somehow remain prominent today. Many of these old academics had little to no engineering or practical skills, let alone the empathy to understand the true nature of 'hunter-gatherers' or the issues surrounding self-sufficiency in a hostile world (one would imagine that thinking and understanding the environment a little more like Ray Mears would have helped them considerably).

As will be revealed later in the book, often when archaeologists are given scientific evidence from carbon dating that contradicts their 'traditionally' held views, it's normally dismissed as an 'anomaly' sadly, this institutional 'dumbing-down' of evidence, is all part of a well-practised archaeological (non-acceptance of new ideas) belief system, that resists any form of unauthorised change, particularly from outside the accepted academic schools of thought, who compete for media attention and financial resources.

This 'strange' approach to the science of archaeology can also be seen when sites are dated. A majority of sites are dated by broken pottery or flint finds discovered within the area. This tenuous link is based on the premise that ALL pottery and flints can be dated by its design or structure. In some sites, it's absolutely correct to say that these types of finds can be a good source of evidence if it is found 'in situ' with other items such as coins or other carbon-dated material.

However, to rely on this as a form of evidence when pieces are found at random can be problematical, as ALL it shows is that this type of pot was used on this site (at some point in history) after this type of pot was made – and not necessarily the general assumption and 'bad science' that the site and this random object are of the 'same' time-period.

For example, during an excavation in the 1920s Colonel Hawley uncovered an 1801 bottle of port planted by William Cunningham from a previous excavation of the site. Using past and current archaeological methodology – Hawley should have dated the Stonehenge as 'Victorian', as technically the bottle was found 'in situ'. Hawkins also found Roman coins in the foundations of standing stones. Still, like the bottle he had more information and knowledge about other 'older' finds found on the site to stop him claiming (unlike other past archaeologists) that it was a Roman temple. Sadly, this is exactly what we do currently with the antler picks found on a site!

Moreover, complete sites are dated just by fragments of pottery without any other evidence, or even random flints, as if knapped flints can be dated with any accuracy. The number can readily see this of so-called 'iron age' encampments found on OS maps. Most of these sites are on hills and have ditches surrounding them; therefore, archaeologists automatically classify these monuments as 'iron age' as the perception is that they are fortifications, built at a time of extreme violence – the iron age. However, there is not one single piece of scientific evidence to support this fanciful claim, yet we have thousands of monuments incorrectly classified as 'iron age' all over Britain. Moreover, this type of unsupported evidence would simply not be deemed acceptable by any other 'science'.

Students of archaeology are taught just facts and figures and not the scientific practices of critical 'primary source' analysis and deductive logic within their courses, which is required to make sense to these fragments of prehistoric information – which sadly leads to blanket acceptance of flawed or tainted knowledge.

I witnessed at first-hand, this kind of prejudice when I submitted my final essay during my archaeology course in the 1990s. The theme was about Stonehenge and highlighted the conflicting evidence throughout the site. This particularly applied to the car park post holes that had been ignored by archaeologists when discovered in the 1960s and in so doing, they missed how this find could have helped to establish the true dating of Stonehenge instead of relying on the 'loose' pottery and antler pick evidence that was accepted as the absolute truth.

I will never forget the comments my lecturer wrote on my marking sheet, which seem even more poignant today as I write this prologue: "Would make the basis of a good book but has no credibility for serious archaeology today". I suppose I should have been happy to have received a pass mark, even if it was only just!

Anyway, back to the plot. I was driving to London via the A303 which takes me passed Stonehenge when suddenly, the day turned to night, and a cold, eerie storm ripped through Salisbury Plain. I watched in the slow traffic as the poor tourists, in their summer clothes, ran as best they could for shelter while the traffic crept to a halt. At that point, my mind started to drift, and I looked around at the grassy fields as they began to become waterlogged.

I was driving past a point called 'Stonehenge Bottom', a deep ravine adjacent to Stonehenge. The hills were now feeding water down to the lowest end of the valley, and water was, very quickly, becoming very deep as it reverted back to the river it once had been. "You idiot!" I said out loud to no-one in particular.

It was a phrase I had started to use a lot in everyday life, as I had become a great admirer of Hugh Lawrie's 'House M.D.' – as I could identify with the same stubborn, rebellious and analytical qualities of the TV personality. If you haven't managed to catch any of these enthralling programmes, I'd highly recommend them as Hugh portrays a medical genius who uses a method of 'Deductive Logic' called 'differential diagnoses' to solve his medical puzzles, in the same way Sherlock Holmes used it to solve other mysteries.

House M.D.

The system lists the conditions found in the patient (evidence found at the site) then lists ALL the plausible reasons for this condition (all possible events that could lead to this evidence) and then applying the Occam's razor principle: "suppose there exist two explanations for an occurrence. In this case the one that requires the smallest number of assumptions is usually correct." And you get your solution.

This method, I've attempted to bring into the science of archaeology, as like medicine it has many puzzles and moreover, the professionals in the field (in my opinion) get it wrong in huge proportions. This can be best illustrated with the £550m annual compensation package the NHS pays out each year for incorrect diagnoses and treatment. It is, therefore, a 'logical conclusion', that the so-called 'experts' get it wrong all the time, especially when it comes to the sciences of archaeology and geology. This is exasperated by the fact that although archaeologists take three years to qualify and five years to obtain a PhD, medical doctors take ten years to qualify and practice, and they still get it wrong.

Meanwhile, back at the car park. The reason for my outburst was that I had driven and walked past this same spot more times than I care to remember, but I had never realised that this was a massive clue to the 'post hole puzzle' I had considered so many years before, in my essay.

I got off the road and returned to Stonehenge. As I entered the old car park, I was guided to the auxiliary parking spaces on the grass behind the tarmac section. There was some chaos, as attendants were busy trying to fence off a large central section of the grassy parking area as it had started flooding. Most drivers found this naturally quite annoying, but I had such a huge smile on my face that I'm sure the attendants must have thought I was insane.

You see, I had been told (by the 'experts') as are all archaeologists that have studied the site, that the Palaeochannel riverbed, where the car park lays on and surrounds the area, was pre-ice age (at least 400,000 years ago if not more) so consequently, the old riverbed has always been mostly ignored.

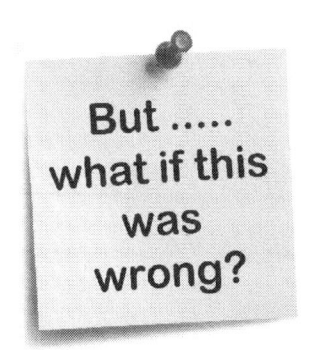

But ..... what if this was wrong?

As I stood in the rain watching the river return to Stonehenge, I asked myself 'why is the car park, still flooding?' – If the experts were right, despite this extraordinarily heavy rainfall, should not be flooding as the 'dry river valley' (in which the car park was situated) had supposedly, dried up hundreds of thousands of years ago, only a significant raising of the water table would cause it to flood now – not this relatively small level of rainfall I was witnessing. Yet the evidence I saw with my own eyes told me otherwise. I knew I had to go back and look at the evidence from the start, and this time, I would question everything, not assume that the 'accepted' theories were correct and would literally leave no stone unturned.

Because, if the experts were wrong, this small piece of the jigsaw would suddenly reveal not only the darkest secrets of Stonehenge but the correct date of the great civilisation that had created the stone monuments of Britain.

Introduction

This book and trilogy has been written to explain and prove a hypothesis that I have been working on over the last 30 years.

In publishing this work, I understand that it represents a fundamental change to not only British history but the history of the world. Consequently, I have not undertaken this task lightly, but there are moments in the evolution of any science – and yes, archaeology is a science - when a new theory will challenge the fundamental beliefs of that science's existing structure, and that is the objective of this book.

These progressive challenges should in no way be viewed as a criticism of the current theories, but a logical succession, creating a more coherent set of beliefs that moves the science forwards and helps everyone involved to develop a greater understanding of the subject. It allows experts to re-examine the subject matter in a new light and can extract the truth from the myth - which has sometimes been responsible for creating false realities.

In my view, archaeology (and in some respects geology) has not been challenged enough over the years mainly to the same extent as we have seen in other better-funded sciences such as chemistry, physics or biology. If these unchallenged acceptances were extended to the real sciences, we would probably still be living in a world without Quantum Mechanics or even Darwin's theory of evolution.

What you will see contained in this book is a newer progressive form of 'deductive' archaeology, which I refer to as 'Landscape Dating'. It allows us to date sites, not only from the findings on the site but critically, from their location in the prehistoric landscape. This science can bring a new interpretation and understanding of the structural complexities and the philosophies of our ancestors.

The evidence for Landscape Dating presented in this book, will allow us to paint a more balanced view of past humanity as an intelligent trading society rather than fur-covered hairy men, running half-naked, chasing deer and mammoths over Salisbury plain – which is owed to the past flights of fancy of Victorian archaeologists and anthropologists. Furthermore, this unique civilisation can be classified as 'advanced' as it invented the boat that allowed it to migrate at a rapid rate and to travel the 'known' world trading, teaching and inbreeding with the local populations ultimately sharing their engineering and philosophical knowledge as shown by the history of the Ancient Greeks and Egyptians civilisations, amongst others.

History of any site can best be seen within the landscape and at the location of the magnificent monuments. When you see henges or stone circles on the edge of cliffs or peninsulas, the power and awe of these ancient monuments are absolutely breath-taking.

As I have examined these ancient monuments in-depth, I have considered them from the perspective of the engineer and as a social philosopher rather than as an archaeologist, and that attitude and style are represented in the context this book. I have tried to lay out my hypothesis in a jargon-free, logical and sensible way with evidence that I hope you will consider being sufficient proof to enable you to reconsider what you currently believe to be accepted history.

But just for the purists, I have also included the required references, to show that there are real science and evidence behind the conjecture. In some instances, I will, in turn, accepted theories on their head, as the evidence can be interpreted in a completely different way to the currently accepted theories.

Other Archaeology books I have read in the past have frustrated and confused me. They either ramble on about the author's friends and endless lunches they have had while researching the book or focus on irrelevant issues. I will do neither in this book – I will simply try to present 'the facts' and my views based on these facts in 'layman's terms' and an informative, interesting manner. It's only by engaging in the evidence that future debates can be progressed and by so doing, our understanding enhanced.

What we must bear in mind is that no evidence is 'absolute' but just the current best interpretation at present, which in science is always open to scrutiny, debate and reinterpretation. I will then go briefly through the evidence to date, as found in detail in the first book of the trilogy 'The Post-Glacial Flooding Hypothesis' that shows that rivers were higher in the past – nothing more and nothing less! And then we will look at the sites around one of the first book's case study the river 'Avon' and the four sites of Stonehenge, Woodhenge (Durrington Walls), Avebury and Old Sarum.

I have always admired writers and recently, during my many university courses, presenters who can take complex subjects and turn them into simple analogies, which allow anyone to understand the concepts without reverting to jargon or technical references. If you have ever studied philosophy or quantum mechanics, as I have, you appreciate how necessary, such tools are to explain concepts and which lecturers do understand their subject and the ones who are just treading water.

Indeed, one of my favourite film scenes is from 'Philadelphia' when Denzel Washington turns to Tom Hanks, who is in the process of explaining a complex legal problem and asks him to "tell it to me as if I was a six-year-old". A sure way of saying, give it to me straight, simple and without convoluted language! Well, I hope this book doesn't quite talk to you as if you're a six-year-old. Still, I will explain some of the complexities and mysteries of

Prehistoric Britain – The Stonehenge Enigma

archaeology in a down to earth, clear and precise manner, and sometimes using analogies when necessary.

> **Tell it to me as if I was a six-year-old**

To help compartmentalise the topic or subject matter, Sherlock will appear to conclude the debate and clarify what I term as 'proof of my hypotheses'. They will be thirty or so proofs which are the basis of the evidence in the formulation of this book; a complete list will be shown in Appendix A regarding the pages the evidence is gathered

A large part of this book is my landscape surveys of Mesolithic and Neolithic Sites in the Stonehenge area. This and other 'case studies' are central to the book as I see them as the 'best evidence' for my hypothesis. Too many good ideas look feasible on paper, but when they are studied in detail, they are shown to be 'just ideas' without actual substance or methodology.

I could have chosen any area in Britain to test my hypothesis, but Stonehenge provided me with more archaeological evidence than any other as it had been the centre of prehistoric interest since the Roman invasion 2,000 years ago. It also has the most detailed analysis of any site in Britain as money has been invested in this location, unlike most other places - and sadly, even then that is still not enough.

It has always been recognised that the post-glacial landscape is still a mystery to both geologists and archaeologist alike, as quoted in the book 'Stonehenge in the Landscape' by Michael Allen "In short, we are dealing with a period from the upper Palaeolithic to the Late Neolithic covering nearly five millennia for which, realistically, we know little from the environment except by assumption and inference from the adjacent area away from the chalk."

Archaeologists have always sadly failed to understand the type of culture that was required to socially organise and manage the large numbers to create these types of structures. For this 'lost civilisation' has enormous consequences for the history of not only Britain but also Europe and the World. We will show you that this civilisation uses (for its time) engineering skills and mathematics way beyond what archaeologists and historians have to date recognised and given credit for their unique abilities.

Enjoy the book, and I hope it will encourage you to go out and re-explore these ancient sites armed with a new vision and knowledge of how our landscape really used to look some 10,000 years ago. For each unexplored prehistoric site still holds great secrets of our 'lost civilisation' past just waiting to be rediscovered. Those who dare to venture forth 'with an open mind' could be actively participating in solving the disentanglement of the greatest historical mystery of all time.

"Lost Civilisation"

Section One – The GEOLOGICAL EVIDENCE

Chapter 1 - The Post-Glacial Flooding Hypothesis

In the first book of this trilogy 'The Post-Glacial Flooding Hypothesis,' we looked at the new mathematical models that allowed us to calculate the amount of water that was released during and after the Last Glacial Maximum just over ten thousand years ago.

These models showed us that a minimum of 8.42 quadrillion tonnes of water was released on the UK at the end of the last ice age. This is equivalent of 98425.2 inches of rain falling on every square Inch of Britain's landmass or the same as - One Inch of rain steadily falling every day for the next 270 years

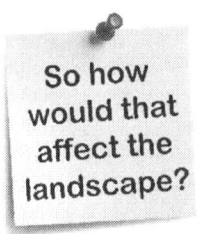

So how would that affect the landscape?

The worst known flooding in British history occurred in 1947 when just six inches of rain (149mm) fell on up to 12" of snow (so a maximum of 15" of rain if melted) over three months. The flooding, which inundated nearly all the main rivers in the South, Midlands, and the Northeast of England, was notable for its origins, geographical extent, and duration.

It was impacting on thirty out of the forty English counties over a two-week period, when around 700,000 acres of land became flooded. Tens of thousands of people were temporarily displaced from their homes, and thousands of acres of crops were lost, and this was just 15 of the estimated equivalent 98,425 inches of water that was shed on the British landscape after the last Ice Age.

Raised Water Table

According to William Donn (Donn et al., 1962). The Fennoscandian and Great Britain ice sheet covered $4.7 \cdot 10^6$ km², which is equivalent to:

- $8.42 \cdot 10^6$ Gigatonnes of water / $4.7 \cdot 10^6$ km², which gives us 1.79 Gt per km²
- 1.79 Gt of water at a penetration rate of 43%, give us 0.77 Gt of water per km²

- 0.77 Gigatonnes of water by U.K. landmass 242,495 km² give us 186,804 Gt of groundwater

This water will be released at a rate of 1 – 12mm per annum and be at a depth of possibly 75km. Therefore, to release groundwater at a depth of 75km at an average rate of 6mm per annum would take 12,500 years – not the 1,200 years previously believed, which is just the surface water from the last stages of the meltwater ice.

This is the reason that rivers (like the Thames) still flow even after months of drought, as the groundwater is constantly leaking into the river, which was at its highest rate at the start of the Mesolithic, just after the great meltwater floods.

Sea-Level Changes

If this model is correct, we should be able to get verification via other empirical evidence, as shown in sea level water rises, to see if it has been constant over the last 12,500 years.

Most geologists and paleoclimatologists, when talking about the end of the last ice age, refer people to the phenomenon called the 'Meltwater Pulse' – which is the rapid rise in sea level (20m) between 13,500 and 14,700

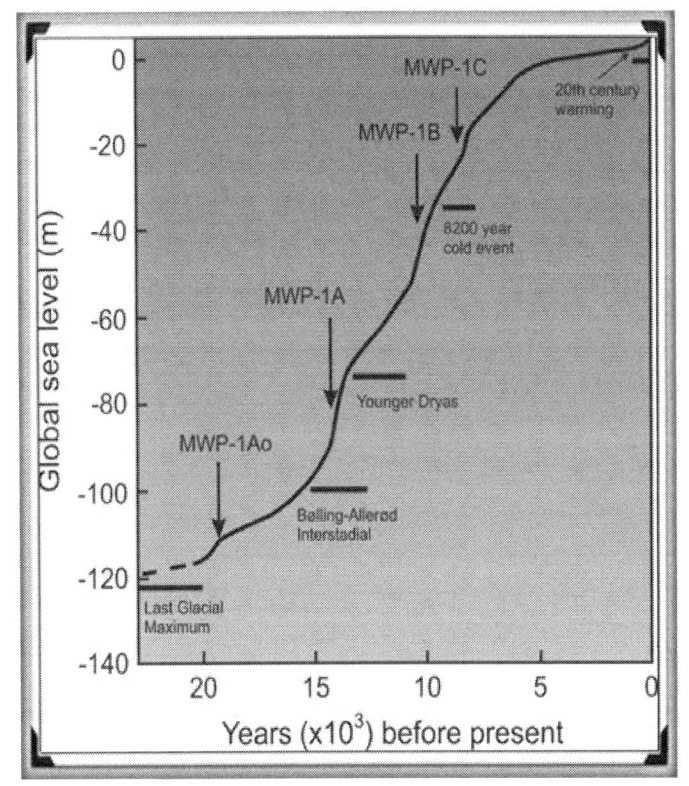

Figure 1- Historical Sea Level Change

Prehistoric Britain – The Stonehenge Enigma

years before present, over a 400 – 500 year period. Although it is a tremendous value, it should be recognised that this 'pulse' as only 16% of the total sea rise since the end of the last ice age.

We have constructed a model of sea-level changes by combining both the Wadden Sea model (Vermeersen et al., 2018) and the NASA sea-level model to calculate the rise in sea level in the North Sea area and the discharge levels from the Rivers that flow into the area over the last 10,000 years since the Last Ice Age (Fig. 1).

Landscape Transformation

When we put all the information about the Holocene together including the vast amounts of meltwater, Ice melt pulses, raised the water table and increased precipitation, then we are left with evidence of increased water activity, volume and consequential levels of Holocene rivers.

Table 1 – Wadden sea level rises and precipitation levels (* Meltwater Pulse)

BCE	Change (mm) over - 500 years	Discharge Ratio rate - compared to today = 1	Adjusted Ratio for Discharge - Pulses	Precipitation levels mm pa
950 AD	50	1	1	450
450 AD	400	8	8	430
50	300	6	6	440
550	400	8	8	440
1050	350	7	7	450
1550	350	7	7	375
2050	400	8	8	440
2550	500	10	10	550
3050	1000	20	20	550
3550	1000	20	20	460
4050	1500	30	30	450
4550	1500	30	30	525
5050	1500	30	30	625
5550	6500	130 *	50	640
6050	4000	80	70	670
6550	7000	140 *	90	630
7050	6000	120	120	600
7550	7000	140	140	400

Figure 2 is based on the above table which shows the Wadden Sea area (part of the North Sea) which indicates how the rising sea levels correlates to river discharge into this area and therefore size.

Therefore the blue 'discharge' line (on the graph) is an indication of the volume discharge and hence the size and height of rivers over the last ten thousand years – the chart uses today's discharge rate (950 AD) representing one unit, to give us a simple visual comparison to previous years as a ratio of size – hence 8050 BCE the rivers were 140 times larger than today.

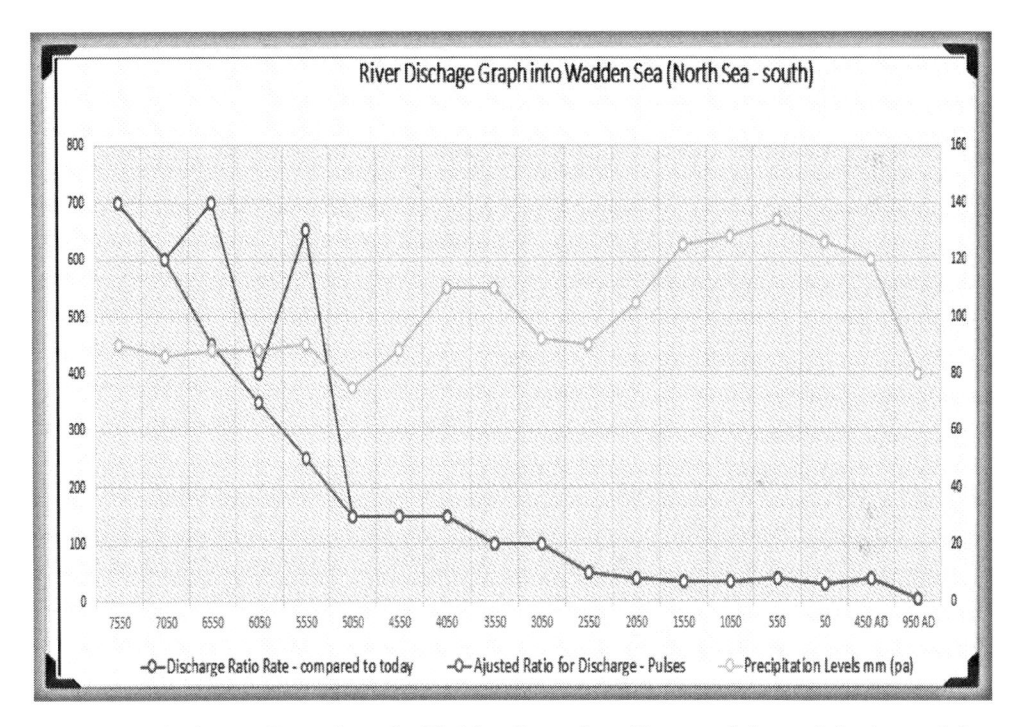

Figure 2 - Discharges Rates from the Wadden Sea – the yellow graph is precipitation and the green is the water pulses above the estimated steady blue discharge from the water table

Other Post-Glacial Flooding around the world

The flooding after the LGM was not only limited to Britain. We have shown in the first book of the trilogy that flooding occurred in Northern America – showing an increase of discharge from rivers such as the Mississippi increasing from today's rate of 16,790 m³/s to 160,000 m³/s just after the LGM, a rise of 853%, clearly showing an increase in river height.

We also see the same river level of increases in Germany and the consequence of these raised discharge rates and water levels in the historical flooding of the Black Sea some 2000 miles from the Ice sheet which turned the freshwater to a salt lake when it overflowed into the Mediterranean.

1. The steady rise in sea levels over the last ten thousand years - proves that water was still sitting on the land in the form of enlarged rivers, which would have kept the landscape flooded for thousands of years after the ice had melted

Britain's Post-Glacial Flooding

In a Lewin and Macklin, 2003 study they showed that 147 channel floods occurred during the Holocene period due to the rise in the water table, which continued up to just 1000 years ago. Moreover, as pointed out within the paper "Constant Holocene sedimentation might be expected to produce straight-line cumulative plots and even probability levels, with deviations representing episodic or increasing/decreasing trends inactivity".

However, the uneven preservation of alluvial units (Lewin and Macklin, 2003) base their 'recorded' alluvial archive in different ways, especially but not exclusively towards later Holocene sediments. Furthermore, 14C dated materials are also likely to appear bunched in relation to 14C production variability, which may or may not coincide with flood production, so that to an extent the spikiness of the illustrated plots represents more complex factors than episodic alluviation alone. These factors need to be borne in mind when interpreting the data presented."

We then investigated the Thames as a case study to see how Britain's largest river was affected in the Mesolithic and Neolithic periods. This was achieved by constructing a discharge model based on the sedimentary data supplied by the British Geological Society's superficial maps of the areas and some borehole core sample.

The conclusion of this study was that the current average discharge of 65.8 m^3/s was increased by 3723% within the watershed area, which allowed us to estimate that at its peak the Thames River discharged 2450 m^3/s (0.0025 Gt /s or 1314 Gt per annum). About the same rate of one of the smaller rivers of North America during the same period, which begs the question as the Thames is the largest river in the country, would it not be affected mostly by the meltwater at the end of the last ice age.

So, have the geologists got the extent of the alluvium flooding correct?

To investigate, we need to look at a detailed excavation undertaken at the edge of the BGS superficial Alluvium flood map, to get some real evidence about what sediments are shown, which will allow us to better understand the dates Geologists have suggested in the past.

If we look at the Cross-Section profile of the Thames, we see that the area of Holocene superficial sediment effect, increases by at least one mile and is terminated by Boreholes TQ47NE344 and TQ58NW141.

Borehole TQ47NE344 – shows 5.95m of "Brown Silty Sand" before hitting Chalk and TQ58NW141 4.42m of "Loamy Sand and Stones" with a base of "sand and Gravel".

This increases the Thames Flood Model from a discharged 2,450 m^3/s to 12,250 m^3/s, which reflects more accurately the North American Discharge Model.

2. Lewis & Macklin's 2003 scientific paper proves that the rivers in Britain have flooded over 100 times in the last ten thousand years - with some of these events lasting over hundreds of years.

Peat (Ultimate Evidence of Holocene Flooding).

The formation of bogs in the UK began 10,000 years ago at the end of the last ice age, when glaciers retreated northwards, leaving behind a landscape of shallow meltwater lakes and waterlogged hollows. An estimated 2.3 million hectares (9.5% of the UK land area) is covered by bog peatlands. [1]

Peat (turf) is an accumulation of partially decayed vegetation. One of the most common components is Sphagnum moss, although many other plants can contribute. Soils that contain mostly peat are known as a histosol. Peat forms in wetland conditions, where flooding obstructs flows of oxygen from the atmosphere, reducing rates of decomposition.

Bogs are the most important source of peat, but other less common wetland types also deposit peat, including fens, pocosins, and peat swamp forests. There are many other useful words for lands dominated by peat, including moors, muskeg, or mires. Landscapes covered in peat also have specific kinds of plants, mainly Sphagnum moss, Ericaceous shrubs, and sedges (see bog for more information on this aspect of peat). Since organic matter accumulates over thousands of years, peat deposits also provide records of past vegetation and climates stored in plant remains, particularly pollen.

Hence, they allow scientists to reconstruct past environments and changes in land use.

Peat forms when plant materia - usually in marshy areas, are inhibited from decaying entirely by acidic and anaerobic (lack of oxygen) conditions. It is composed mainly of marshland vegetation: trees, grasses, fungi, as well as other types of organic remains, such as insects, and animal remains. Under certain conditions, the decomposition of the latter is inhibited, and archaeologists often take advantage of this.

Peat layer growth and the degree of decomposition (or humidification) depend principally on its composition and on the degree of waterlogging. Peat formed in very wet conditions accumulates considerably faster and is less decomposed, then that in drier places. This allows climatologists to use peat as an indicator of climatic change.

Unlike sub-soils, such as head and alluvium, most peat bogs can be accurately carbon dated - this is central to understanding post-glacial flooding as the flooded areas of Britain would be major contenders to accumulate marshes and bogs that would create the peat sub-soils of today (Fig. 3).

We can use peat not only to find the Holocene wet areas and raised river levels – but moreover, we can also use them to identify the size and flow of the rivers during the Mesolithic and Neolithic period.

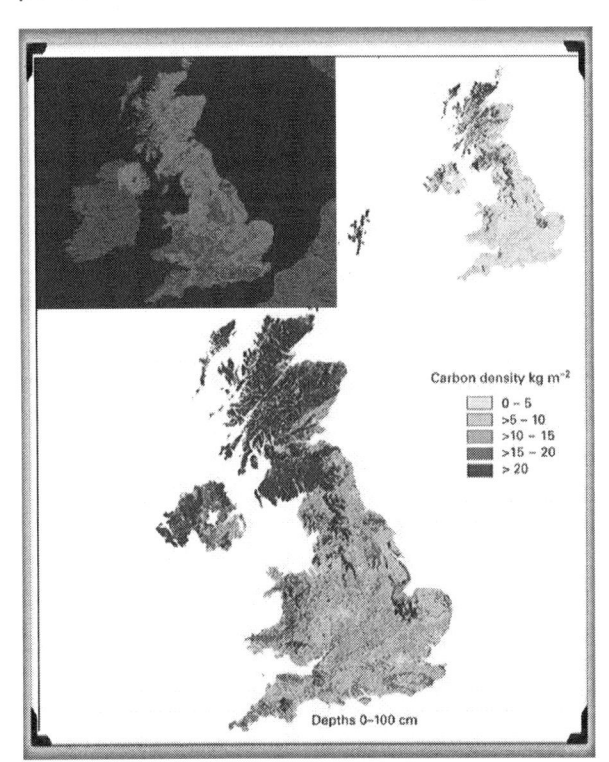

Figure 3- Peat growth - reflecting the post-glacial flooding of Britain (blue map)

Blanket bog occupies approximately 6 % of the area of the U.K. today. The Holocene expansion of this hyperoceanic biome has previously been explained as a consequence of Neolithic forest clearance. However, the present distribution of blanket bog in Great Britain can be predicted accurately with a simple model (PeatStash) based on summer temperature and moisture index thresholds, and the same model correctly predicts the

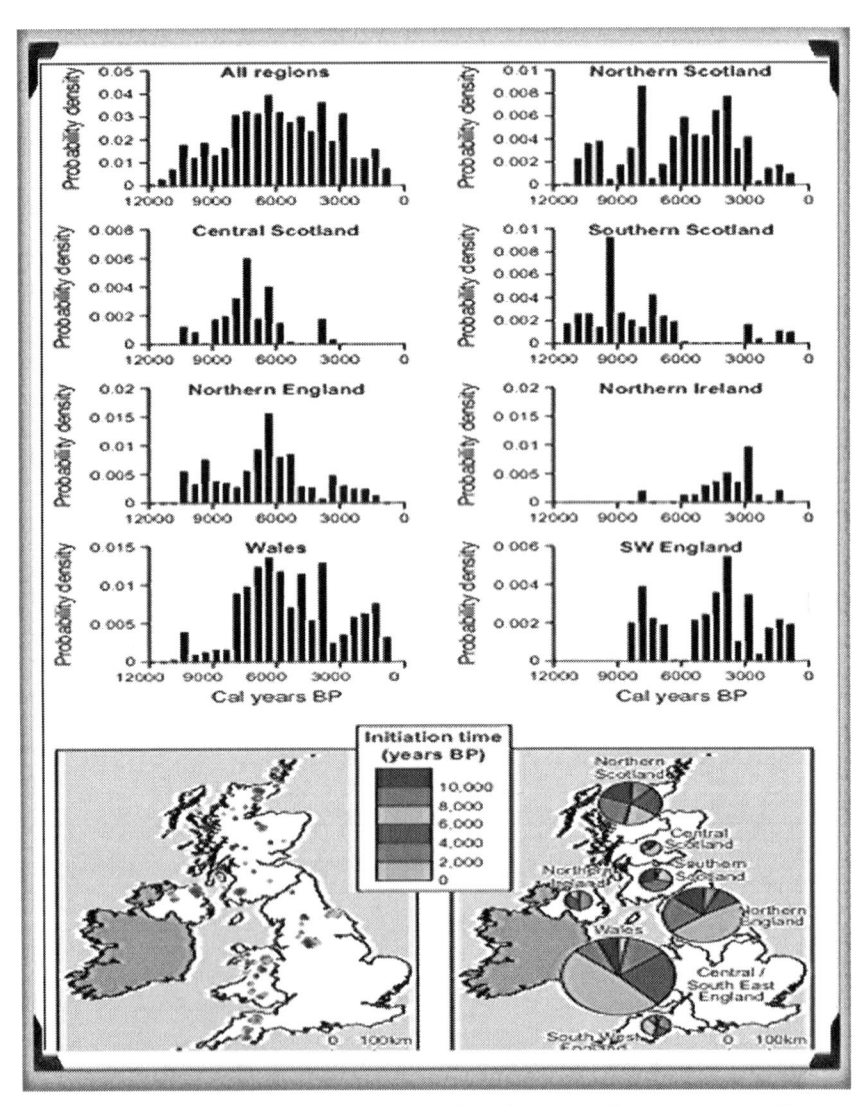

Figure 4 - Carbon dated peat samples showing when these peat formations were formed

highly disjunct distribution of blanket bog worldwide. This finding suggests that climate, rather than land-use history, controls blanket-bog distribution in the U.K. and everywhere else. (Gallego-Sala et al.,2016).

The maximum rate of peat production is not as one would expect directly after the meltwater flooding at the end of the Last Glacial Maximum, because if the waters subsided quickly, then its peak Peat rate would occur in the early Holocene period. But what we see, is that the peak growth is 4000 to 6000 years later, as we see in Scotland (fig.4), the reason for this, is because the rivers were at their highest and fastest, early in the Holocene - not allowing the right environment for the growth of marshes and bogs. It is only when the rivers start to subside, that peats beginning to form, which is only interrupted, by occasional flooding, due to precipitation towards the end of the Neolithic period, and the onset of farming.

3. Peat is a product of wet marshy ground and plant growth - this proves not only the extent of the Post-Glacial Flooding, but moreover, the dates of these episodes

Prehistoric Britain – The Stonehenge Enigma

Case Study - River Avon

The Quaternary deposits in the Avon valley include clay-with-flints, head, gravelly head, river terrace deposits, brickearth, alluvium and occasional peat. Clay-with-flint is a residual deposit created by modification of Palaeogene sediments and the solution of the underlying chalk, deposited considerably earlier than the river terrace deposits.

The exact age is uncertain, but clay-with-flint deposits in south-west England are likely of Pleistocene age (Gallois 2009). Clay-with-flint is mainly found on the flats of hilltops. Older head deposits, associated with clay-with-flint sediments, formed through solifluction and solution of the latter and the underlying bedrock. It is often found on the upper valley slopes. Further down the valley 'head gravel', 'gravelly head' and 'head' are found, deposited by fluvial transport, hill wash, hill creep and solifluction (Barton et al. 2003; Hopson et al. 2007).

The fluvial deposits in the area form a flight of 14 river terraces. The highest terraces, up to 100m above the Avon valley floor, spread up to 12km wide from the present-day river axis. The lower terraces in the Avon catchment are 3km to 6km wide and are found alongside and below the present-day river (BGS 1991, 2004, 2005). The massive extent and limited altitudinal separation between the highest terraces point to the draped deposition of these terraces over the landscape (Clarke and Green 1987).

The terraces are of relatively constant thickness along the valley. This is typical for systems where sediment overloading from upstream and input from tributaries to the main valley occurs (Blum and Törnqvist 2000). This is probably combined with lateral erosion and redeposition of fluvial sediments (Brown et al. 2009a, b).

This mechanism could explain the progressive restriction of floodplain width between each erosion-aggradation phase (Brown et al. 2010). The high number of terraces may indicate that terrace formation in the Avon valley cannot directly be linked to MIS cycles, as suggested in the model of terrace formation developed by Bridgland (2000).

The Avon terraces, the pre-Quaternary geology is briefly discussed In a publication 'Crustal uplift in Southern England: evidence from a river terrace records' Illustrated that there were several terraces from the river Avon still visible in the Hampshire basin which they called T5 - T10.

'Little has been done to determine the age of either the terrace sequence or the older River Gravels in the Avon Valley'.

'However, interglacial sediments within the two lowest terraces of the Solent have been assigned to OIS 7, and OIS5e (Allen et al., 1996) Organic Remains of probable Ipswichian(OIS 5e) age (Barber and Brown, 1987), and probable early Devensian age (Green et al.,1983) have been described from sediments underlying low-level terraces within the Avon valley, but at higher elevations in the valleys of the Avon and its tributaries, no organic remains have ever been described'.

This dating of River terraces is more confused when a recent publication called: 'Pleistocene landscape evolution in the Avon Valley, southern Britain: Optical dating of terrace formation and Palaeolithic archaeology' by Egberts et al., 2019. Produced a set of results that questioned the way previous geologists have dated these river terraces.

The diagram in Fig.5 presents the OSL results per terrace and in relationship to the MIS stages. The schematic valley cross-section is shown in Fig. 6 is also based on the 3Dmodel of the superficial geology of the Avon valley, built in Rock works based on BGS

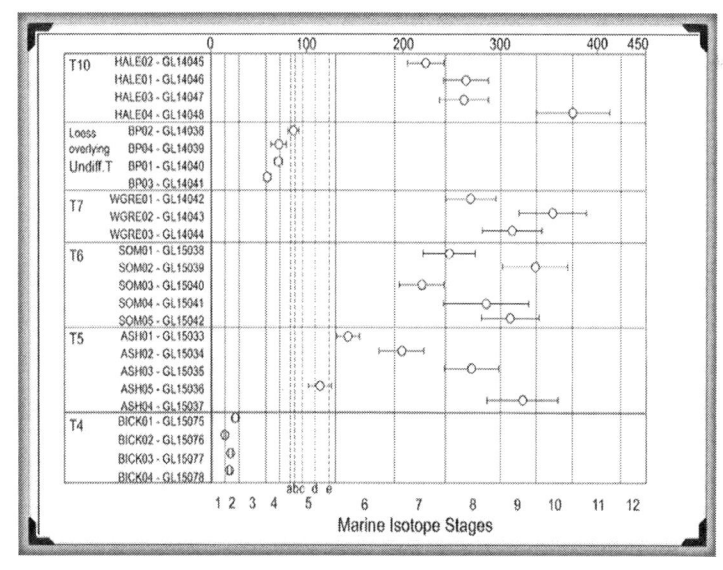

Figure 5 - OSL Results Avon River

borehole data. The OSL ages for T10-7 suggest deposit during or before MIS10/9 (Fig. 5 – including the LGM). They are broadly in agreement with, but potentially offer a refinement of, previously proposed relative chronologies used for dating the archaeological record of T7 and the calculation of regional uplift and incision rates.

The first observation you can make from these results is that they are 'inconsistent' at best and almost random at worst? It is clearly not what was expected by the team as the supposed oldest terrace at the top T10 (at the height of 102m OD. Fig 6) was laid according to the OSL dating method) over a 200,000-year period. This is compounded with T7 terrace (58m OD) being dated BEFORE T10?? But the most compelling evidence of the problems (with this old dated terrace hypothesis of yesteryear) is the Loess Terrace at (77m OD – Undif. T) which was laid during the LGM, as was T4 which has the youngest dates.

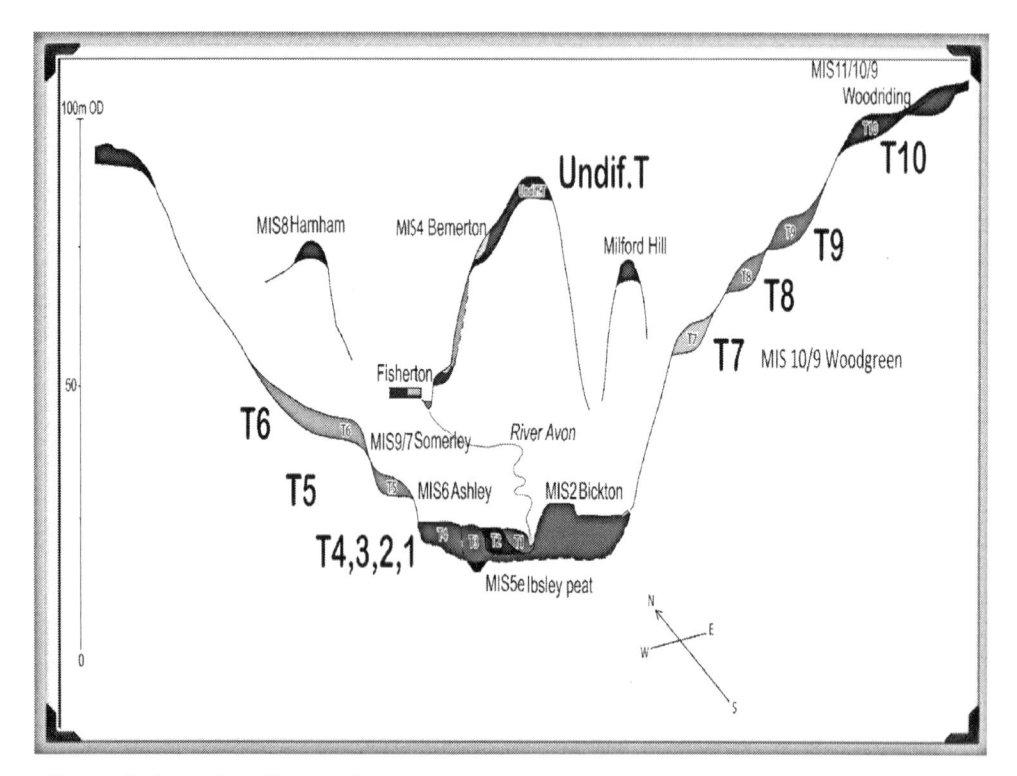

Figure 6- Avon River Terrace Levels

The authors attempted to explain this remarkable result by suggesting "Therefore, more plausible explanations for this discrepancy between the age estimate of T4 at Fisherton and that at Bickton are either that T4 at Bickton includes sediments 'reworked' during more recent fluvial processes or that T4 is a 'compound' terrace exhibiting differing depositional behaviour in the upper and lower catchments."

When we look at this new OSL method of dating we are not fully assured of its accuracy - as seen by the dating of sediment sample GL 14039 which was dated as 70ka +/- 8, and sediment sample GL14041 at the same level was dated 58ka +/- 4 and also sample GL14038 dated 86ka +/- 6 and sample GL14040 dated 70ka +/- 4, again at the same soil level.

Moreover, there are not only questionable dates at the same level (almost within the error limits) but the amount of sediment laid down below the topsoil - the first two samples 62ka for the 83cm depth (1.33 cm per 1000 years) and then just 16ka for another 70cm (0.23 cm per1000 years).

This would therefore question the accuracy of the OSL dating method. If history is repeating itself, as with radiocarbon dating, then over the next 50 years, these results will be more accurately defined. But what these samples do show is that dating these levels by visual evidence alone is not accurate as the report also confirms.

This is verified in a 14C v OSL dating paper (Gaigalas, 2000) when they concluded on their results "The observation of an anomaly high OSL age (from 39+/- 4 to 40 +/- 2 ka) for sands which covered the peat layer with 14C dates 24,430 +/- 210 of organic detritus, 27,800 +/- 340 of carbonate tuff.... Strongly suggests that these sands were exposed only for a short time."

This showed that the OSL was as much as 30% to 40% older than carbon dating. This is confirmed in the dating range in Fig.60 and illustrates that the Undifferentiated Terrace could easily be dated to the LGM.

What also was missed by the report was the evidence as previously shown in our case studies in this section was the number of river flooding that occurred in the Holocene and consequently must have flooded some of the older river terraces. We suspect that is why the terraces between T7 and T10 are of river silt and dates that are out of sequence to the above and below terraces.

"There are obvious problems with uplift modelling based on relative altitudes of terrace deposits and the use of the Palaeolithic record as a chronological marker, and indeed the age proposed by Maddy et al. (2000) and Westawayet al. (2006) for T7 (Woodgreen Palaeolithic site) is not in agreement with our chronometric date of 389-243 ka".

This apparent problem is compounded by the fact we have also shown in this section is that during the period 389 - 243ka the sea level analysis shows that the ice during this period was of a LESSER extent that the last LGM and therefore would affect the river terraces less rather than more!

Moreover, what we agree is the sentiment that "The reinvestigation of archaeological sites in the Avon valley shows that terrace deposits offer an opportunity to provide a valuable relative chronological framework but that in conjunction with chronometric age control and accurate height and deposit thickness modelling, a far better appreciation of the complexities of the system and diachronic evolution can be achieved. The more detailed understandings of landscape evolution which can be realised have direct implications for our interpretations of hominin landscape use, behaviour and predictive modelling of Palaeolithic sites".

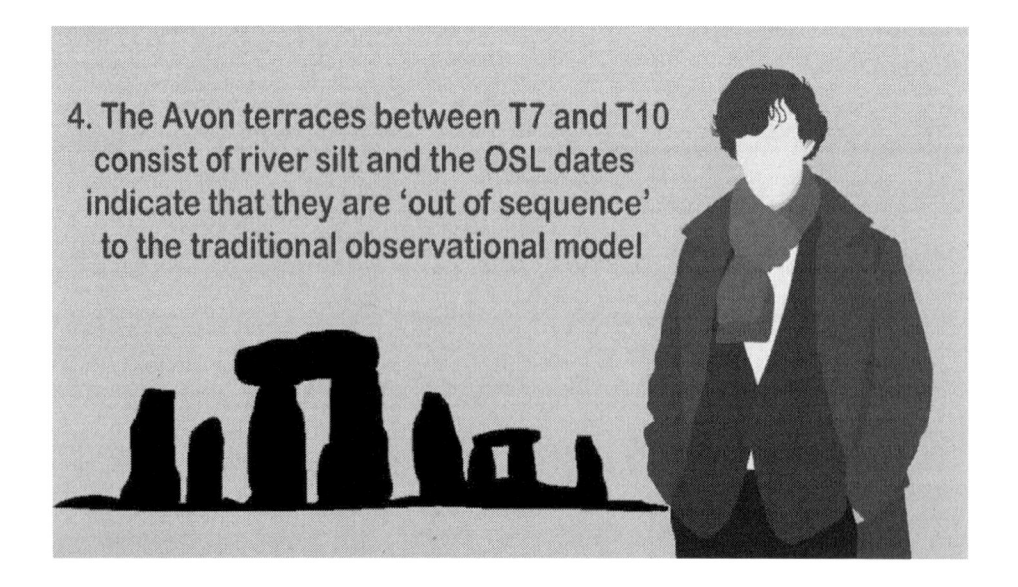

4. The Avon terraces between T7 and T10 consist of river silt and the OSL dates indicate that they are 'out of sequence' to the traditional observational model

Prehistoric Britain – The Stonehenge Enigma

Finally, archaeologists and geologists resist the fact that the river Avon was in Stonehenge Bottom during the Mesolithic and Neolithic period. They insist that there is no evidence in the form of Alluvium or Colluvium in sufficient quantities to support my hypothesis. This objection has a simple solution as Julian Richard's suggested in his book 'The Stonehenge Environs Project': "colluvium sediments may have been removed or thinned by the action of seasonal streams or higher water tables in the past".

Macklin, as we have now seen in this section has identified over one hundred Holocene river floods, twelve of which lasted hundreds of years, that would have contributed to this lack of alluvium or colluvium at Stonehenge Bottom. Moreover, the sources of the rivers that lay this sediment over the centuries of water flow, rely on massive precipitation entering the rivers, cutting through rocks and valleys making them flow at extreme levels which create this erosion and consequential sediment. However, the source of Palaeochannel water are natural springs found locally underground and therefore would not contain the same alluvium levels as active flowing rivers - resolving this dilemma.

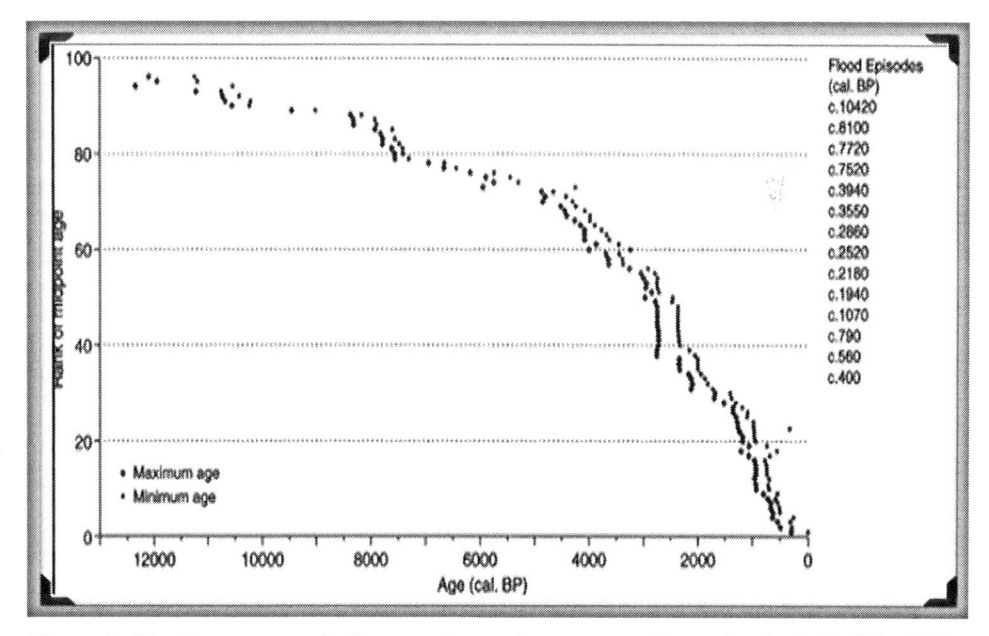

Figure 7- Flood events over the last ten thousand years according to Lewis & Macklin 2003.

Prehistoric Britain – The Stonehenge Enigma

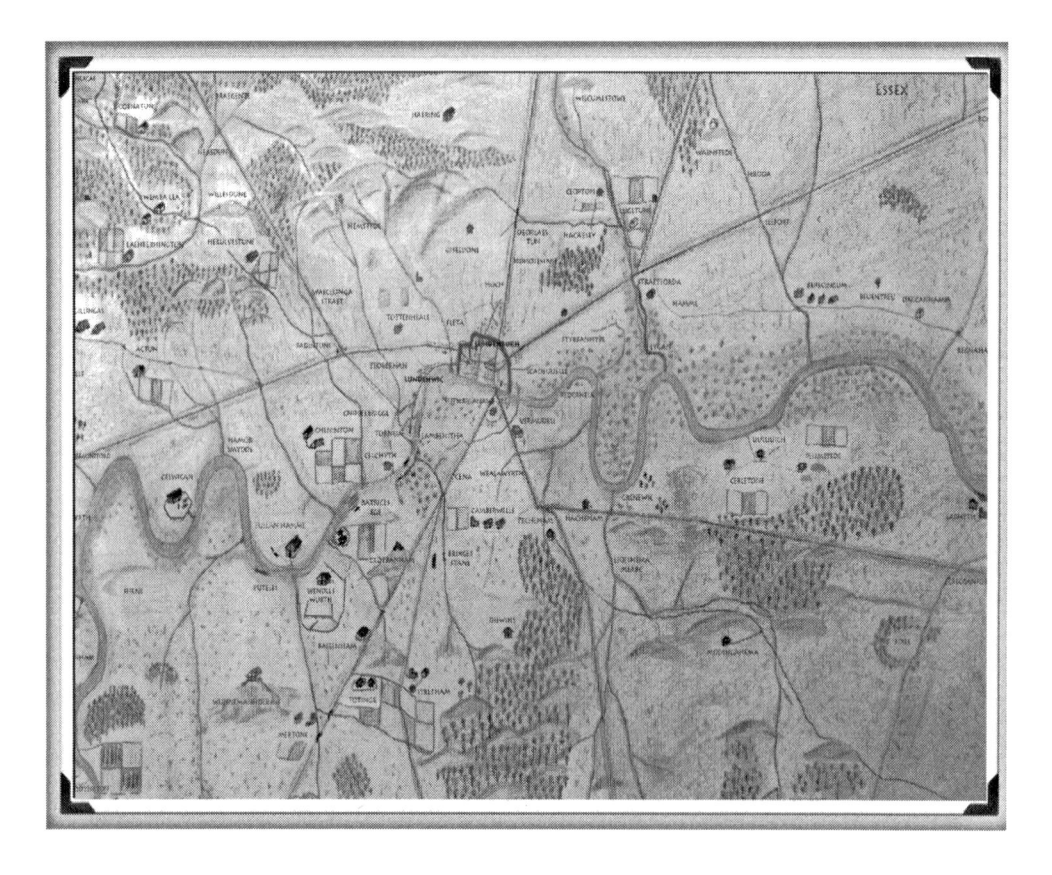

Figure 8- Anglo- Saxon map showing the extent of the flooding even in recent years

Section Two - Archaeological Evidence

The following section looks at the existing archaeological evidence within prehistoric sites in Britain to see if there is a further affirmation to prove my hypothesis. Surprisingly, the most undeniable proof comes from past archaeological excavations. Primary source materials through excavation and findings are always open to reinterpretation, especially in both archaeology and geology, as in most cases, there is a little 'other' evidence to support the original theories. However, geology is now changing as it attempts to incorporate the new technique of Optical Dating methods (as we saw in the previous chapter) in the same way as carbon dating revolutionised archaeology. But yet even with a method of confirming dates, the samples used can also be called into question and the results even more so, as objects are never fixed in time or location.

Now we have established that there is compelling evidence of higher prehistoric rivers, as shown on the superficial sediment geological maps of Britain, we must now look to see if we can find more realistic dates for the sites that sit on the edges of these waterways. The most effective way in establishing how these raised groundwater levels affected our ancestors is to look at the landscape features constructed by this civilisation, to see if we have evidence of this groundwater within their constructions.

We have concentrated on the River Avon region, as it is the only area in Britain that provides sufficient detail to be able to test my hypothesis. Nevertheless, I have also found similar evidence throughout Britain, perhaps less detailed but firm evidence, which will also be in part included as discussion points.

Chapter 2 – Stonehenge Phase I

Looking at the most important prehistoric site in Britain, Stonehenge, we are asked by archaeologists to consider that it is an astronomical calendar showing the rising and setting of the Sun, Moon, etc. This assumption may be partially correct, but why would you place the site in an area were trees would obscure your view - if you wish to study the sunrise and sunset, with any great accuracy, would you not locate your site at the highest point available?

So why was Stonehenge built where it is, rather than at the top of the hill just 500 metres away that is 30 metres higher - especially considering that the builders took the trouble to get stones from 200 miles away in Wales, for what possible reason would they stop short of obtaining the best setting?

As there is no observational advantage to placing the site in this location, we must therefore conclude that it was access to the area that was of paramount importance. If we look at a standard Ordnance Survey (OS) map of Stonehenge, it outlines the landscape and topology of the surrounding area by showing the contours of the hillsides. But it does not give you a clear idea of how Stonehenge sits in the landscape; for that, we need to look at a profile of the area.

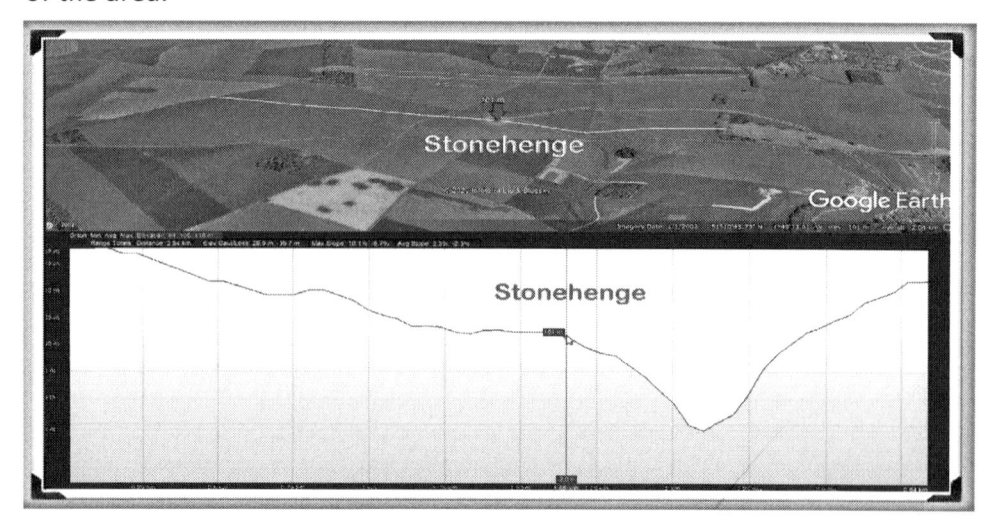

Figure 9 - Profile of Stonehenge (east to west) and the Palaeochannel that it sits beside.

Prehistoric Britain – The Stonehenge Enigma

Amazingly these profiles of Stonehenge show that it was built on the shoreline of a vast river complex. We can see this evidence on any elevation map, where we find that Stonehenge is sited halfway up a 'Dry River Valley' (Palaeochannel) known as 'Stonehenge Bottom'.

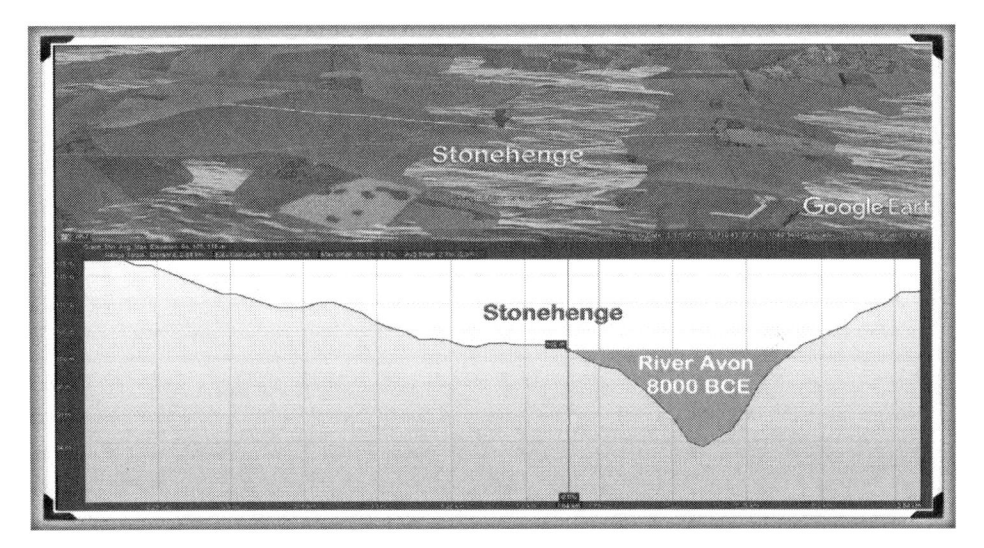

Figure 10 - Stonehenge with the River Avon as it would have looked in 8000BCE.

Our hypothesis and case study on the river Avon indicates that the groundwater tables during the Mesolithic and Neolithic periods were as high as river terrace T9 (Egberts et al., 2019), which was 100m high. This would mean that the river Avon would have filled the dry river valley with groundwater 30m above the existing groundwater table – when this happens, the profile changes dramatically.

And so suddenly, the impossible becomes possible, the implausible becomes credible, and myth becomes fact, for these profiles can only indicate one conclusion – Stonehenge was built on the side of a hill surrounded by water!

These amazing features are not just found on a single side of the monument; we can go around the whole circle to see these watery features. I believe these profiles tell the entire story of Stonehenge. A picture is said to paint a thousand words; these pictures show that our most famous ancient monument was once a magnificent feature in the landscape on the edge of a peninsula, surrounded by water. Now that we have shown that water existed at the Stonehenge site during Mesolithic and Neolithic times, we can re-sequence the events and building phases.

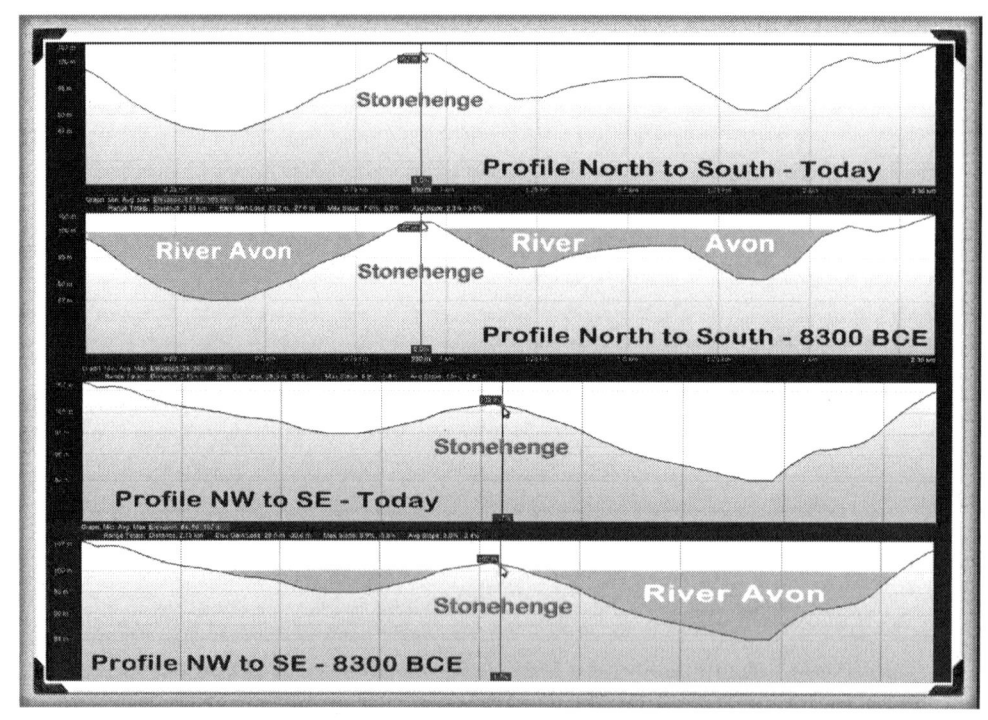

Figure 11- Profiles of Stonehenge showing the River Avon around the Stonehenge Peninsula

5. The location of Stonehenge at the edge of a Palaeochannel - (Dry River Valley) proves that the environment was flooded at the time of construction

Prehistoric Britain – The Stonehenge Enigma

The Ditch / Moat

If groundwater was contemporary in the past, then some evidence should still be present. Consequently, one of the more interesting facts found when studying any prehistoric site is that the constructors seemed to spend a disproportionate amount of time digging ditches to surround their monuments, whether around henges or barrows.

This practice would be considered strange, even if the prehistoric builders had practical and modern, labour saving tools. However, our ancestors only had the benefit of stone tools, bones and antler - making such excavation exceptionally slow, cumbersome and therefore even more bewildering.

Looking at Avebury (a henge monument), as an example, the most conservative archaeological estimation, suggests that the ditches surrounding Avebury, would have taken 1.5 million-working hours to build. That's equivalent to 100 people working 12 hours a day, every day, for 3.5 years. In comparison, building a wooden palisade using the same tools, would have taken less than one month – merely 2% of the time and exhaustion.

Current archaeological theories surrounding these ditches maintain that they were used either as defensive fortification and/or a landscape feature to keep out/in animals or and even more recently, bizarre interpretations such as a 'ceremonial' feature to ward off evil spirits.

All this shows is the levels of desperation the archaeologists have descended into in recent years in an abortive attempt to understand such basic structures, such as a moat. These quaint ideas strike me as somewhat flawed as a ditch is significantly less effective than a palisade (a long line of sharpened wooden stakes planted into the ground), which would have been considerably more straightforward, quicker to construct and more effective. As for evil spirits would not a neat little 6-inch channel achieve the same symbolic purpose as a huge five metre ditch?

Lt-Col William Hawley, was one of the amateur archaeologists, employed by the Ministry of Works to undertake excavations at our famous monuments

Stonehenge and Avebury in the 1920s. Unfortunately, he was not the most 'careful' of archaeologists. This was a view shared by colleagues such as Atkinson, in his book, 'Stonehenge' 3rd edition, London 1979 – where he suggests that Hawley's methods were somewhat 'inadequate'.

Despite this accusation of carelessness, he was still able to find some strange features, which can clearly be seen as evidence of a moat. For example, below a layer of chalk rubble infill (chalk which would have fallen naturally into the moat when it was disused) under a layer of flint, he discovered 'foot-trampled mud' (Cleal et al., 1995,p.68) – found in an area of chalkland which has no natural mud/clay, with an associated 'layer of struck flint' – which he found in many segments.

Now this, in itself, sounds quite interesting, if not conclusive as evidence of the existence of a moat, until you look for other landscape features with similar foundations which when analysed, start to build up a much more conclusive picture. Such landscape features can be found in 'dew ponds'.

Figure 12 - Typical Dew Pond as found in Wiltshire

A dew pond is an artificial pond usually sited on the top of a hill, intended for watering livestock. Dew ponds are used in areas where a natural supply of surface water may not be readily available. The name dew pond (sometimes cloud pond or mist pond) is first found in the Journal of the Royal Agricultural Society in 1865. Despite the name, their primary source of water is believed to be rainfall rather than dew or mist.

The mystery of dew ponds has drawn the interest of many historians and scientists, but until recent times there has been little agreement on their early origins. It was widely believed that the technique for building dew ponds had been understood from the earliest times, as Kipling tells us in Puck of Pook's Hill. The two Chanctonbury Hill dew ponds were dated, from flint tools excavated nearby and similarity to other dated earthworks to the Neolithic period.

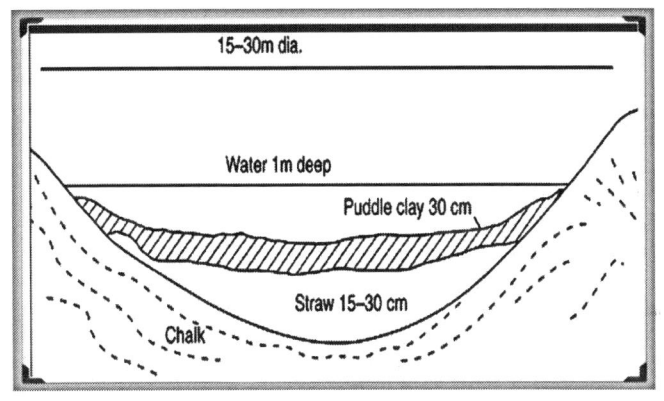

Figure 13- Profile of a typical dew pound construction

They are usually shallow, saucer-shaped and lined with puddled clay, chalk or marl on an insulating straw layer over a bottom layer of chalk or lime. To deter earthworms from their natural tendency of burrowing upwards, which would in a short while make the clay lining porous, a layer of soot would be incorporated or lime mixed with the clay. The clay is usually covered with straw to prevent cracking by the sun and a final layer of chalk rubble or broken stone to protect the lining from the hoofs of sheep or cattle.

In 1877 Mr H. P. Slade discarded the term " dew-ponds " in favour of " artificial rain-ponds," and scouted the idea that dew had any part in filling ponds at all. His remarks dealt practically with one pond, the greatest diameter of which was 69½ feet, which was constructed in 1836 at the cost of £40. It was bedded in the Thorpe Downs, near Loughborough, on the Berkshire Hills, at the height of 450 feet above the level of the sea. Being " fed from the heavens," this fact probably gave rise to its being classed as a dew-pond. The basis of this pond was stated to be, first a layer of thick clay (mixed with lime to prevent the working of earth-worms), second, a coating of straw, " to prevent the sun cracking the clay," and, thirdly, a layer of loose rubble. Moreover, during an interval of 40 years, till 1876, the pond had only once been dry.

> So, was it a dew pond liner that Hawley found at the bottom of the ditches at Stonehenge?

I believe so. Nonetheless, Hawley can be forgiven for not recognising that this clay lining feature being used to stop the lying water being absorbed through the porous chalk into the bedrock. Because he was not looking for a moat, as he was incorrectly informed by his geologists, that the surrounding area, was perceived to have been dry for over half a million years and therefore did not have a raised water table in the past.

Hawley also found evidence of what he called a strange 'dark soil layer' which existed within the primary fill, in many parts of the ditch I would strongly suggest that this 'dark soil layer' consisted of decayed remains and sediment, possible the hay which is traditionally lined with the clay to stop cracking. Moreover, over time, organic matter would have naturally floated to the bottom (like a pond), especially if they had not been cleaned regularly. This would naturally have left a lining of dark soil at the bottom of the moat was it fell into disuse and became dry

By 1923 Hawley reported that this 'ubiquitous dark layer' was found throughout his excavations, sometimes up to 8" thick, suggesting its existence in water would have been for some considerable length of time, and it was resting directly at the bottom of the moated ditch. This 'Dark Layer' was also observed by Atkinson in 1954 when the recut a piece of

Hawley's trench (segment 98) and found the same dark layer - not flint this time, but a stone layer. Moreover, he described the soils above as loamy (sand and clay) (Evans et al., 1984, 7-30) and that this layer (like the construction of dew ponds) was "often associated with a 'layer' of struck flint, which was found in many segments" (Cleal et al., 1995, p.68), to protect the clay lining.

There it has now been established that Stonehenge had, at some stage, a layer of waterproofing, the 'layer of foot-trampled mud' plus a 'layer of struck flint' added to the ditch. It's also been established that this ditch was, at some point, filled with water for quite some considerable amount of time, as evidenced by the deep 'dark layer' sediment.

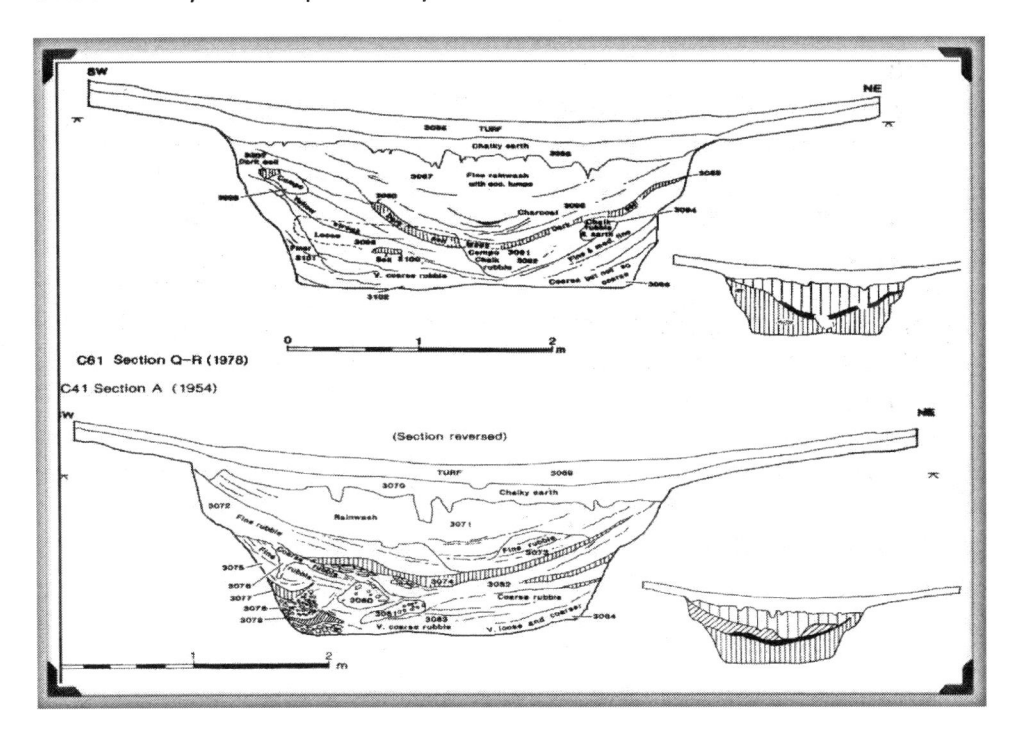

Figure 14- Hawley's Ditch excavation and the 'dark matter'

This use of the ditch as a moat is escalated in Hawley's finding of other moats that surrounded the north and south mounds, which 'connected' to the Stonehenge moated ditch. On the shallow associated banks of the ditches, he finds lots of what he calls 'yellow marl' – "there was a quantity of the yellowish marl within the ditch and about the site of the palisade" (Cleal et al., 1995, p.278) - Marl was originally an old term loosely applied to a variety of materials, most of which occur as loose, earthy deposits consisting chiefly of an intimate mixture of clay and calcium carbonate, formed under freshwater conditions; specifically an earthy substance containing 35–65% clay and 65–35% carbonate. (Pettijohn, F. J. (1957). p.410)

As this marl had fragments of Blue and Sarsen stones within it – this clearly shows that 'freshwater' was in the moat and present at the time of construction.

6. Hawley found evidence of a 'water sealant' at the bottom of the Stonehenge ditch, which he described as 'foot-trampled mud' in association with a 'flint layer' – proving that water was planned to be in the ditch.

But that's not ALL!!

If you look at remains of the Stonehenge moat today, it appears very shallow and uneven, but when excavated, it looks very different. It is, in fact, a series of 'individual pits', which, in places, are connected by shallow walls.

This opens up a series of fascinating unanswered questions:

Prehistoric Britain – The Stonehenge Enigma

- Was the ditch half-finished, for the pits differ in size, shape and depth, or perhaps they were 'dodgy Welsh builders' who did not know what they were doing?

- If the ditch is indeed defensive or symbolic as some archaeologists suggest, why not pile the chalk on one side rather than both sides?

- Why are their seats or shelves left in the ditch?

- Why are there stone holes at the bottom of the moated ditch?

The ability to build defensive structures was available to our ancestors. Still, on this occasion, they decided not to use it, as clearly it was made for another purpose, and that purpose was as a groundwater filled moat.

The only reason you would cut the ditch down to different levels is to search for the groundwater level under the chalk bedrock. As chalk is a porous substance and water travels freely through it, the groundwater table over an area like Stonehenge can vary by a metre or so depending on the makeup of the chalk, as water runs through the fault lines in the chalk strata, leading to varying groundwater levels over an area.

7. Hawley found evidence of a 'dark layer' in most of his ditch excavations, proving the presence of a moat with water decayed organic matter and sediment

> Bearing this in mind we can now answer one of the most frequently asked questions about Stonehenge – why was it built on Salisbury Plain?

This variation of groundwater tables would also explain why the builders left shallow walls and why none of the walls goes up to the surface – so the water could flow between the individual pits.

There are TWO answers to this question.

First, CHALK

Our ancestors needed a place with a chalk sub-soil as it has two exceptional properties – it's porousness and its resistance to dissolve in water.

The problem with chalk is that it's difficult to excavate, in fact almost impossible. So, if Mesolithic Man wanted an easy time and needed a large defensive ditch, he would have chosen a site with soft soil, unless he's insane or had nothing better to do for the next few years or so!

These builders were attracted to chalk and its unique characteristics. Not only is it porous, but it is SLOW porous, which means that a pit or hole below the local groundwater table would gradually fill with or empty with water at a consistent rate. In addition, because it's part of the limestone family, it would not crumble and dissolve.

If these moats are used in conjunction with natural groundwater reeds (Phragmites australis is one of the main wetland plant species used for phytoremediation water treatment) placed on the shelves within the ditch, the result is pure, clean, freshwater good enough to drink comparable to modern tap water. This type of water purification would not be seen in Britain for another 8,000 years. It would also leave Hawley's unidentified 'dark layer'.

The second reason is River WATER

We have seen from the previous Geological Section that the groundwater tables were far higher than we experience today, due to the meltwater raising the water table. For a site like Stonehenge, this would mean that the monument would have been surrounded by groundwater on three sides.

This high groundwater would permeate into any pits or ditches dug below the water table, and this water would be FILTERED of debris. Therefore, the ditches that surrounded Stonehenge were deliberately cut by our ancestors below the groundwater table in order to allow them to fill with filtered, clean (and if reeds were added) drinkable water.

It is commonly agreed amongst both geologists and archaeologist that 'dew ponds' could be used in areas without natural springs for drinking water so why didn't our ancestors simply build a "dew pond"– why go through the enormous and challenging task of building a 100-foot ring ditch full of freshwater pits?

Moreover, from the archaeological evidence I would suggest that the active moat from the start of the Phase 1 period at Stonehenge (when the water table was at its highest) and the river Avon was 30m higher than today, changed as the river levels dropped in the Neolithic Period, so did consequently, the height of the Moat. Therefore, this civilisation decided to line the moat with clay and flint to keep the waters high and preserve its use until eventually, it was impossible to preserve and at this point Phase 2 of the site, involving the introduction of the massive sarsen stones and construction of the avenue, as they adaption the site and purpose began.

However, the mystery of this ring ditch/moat deepens when you look at the other ditches in the prehistoric world, which shows that the ditch is not a single cut, but a series of individual pits interlinking to each other, with walls and seats cut into the chalk – which is not seen anywhere in the prehistoric world.

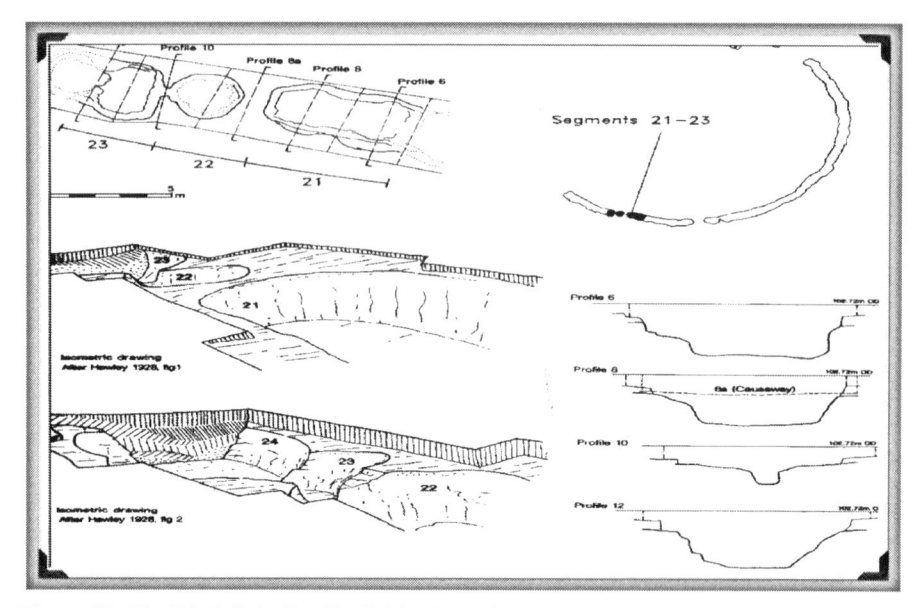

Figure 15- The Ditch is built of individual pits that seek to find the water table below the surface – Hawley 1922.

8. The Stonehenge Ditch was constructed of individual pits with seats and internal walls - the only reason you would build such a structure is if it was a moat of water

The Prehistoric Health Spa

Timothy Darvill, Professor of Archaeology at Bournemouth University, has revealed research that he believes shows that Stonehenge was an ancient healing place. In his book, 'Stonehenge: The Biography of a Landscape' the Professor cites that human remains excavated from burial mounds near Stonehenge reveal that many of the buried had been ill before their death.

Darvill also suggests that these remains are not those of local people but of people who had come travelled from far and wide. For example, the Amesbury Archer, the name given to one of the remains identified, originated from what is now known as Switzerland. The Professor believes that Stonehenge would have been predominantly used during the winter solstice when our ancestors believed it was occupied by Apollo, the Greek and Roman God of healing.

However, I would suggest that it was not the gods alone at Stonehenge that encouraged people from across the known world to travel such vast distances. It was another feature of Stonehenge that still survives today – the legendary Bluestone.

Bluestones are unexceptional, igneous rocks, such as Dolerite and Rhyolite. They are so-called because they take on a bluish hue when 'WET'. Over the centuries, legends have endowed these stones with mystical properties.

The British poet Layamon, inspired by the folklore accounts of 12th Century cleric Geoffrey of Monmouth, wrote in 1215:

The stones are great
And magic power they have
Men that are sick
Fare to that stone
And they wash that stone
And with that water bathe away their sickness

As this ancient poem very obviously shows, the sick would BATHE away their illnesses. I find it surprising that Professor Darvill never linked this revealing poem to his hypothesis. Recently, findings by Professor Mike Parker Pearson of Sheffield University have revealed a smaller version of Stonehenge, confirming the link between Bluestones and WATER.

The BBC reported that:

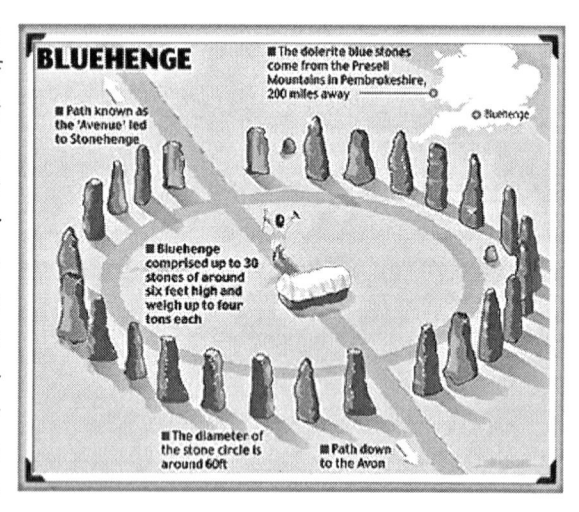

'About a mile away from Stonehenge, at the end of the 'Avenue' that connects it to the River Avon, archaeologists have discovered a smaller prehistoric site, named - appropriately, after the colour of the 27 Welsh stones it was made of – 'Bluehenge'. The newly discovered stone circle is thought to have been put up 5,000 years ago - which is around the same time work on Stonehenge began - and appears to be a miniature version of it.'

Another interesting aspect of the moat at Stonehenge discovered by Hawley was the number of 'craters' found at the bottom of the moat. These craters were large enough to have accommodated quite large Bluestones. In fact, Hawley in one particular part of the moat found a two-metre wide hole which he described as a post hole – this, however, is too big for a post, but it could easily have been a stone hole as its size and shape was similar to the remaining standing Bluestones we see today in front of the Sarsen Stone circle.

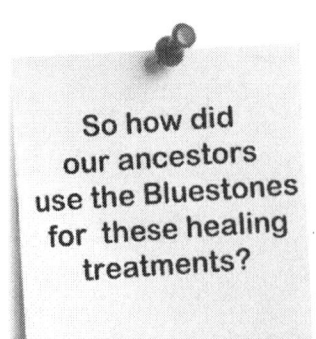

> So how did our ancestors use the Bluestones for these healing treatments?

Prehistoric Britain – The Stonehenge Enigma

It should be remembered that Bluestones aren't the same size as the Sarsen Stones, they're much smaller – in fact, an average visitor to the Stonehenge monument may quite easily scan over them without really noticing their presence. Archaeologists currently believe that their small size is because they are what remains after the damage by souvenir hunters over the years.

But I propose that they may well have been small when brought to Stonehenge originally, for they have little to no building quality, but as a healing agent to be placed at the edge and in the moat, to initiate their medical remedy. As an indication of how these stones were initially used, archaeologists have identified a colossal amount of Bluestone chippings covering the entire site at Stonehenge, 3,600 in fact, so many they call the soil surrounding which contain these shards 'The Stonehenge Layer'.

I would suggest that just as we enjoy adding a variety of salts to our baths today, so did the Mesolithic people – they would have added a small amount of Bluestone chippings into the moat as he bathed. By chipping the Bluestones, revealing the inner core, their healing qualities would have been enhanced.

The traditional view of why these quantities of Bluestone chippings are abundant is because they were 'worked' upon and re-shaped to fit the holes, which had already been prepared. This seems completely illogical - why would anyone in their right mind undertake the gruelling task of working on this exceptionally hard stone to fit into the holes, when it would have been so much easier to have dug the chalk soil first to accommodate the shape of the stones. Another traditional view is that the many chippings found were remnants from 'dressing' by re-shaping of these Bluestones.

> Why are Bluestones so inconsistent and variable with different sizes and different shapes?

We are aware that the more massive Sarsen Stones were dressed on the inner side of the stone circle, as the flake marks are still visible - but no evidence to date that the bluestones also were dressed.

Prehistoric Britain – The Stonehenge Enigma

Given that archaeologists believe that the Bluestone chips exist only because of the re-working by our ancestors or the results of Victorian souvenir hunters, it would be interesting to compare their number (3,675) to the number of chippings discovered from the softer, easier to break, more famous and more plentiful Sarsen Stones, which we know were re-worked.

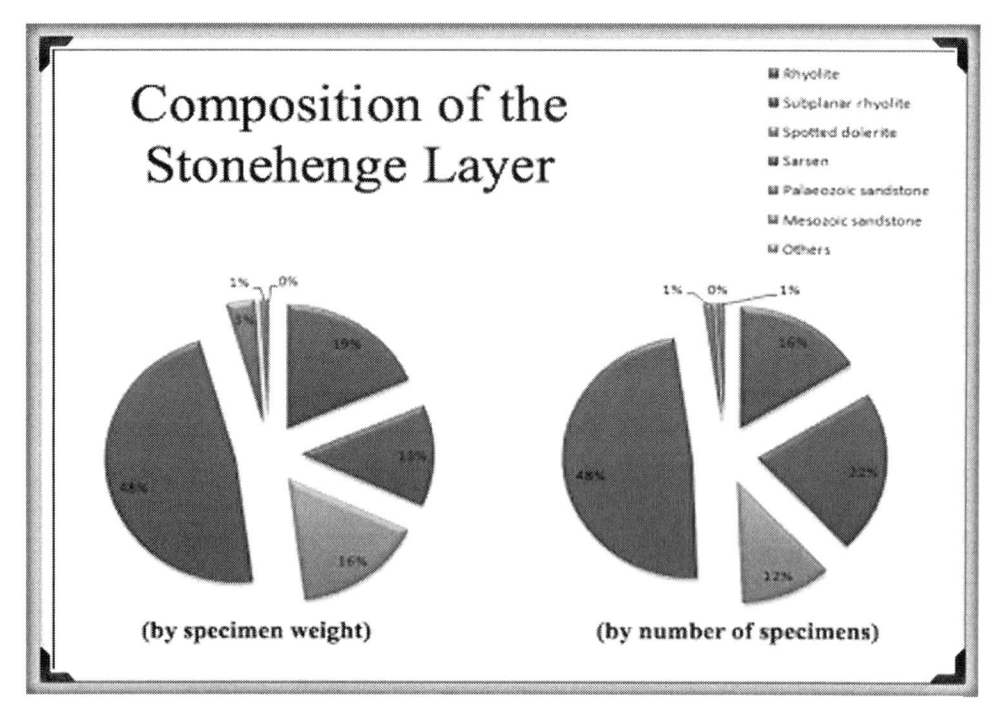

Figure 16- Stonehenge Layer showing disproportionate number of chippings

You would think, proportionately (251 cubic metres of Sarsen Stones v 28 metric metres of Bluestones), there would be a lot more Sarsen stone chipping to Bluestones – but you would be wrong!! Only 2,173 Sarsen Stone pieces have been found despite there being over nine times more Sarsen Stones than Bluestones.

So, assuming that there would have been a similar level of interest in Blue and Sarsen Stones by souvenir hunters, and a similar amount of re-working of the stones by our ancestors, you would expect to find at least 30,000 Sarsen Stone fragments, but has already shown a paltry 2173 have been discovered. Or if 2173 Sarsen stones pieces were the norm for both re-working and souvenir hunters – they should have found only 240 bluestone fragments and not the 3675 (Cleal et al.,1995, pp. 379 – 387).

I can therefore very confidently conclude that the Bluestones were deliberately broken up to be used in the moat. Our ancestors are likely to have believed that once the outside covering of the Bluestones had been thoroughly exhausted, the beneficial properties would be diminished, and so they were abandoned.

This is confirmed by Tim Darvill and Geoffrey Wainwright's who stated "Our excavations within Stonehenge in 2008 confirmed what earlier excavations had hinted at: namely that the Bluestones started to be broken up and chipped away more or less from the time they were set up in each successive arrangement." [2]

The concept of a prehistoric man bathing away his ills may seem absurd to some, but throughout history, it has been shown that humanity has been attracted to this type of treatment. It became commonplace in Britain during the Roman Empire some 2,000 years ago when every large villa had its own spa.

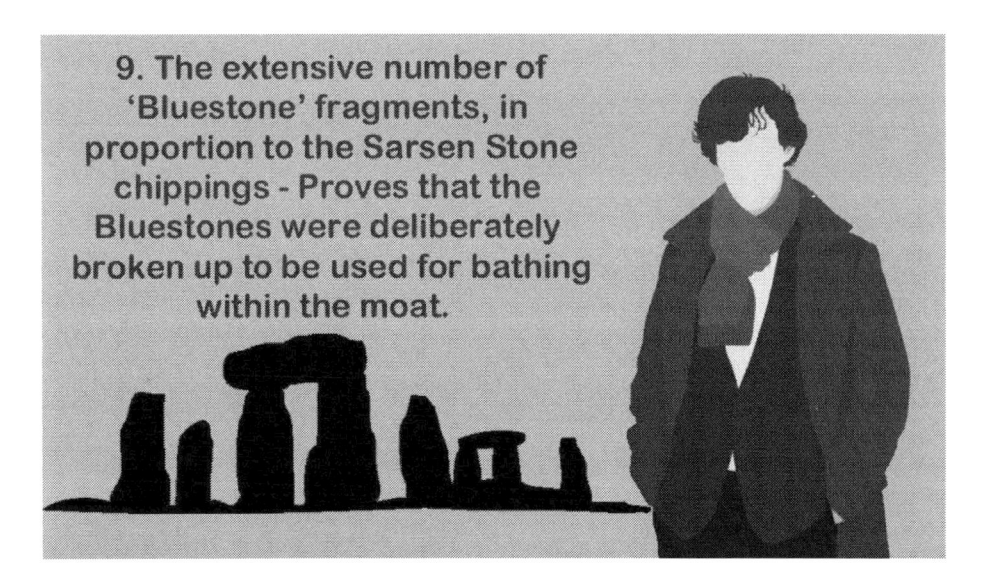

9. The extensive number of 'Bluestone' fragments, in proportion to the Sarsen Stone chippings - Proves that the Bluestones were deliberately broken up to be used for bathing within the moat.

So, is it a giant leap to imagine that the origin of such activities could have been introduced at an early period?

When in the Bronze Age the moat at Stonehenge had eventually dried up and could no longer be used as a spa, these smaller Bluestones were abandoned and became scattered throughout the site. The larger Bluestones at the bottom of the dried moat were probably removed to the stone circle, explaining the considerable variation in shapes and sizes of stone that we see at the Stonehenge monument today.

Aubrey Holes

What is not yet known is if the moat water levels were constant or did it only fill twice a day like the tides or at certain times during the Lunar year?

It is also possible that the engineering of the ditch was so precise, that the water would surge around it over strategically placed barriers (internal walls) to produce a spectacular waterfall effect throughout the entire 320-foot diameter at times of ceremony when the sick would then take to the healing waters? Alternatively, the moat could have been used on a daily basis when full – we simply don't know.

Gerald Hawkins, an American astronomer, published the results of an intense study of Stonehenge's astronomical alignments in Nature in 1963. In the article, he described how he had used a computer to prove that alignments between Stonehenge and 12 major solar and lunar events were extremely unlikely to have been a coincidence (Castleden, 1993).

His book, Stonehenge Decoded, containing the fully developed theory, appeared in Britain in 1966. He described how he had found astronomical alignments among 165 points of Stonehenge, associated purely with the Sun and the Moon, and not with any stars or the five naked-eye planets (Mercury, Venus, Mars, Jupiter or Saturn).

Moreover, he discovered that lunar eclipses could be predicted through a system of moving markers around the circle of Aubrey Holes (a series of 56 holes situated around the Stonehenge moat, which archaeologists believed originally held the Bluestones).

Anyone who has ever tried to make a model of how the Sun and Moon move around the Zodiac will end up, most likely, with a circle of 28 markers around a central earth. Moving a 'Moon-marker' one position per day and a 'Sun-marker' once every 13 days provides a calendar, accurate to 98%.

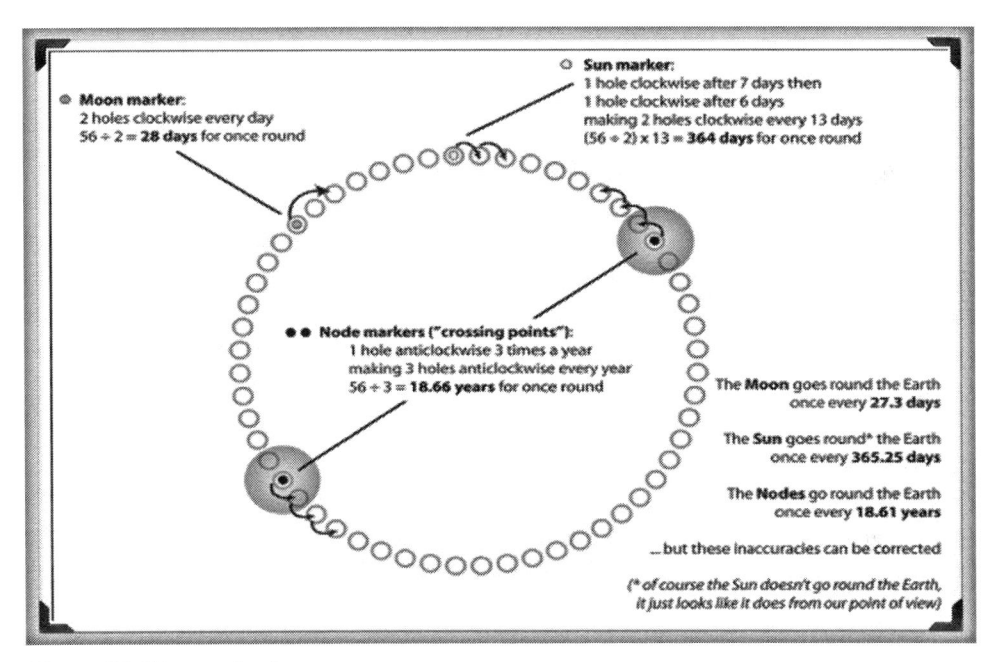

Figure 17- Moon calendar

Every year, for about 34 days, the full and new moons occur near the Sun's path (the ecliptic) and eclipses result. These two occasions, 173 days apart, move backwards around the calendar taking 18.6 years to complete a revolution. The precise two points where the moon crosses the apparent path of the sun through the zodiac (the ecliptic) are the lunar nodes, as mentioned above.

Prehistoric Britain – The Stonehenge Enigma

By doubling the sun-moon calendar to 56 markers, we can obtain an accuracy of 99.8% and meet the handy convenience that 18.6 x 3 is almost the same as 28 x 2. Now, a 3:2 ratio enables eclipses to be predicted to high accuracy.

This complex computation could be calculated through the 'Aubrey Holes' features at Stonehenge. By merely moving one marker, once a day and another marker every 13 days, not only could the spring high tides (by when the marker reaches a particular stone) be predicted, but the Solar and Lunar eclipses could also be calculated with great accuracy – a stunning achievement for so the called primitive Stone Age Man and probably beyond most readers of this book, even with our cherished education system.

Recent scientific papers have revealed that there is a direct correlation with the moon's phases and the water table (Singaraja et al., 2018). Which proves that our ancestors cut pits into the surrounding circle of Stonehenge, these pits would have filled with water at some point of the year either, all the time, twice a day or on high tides during the Lunar year which was calculated via the Aubrey Holes that held these sacred stones.

10. The 58 Aubrey Holes show that stonehenge was initially closely connected with the moon and its direct effect on both the tides and associated water table levels - this proves that the ditch was a moat fed by the same water table.

Many of the diseases and illness of today did not exist in prehistoric times, the weak and deformed would probably die at childbirth, and the mortality rate of children was probably high. So only the strong would generally live to an age where bathing was necessary - but what would be the common ailments that this process could cure?

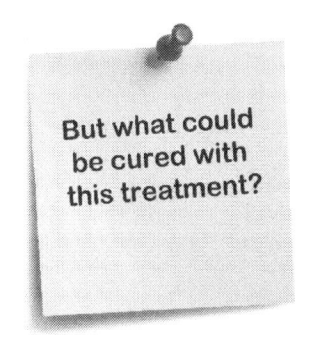

But what could be cured with this treatment?

The most typical form of death in prehistoric times would be infections from either injuries or simple cuts that are infected. We have cupboards full of antiseptics, but they did not. The last book of the trilogy 'Dawn of the Lost Civilisation' will show how this society used surgery for brain injuries, dentistry and the amputation of limbs. The only way to survive many of these procedures would be with antiseptic, and the best natural source is rock salt.

As strange as this sounds, saltwater is a highly effective antibiotic. Apart from organisms evolved to live in salty water, it is highly lethal to a large variety of common microbes. Next time you need to treat a sore throat, try gargling twice a day with a solution made from a teaspoon of common table salt dissolved in 300ml of lukewarm water. You will be amazed at the efficacy of this basic treatment. It goes without saying that saltwater can be used as a typical treatment for other bacterial infections - just apply to the affected part for a few minutes at least twice a day.

Do we need to look at how these unusual pits within the construction of the moat at Stonehenge, helped with this bathing process?

What we see from the excavations is a series of individual pits with seats and stone holes at the base of the moat. Were the stones therefore placed at the bottom of the pit and you sat with your feet by the stone?

Was it then you would 'chip off' the flakes releasing the treatment or was the flakes broken off the stones that surround you then just thrown in like bath salts?

Consequently, still a lot of investigating to do!

Were some parts of the moat salty, for treatment and other pits with clean water separated by these chalk walls?

Or were these stones heated on fires first to help the waters and make bathing more effective – indeed, Hawkins found evidence of fires in the pits at the end of the moated ditch (segment 100).

Bluestones

The most compelling evidence of the rise in water tables during the prehistoric period can be found in the old car park of Stonehenge. Ignored by visitors who used to casually park their cars in close proximity to the stones, three giant circles (similar to mini roundabouts) were painted on the floor.

These painted circles showed where post holes were discovered, when the car park was first constructed, each measuring at least 1 metre in diameter. Interestingly, and somewhat ironically, the reason the original car park was built at this location is because archaeologists believed that this area had no historical relevance – which is far from the truth. During excavations for the building of the carpark, three pits were discovered which contained pieces of bone and fragments of

Figure 18- Stonehenge Old Car Park One Metre Post Holes

charcoal - the pits had evidently held large wooden posts. When this pine charcoal were carbon dated it was found to be some 10,000 years old, over twice the age of any other structure at Stonehenge.

Traditional archaeology describes these posts that would have been placed in these post holes as 'totem poles'. However, if this were true, why would the Mesolithic people needed to struggle with using giant trees, over 1 metre wide, for the simple purpose of erecting ritual 'totem pole'? As our ancestors only possessed flint axes and fire, it would seem more plausible that smaller trees would have been utilised (as seen in North America) to create these 'totem poles', rather than the giant metre wide variety.

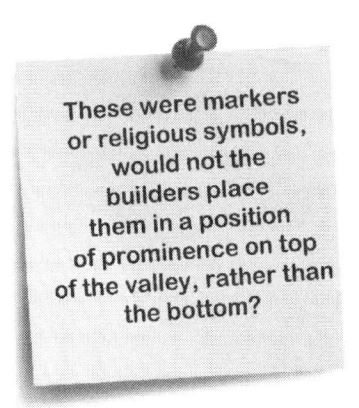

> These were markers or religious symbols, would not the builders place them in a position of prominence on top of the valley, rather than the bottom?

The old car park is 10m lower than the Stonehenge site and recent radiocarbon dating by Darvill and Wainwright's excavations in 2008, have confirmed from charcoal remains (inside the Sarsen Circle) that the area on which the Stonehenge monument is situated was in use by 7200 BCE and this was confirmed a couple of years later by a team from the Open University, who found an OX tooth, from 'feasting' in a nearby site called 'Blick Mead' that was also dated during the 7th millennium BCE at 6250 BCE, emphasising that this area of Stonehenge was for other purposes, rather than an isolated site with marker posts.

If my hypothesis is correct, these post holes housed posts which had no ritual connotations, as associated with 'totem poles', but were in fact functional mooring posts for boats. They were utilised for unloading cargo, and they could be used as simple lifting devices, created by placing a similar-sized tree trunk (cross beam) across the top of two posts, secured with the use of a simple mortise and tenon joint, as used on the Stonehenge lintels.

This lifting device could have been used to raise stones from boats during high tide by merely tying the stones to the cross beams. As the tide receded,

Prehistoric Britain – The Stonehenge Enigma

the vessel holding the stone would naturally lower in the water, lifting the stone 'like magic' into the air. This is the first example of a hydraulic lift, which shows the level of sophistication in our ancestors thinking. The stone could then be lowered to either a sledge or rollers placed under the cross beam for the 50m journey to the top of the hill.

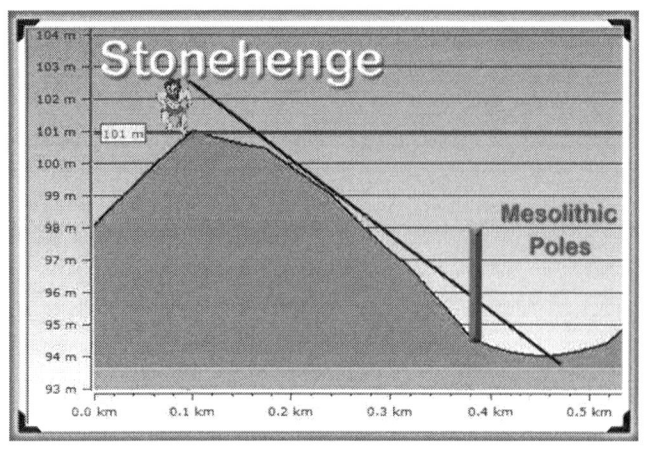

Figure 19 - 'Totem Poles' - place at the bottom of the Dry River Valley

Archaeologists have always calculated that in order to obtain the Bluestones, our ancestors had taken a very long and dangerous boat trip around the coast of South West Britain to an outlet in the South coast that allowed boats to travel up the River Avon or to the banks of Somerset in the North, and had then dragged the stones some 50 miles South, to their resting place in Salisbury Plain. Or some have even imagined dragging these 4-tonne stones on sledges over 200 miles through woods, forests and over rivers.

The post-glacial flooding hypothesis now enables us to understand how they could have easily travelled on the direct water route between South Wales and Somerset to bring these stones to Stonehenge and how easy it was for them using tidal hydraulics to place these stones carefully on to boats for the journey. Validation of my theory was found in a post hole discovered in an extended part of the visitors' centre in 1989 by the company, Wessex Archaeology.

The dating obtained from this post hole confirms the 1966 dates to be accurate, to the embarrassment of the archaeological establishment.

Figure 20- A 'lifting device' that could raise Bluestones out of the boats on to sledges

The Lost North-West Entrance

Based on my hypothesis, there should be some evidence of a 'lost' processional walkway on the North West side of the monument, towards the original ancient shoreline and mooring station, which would have acted as a natural entry route to the site. Archaeologists have discovered a series of holes (known as Q & R holes) in a semi-circular shape at the centre of Stonehenge, which predates the current Sarsen Stones. The most interesting aspect of this semi-circle is its alignment in a North-Western direction.

In astronomical terms, this is very important as it faces the general direction of the midsummer moonset - highlighting the relationship of the moon to the site, as opposed to the sun as many 'druids' would have us believe. This connection is reinforced as the construction of the site may be based on the tidal waters, which in turn, are dependent on the position of the moon reflected by the location of the Bluestone calendar and place marker, as discussed earlier in the chapter.

One of the greatest archaeological mysteries of the Mesolithic and Neolithic periods is the lack of human remains.

We know that the population would have been relatively small during these periods in history, but the lack of graves has forced archaeologists to investigate non-burial alternatives. One of the favoured alternative methods to burial is known as 'excarnation'. This process was commonly practised by Native American Indian tribes, and it involves the corpse to be left open to the elements to decompose – a symbolic process of returning the body to mother earth.

The larger bones would then be collected together and buried with other members of the tribe or family in vaults or tombs. We know that such groups of bones have been found in the Long Barrows surrounding Stonehenge, but to date, no dedicated excarnation sites have been found, until now.

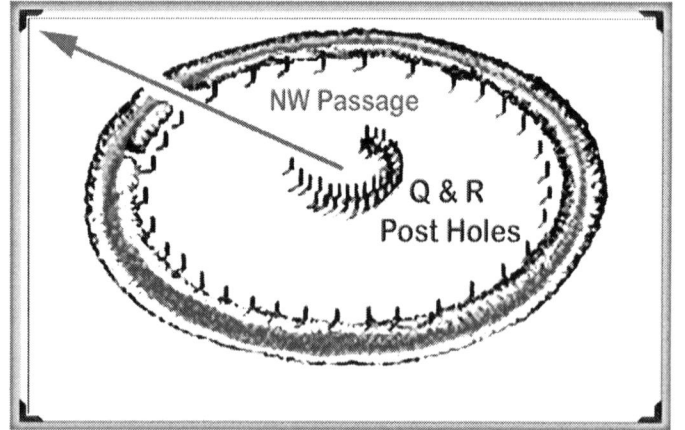

Figure 21- NW passage with Q & R Dolman Holes for Excarnations

Looking at these Q & R post holes, these form a pre-Sarsen semi-circle at Stonehenge. If you look closely, they consist of two parallel sets. Moreover, they emulate not a 'horseshoe' as the archaeologists normally refer to such objects, but a 'crescent moon' for obvious reason, in preparation to the journey to the land of the dead. Another point of interest is the distance between each stone in each individual set, which is approximately 2 metres. The 2 metres (6 foot) spacing of these stone holes should seem familiar as it's the same length as an average coffin or grave pit. As this was a monument to the dead, it would seem appropriate that it would be designed in such a way as to allow bodies to be positioned at its centre, aligned with the setting moon.

It's likely that the platforms upon which the dead were laid were either wooden or a stone slab – as we see from other prehistoric monuments known as 'Dolmens' which archaeologists have still to identify their purpose. Moreover, a resistance survey was taken in May 1994 clearly shows a path leading from the centre of the monument to the car park post holes, past the expected location of Aubrey Hole 40 – the lack of evidence for this post hole may also indicate that there once existed a pathway that passed to the North West on the original plan of the site.

Palisade

With the non-descript name of WA 9421 or the Palisade Ditch, yet another mysterious even lesser publicised feature has been found which does not fit the current expert theories. This Palisade ditch lies in the North-West part of the site, between the Stonehenge monument and the visitor's car park and runs across the site running in a South-West to North-East direction. It spreads from Stonehenge Bottom to Stonehenge Down. From the depth of the postholes, it has been calculated, by archaeologists, to be relatively high and would create the ideal barrier or entrance to the monument, as the interior would have been hidden to outsiders on the land, until entering through the Palisade.

Pollard and Pitts suggest that the posts of the Palisade were about 20 feet high (Pollard and Pitts 2008). The Vatchers (Cleal 1995, 155) reported that the average posthole depth in the subway section of the Palisade was just over 4½ feet. Whittle (1997, 154) used a multiplier of 3.5 for estimating the above-ground height of the West Kennet Palisades in Avebury, suggesting a height of nearly 16 feet not 20 feet for the Stonehenge Palisade.

The most recent theory by 'the experts' and a recent paper in 2020 by Lionel Sims from the University of East London, hypothesis's: "This new model suggests that by the Palisades design of interrupted obscuration and the agency of skyscape knowledge in a planar stationary geocentric earth cosmology, a ritual purpose of the Stonehenge monument complex was to simulate a journey through the underworld" – also known as "mumble jumble", for academics who don't have a clue?

Figure 22- Path (orange) of the wooden Palisade to cut of the island from land animals

As my hypothesis has shown that three sides of the monument were cut off by water, the palisade would have effectively created a barrier between two bodies of water cutting off the entire monument, apt for a sacred site, dedicated to the dead.

Moreover, to keep wild animals from eating the corpses laid out on the slabs, the palisade extended down the water's edge to the North West and was later extended to the Avenue when the waters fell during the Neolithic Period. This clearly indicates that the use of the site as an excarnation facility must have stayed relevant for over 5,000 years, as they increased the palisades length to match the water's falling levels.

Figure 23 - How the palisade would have looked

The palisade cuts not only the peninsula off from the mainland but encloses a second peninsular containing some of the most important Long Barrows at Stonehenge - adding more evidence to the belief that the site was created for the sick and the dead who were then buried on the same isolated island peninsular if the treatment was unsuccessful.

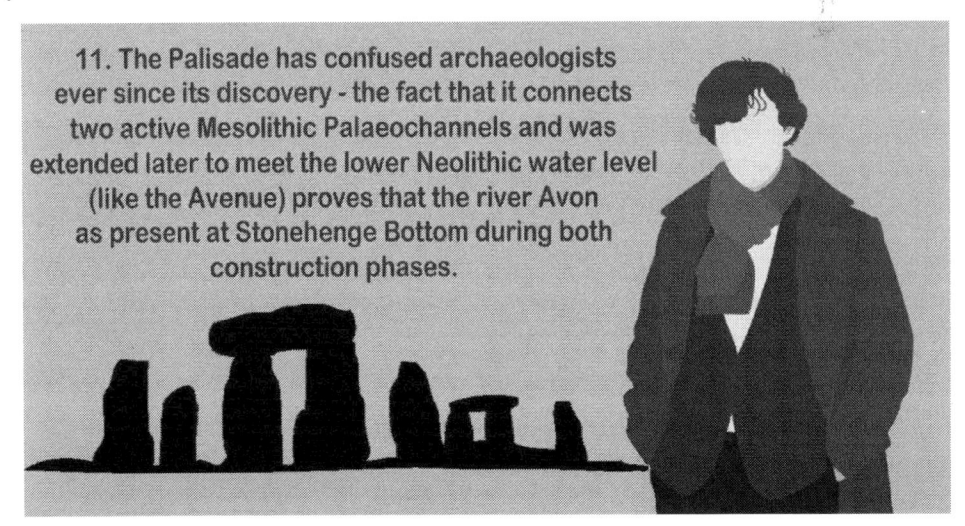

11. The Palisade has confused archaeologists ever since its discovery - the fact that it connects two active Mesolithic Palaeochannels and was extended later to meet the lower Neolithic water level (like the Avenue) proves that the river Avon as present at Stonehenge Bottom during both construction phases.

Prehistoric Britain – The Stonehenge Enigma

CASE STUDY - An inconvenient truth

A recent paper by the University of London, Southampton, and Manchester; about the discovery of the quarry that provided the 'bluestones' for Stonehenge at Craig Rhos-y-Felin (Mike Parker-Pearson et al., 2015) caught the eye of the world by archaeologists announcing Stonehenge was initially built in Wales and was then transferred to Salisbury Plain 500 years later.

The 'Craig Rhos-y-Felin: a Welsh bluestone megalith quarry for Stonehenge' was a report published in December's Edition of Antiquity Magazine 2016, it stated that a series of radiocarbon dates were found on the site next to a 4m long monolith (ready for transportation) made of a rock which was microscopically identified as the same bluestone as the rocks that surround the existing Stonehenge site. Moreover, the report's authors had decided that just two random sample dates (the two closest to their own well-publicised hypothesis on Stonehenge's construction date) would be headlined and advertised to the mass media.

Figure 24 - Craig Rhos-y-felin Quarry

In spite of these 'limited' published radiocarbon dates, the archaeologists still had an obvious problem, as the dates were still 500 years older than the proof, they were hoping to find. So, they had to invent a new 'story' to compensate for this 'poor science' and so stated the speculation, in their report, that the monument was initially built in Wales then moved at a later date. This will no doubt be followed by another story in a few years' time (archaeologists love to do the lucrative lecture tours on limited 'titbits' of information) finding remains of a few small bluestones within a short distance from the quarry site and claiming them as evidence of the original Stonehenge – this would probably be followed by an even more lucrative lecture tour.

Nevertheless, if we take an unbiased and more analytical view of the report, we find something very different from the media claims and much more scientifically interesting.

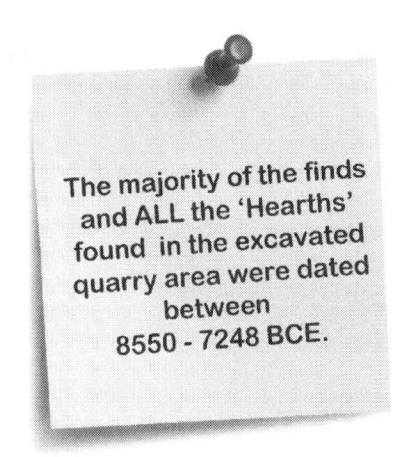

> The majority of the finds and ALL the 'Hearths' found in the excavated quarry area were dated between 8550 - 7248 BCE.

What was contained in detail within the report but overlooked, was the fact that a considerable number of Mesolithic carbon dates (fourteen compared to just two Neolithic dates the report headlined) were obtained from actual human-made hearths which were much, much earlier in history compared to two random nutshells found in an 'occupation area' - which could have been scattered by animals or even the weather?

These earlier and more frequent dates are from hearths rather than just random nutshells and were entirely overlooked by the team, as it was 'perceived' to be too early to have a connection to Stonehenge. Nevertheless, this connection was well established some fifty years ago and was reported in a press release I released in August 2011 - entitled 'The Stonehenge Enigma; an inconvenient truth':

Prehistoric Britain – The Stonehenge Enigma

The article shows that English Heritage did their utmost to conceal the truth about the real 'probable' date of Stonehenge being 5,000 years earlier than their current position. This scientific evidence was based on radiocarbon dating of the three giant post holes found in the visitor's car park during its construction in 1966.

At the time the wooden charcoal remains of the posts (found at the bottom of the post holes) were labelled Neolithic in origin to support the accepted antler pick dating hypothesis and was placed on a shelf probably for eternity.

The report from the 1966 excavation reads: "It is unfortunate that no dating evidence was obtainable from the three holes in the form of pottery. Certainly, the holes themselves would appear to be Neolithic in character, very similar to others excavated of this period..... comparable traces of posts

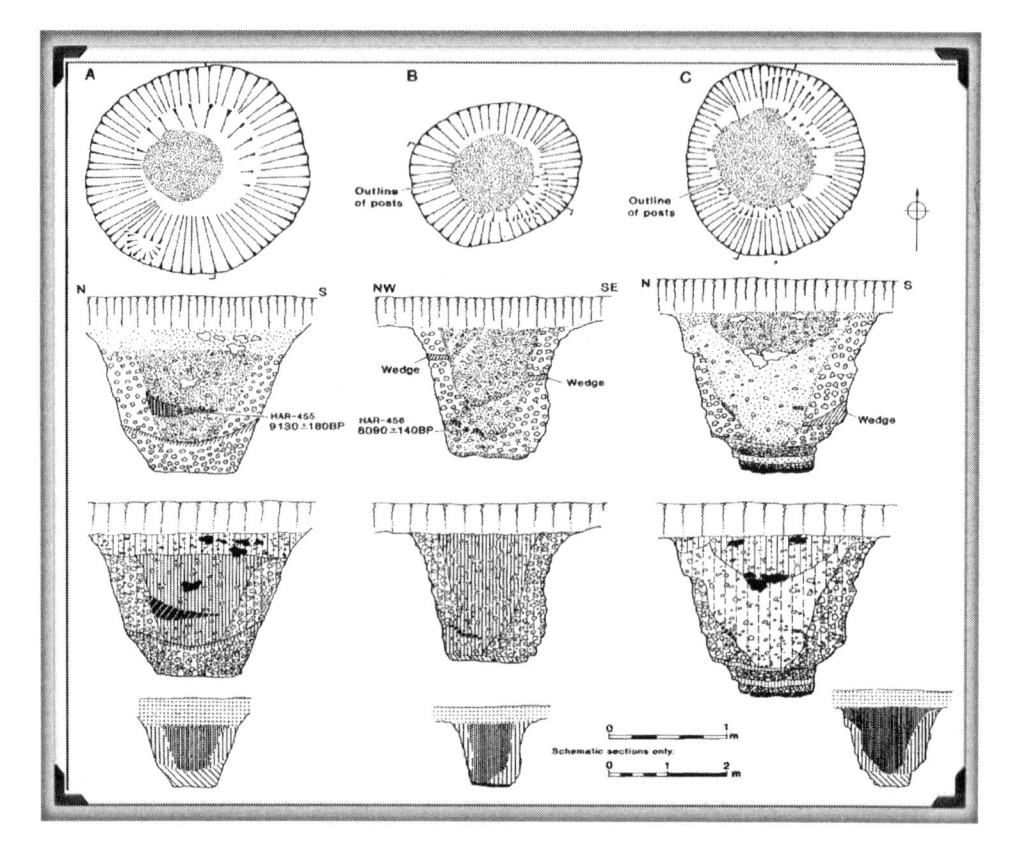

Figure 25- Old Car Park Excavation in 1966

have been found in a Neolithic context... such as King Barrow Wood" Lance and Faith Vatcher. [3]

Moreover, the charcoal deposits were sent to their laboratory, and the results were: "It is surprising, in the view of the chalkland environment, that most of the charcoal should be pine. Pine has, however, been found at other sites where it would not be expected, notably Woodhenge" - but even so, these samples were not requested to be carbon dated.

Fortunately, some years later an inquisitive PhD student writing a thesis on the Stonehenge environment found these samples and concluded that they could not be Neolithic, as claimed by the archaeological community, as they were from pine trees which pollen analysis had concluded were 'extinct' in this area at this time of Stonehenge's supposed construction.

The officials (of the Historic Buildings and Monuments Commission, which was later renamed English Heritage) were dismayed when they found out that their 'experts' were wrong, and the student was absolutely correct (yet sadly, never gave her a deserved job!!) in her assumption as the carbon dating placed them at the start of the Mesolithic of 8860 to 6590 BCE just after the last ice age. Furthermore, what happened to the pine Woodhenge samples as indicated in the lab report of 1966 – which to date have not been carbon dated, are they also Mesolithic and not Neolithic as their original unscientific estimation, if so, what is the real age of Woodhenge?

Consequently, rather than then admitting their fundamental error and re-opening the site to look for more holes and dates to get to the bottom of this unique mystery (which would have been the case for most credible scientific disciplines) they came up with a remarkable and unproven story that these were random 'totem poles' placed by wandering 'hunter-gatherers' which did not relate to the Stonehenge site just 50m away. But was a sheer coincidence, which should be totally ignored.

If the missed carbon dating of these Mesolithic posts didn't spark an enquiry into the dating of Stonehenge, then another similar discovery three years later in 1988-89 should have done, as Wessex Archaeology, were employed to undertake an investigation of the area next to the Old Car Park and the construction of the Visitors Centre, opposite Stonehenge. They reported a series of stripes under the surface (they thought was periglacial) and a single pit WA9580 which was on the line of the other posts found in 1966, in the area of the old ticket office.

Within the pit they found (no doubt to the dismay of EH) yet another Mesolithic post hole that match the dates of the 1966 findings. Moreover, what they also found should have

A piece of Bluestone was found in a Mesolithic post hole - 5,000 years before the site was supposedly built?

transformed the current dating of the Stonehenge site. 40cm below the top of the pit they found 'a single piece of rhyolite (62g) within context layer 9581 at the same stratification level of 9585 carbon dated at 7737 – 7454 BCE.

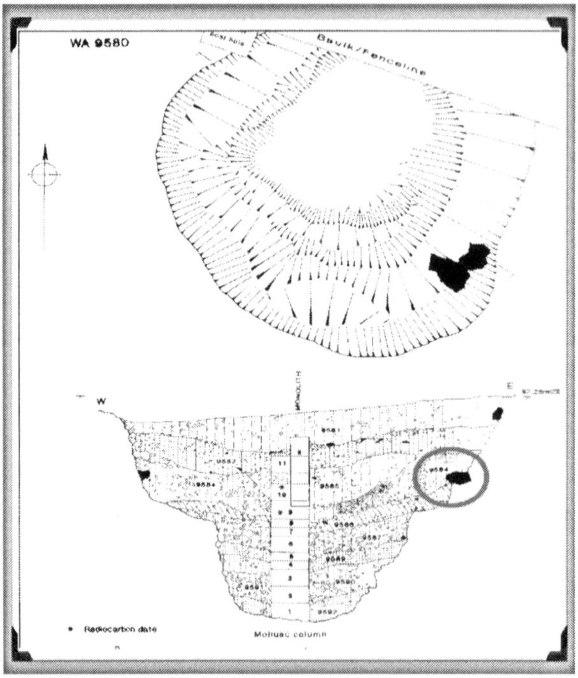

Again EH attempted to supress this finding by suggesting that 'this layer was not earlier than, and was probably contemporary with, the dressing of the Bluestone' – which might be so if the bluestone was not BELOW context layer 9582 which was dated 7595 – 7178 BCE.

Archaeologists have also found charcoal (OxA-18655) from fires in the centre of the Stonehenge monument, found in the Hole socket of

Figure 26- WA 9580 excavated in 1988 which found a Bluestone in the soil 5,000 years before the current EH published date.

> So, why did they not search for more post holes - when the old car park was dug up?

Stone 10 dated 7330 – 7060 BCE (same as the Mesolithic post holes) but again the news was suppressed from the mass media. Then less than a mile away at the top of the hill that overlooks Stonehenge a site called 'blick mead' was excavated by the Open University, they found evidence that people were living and feasting at this same earlier Mesolithic period yet this 'totem pole' myth is still firmly entrenched in EH's view of our prehistoric history through their exhibitions and many costly guidebooks.

Moreover, recently the Stonehenge site has had a significant transformation as it has closed the B-road that went past the stones and gave access to the old visitor's car park - which was now moved a mile up the road to the new multi-million-pound visitors centre. Consequently, the old tarmac was removed and was replaced by grass to make it look more like it did at the time of Stonehenge's construction.

Now one might imagine that if you were going to remove the tarmac from the old visitor's car park (knowing you have found something quite

Figure 27- Tim Daw's unpublished photo of another post in the Old Visitor's Car Park – 600mm to 700mm wide.

extraordinary underneath in the past), you would take this 'once in a lifetime opportunity' to excavate the car park fully to see if you can find any more evidence about the Mesolithic Period of Stonehenge's history?

Tim Daw was a warden at Stonehenge, and he has always been active in taking pictures on the site as he worked on a day-to-day basis at Stonehenge and published them on his blog site. Last year, he found patch marks by the centre upright stones that were identified as the possible missing circle stones of the Inner Circle; therefore, his contribution to the investigation of Stonehenge has been immense.

Tim also took some shots of trenches dug during the reinstatement of the grass over the old visitor's car park and found something quite remarkable - but he was not allowed to publish (his pictures of the trenches) as EH had warned him that his unauthorized blog activities had to stop or else.... three guesses why this happened? Now Tim is a man of principal resisted and resigned so continuing his blog work, and as a consequence, these new 'unofficial' pictures have been made available, showing, even more, post holes are under the car park.

Figure 28- Newly discovered Post Hole D

Tim's newly discovered post hole is on the line of four other known 1966 post holes. Moreover, it supports my hypothesis, that they are all on the shoreline of the River Avon at about 8000 BCE. Furthermore, the fact that rivers in Britain were much larger in the past than today effected on not only the River Avon - but the River Nevern, at Craig Rhos-y-Felin which the current 'Brynberian Stream, (which feeds the Nevern) is only 20m away, from the newly identified quarry site.

During the Mesolithic period, the newly quarried stones could be placed in boats on the shoreline of the quarry in Wales and could be sailed almost directly to Stonehenge, via just two or three enlarged rivers. And not over the longer sea route, some archaeologists have considered.

This report also goes into great depth in the analysing of the Stone structure of the bluestones from other Preseli sites such as Carn Goedog, Cerrigmarchogion and Craig Talfynyydd, Carn Breseb, Carn Gyfrwy and finally Carn Alw areas. All of which have streams and rivers connecting them with the River Nevern – unfortunately, the archaeologists only can conceive this connection is of a 'religious' order rather than something quite functional. Yet, archaeologists do seem able to consider the existence of a hypothetical road system which Mike Parker-Pearson's calls his 'ox-cart' route, that follows the current tarmac covered A40, but sadly doesn't take into account the woods, swamps and even forests of that period, which would make road passing almost impossible.

Nevertheless, this should be no surprise to readers of the Craig Rhos-y-Felin report as it is full of inconsistencies and logical inaccuracies as the layout of the site were never taken into consideration. My analysis of the area shows that the 'Brynberian Stream' by the rocky outcrop was much larger in the past - such as in the period directly after the last ice age. The flooding of this area is well known to geologists as they have found sandy deposits are in the excavation sub-soil. Sadly, the team seems to have created a false assumption that these floodwaters are from 'ice melt' which rapidly disappeared after the ice age into the sea.

Figure 29- Craig Rhos-Y-Felin as it would have looked in the Mesolithic period

We have shown in the first book of the trilogy 'The post-glacial flooding hypothesis' that this is a false assumption. If this was true, the sea levels would have risen rapidly to a couple of meters short of today's sea level then plateaued for thousands of years – but this is not the case as the scientific ocean evidence shows that the 'seepage' into the seas took many thousands of years to occur and hence Doggerland off the East coast of Britain, took almost ten thousand years to disappear under the North Sea.

We obtain this confirmation within the report that an old river ran around this quarry as long ago as 5620 – 5460 BCE and possibly up to 1030 – 910 BCE.

"Most of the site was then covered by a layer of yellow colluvium (035), dated by oak charcoal to 1030–910 cal BC (combine SUERC-46199; 2799±30 BP and SUERC-46203; 2841±28 BP). This deposit is contemporary with the uppermost fill of a palaeochannel of the Brynberian stream that flowed past the northern tip of the outcrop. Charcoal of Corylus and Tilia from the basal fill of this palaeochannel dates to 5800–5640 cal BC (OxA- 32021; 6833±40 BP) and 5620–5460 cal BC (OxA-32022; 6543±37 BP), both at 95.4% probability."

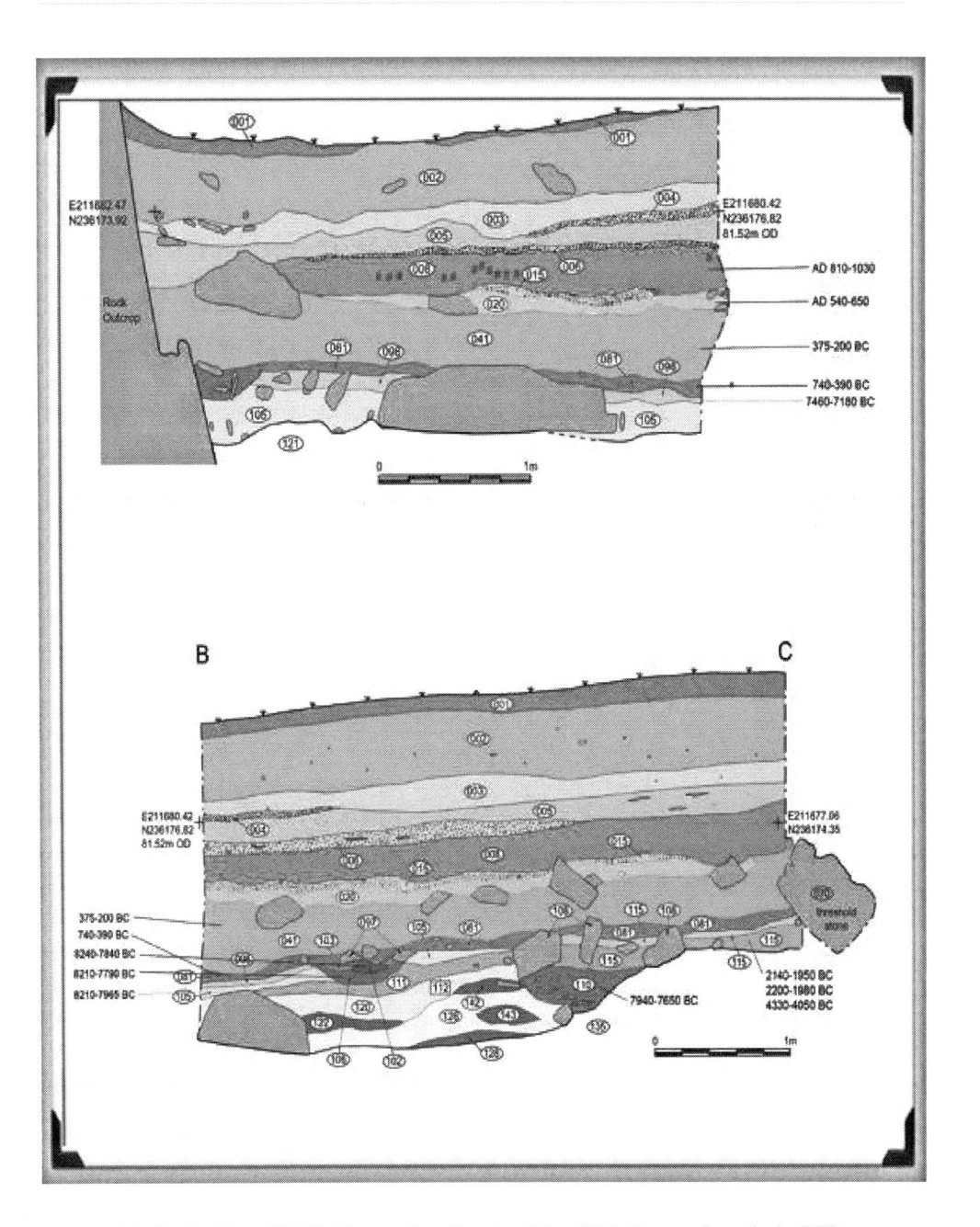

Figure 30- Craig Rhos-Y-Felin Excavation showing Mesolithic human hearths in RED

Consequently, what the report is trying to tell us, is that an enlarged stream that feeds into the River Nevern was flowing at during the Mesolithic Period up to the quarry outcrop rocks, and it remained there just a few metres away even up to 1000 BCE. Therefore, the apparent system of transport for these large newly quarried stones to their final destination at Stonehenge, as we have seen in other countries with their stone constructions like Egypt – was via a boat.

Moreover, the site layout also gives a clear indication of when the stone was genuinely quarried. There is a single monolith ready for transportation by the river on the east side of the site and the hearths which are human-made are a few metres south of this monolith – where you would expect them. The problem for archaeologists is that these are Mesolithic hearths, and they're not just one but three hearths dating from 8550 – 8330 BCE; 8220 – 7790 and BCE 7490 – 7190B CE and yet the report quite clearly states:

"There is no evidence of any Mesolithic Quarrying or working of Rhyolite from this crop".

This is an astonishing unscientific claim - for how they would know what tool marks are either Mesolithic or Neolithic (would they not be using the same tools?) And secondly, what do they think they were doing there at the quarry during these 1300 years?

Moreover, we can now see the massive connection between the quarry site and Stonehenge with over twenty C^{16} dates and correlations to my hypothesis – compared to just two samples the 'experts' are currently claiming (which are 300 – 500 years older than current estimations).

Consequently, we can narrow down the exact date for the construction of Phase I of Stonehenge (bluestone placements in the Aubrey holes) by looking at the overlapping dates and using the latest carbon dating curve (intCal20) to obtain most accurate date variation, and calculating the mean average probable dates.

Table 1- Matching Carbon Dates

Stonehenge Old Car Park		Craig Rhos-Y-Felin (Quarry)	
Post Hole A	HAR-455 (8825 – 7742)	SUERC-50761	8550 - 8330
		OxA-30507	8471 – 8285
		OxA-30548[1]	8286 – 8163
		SUERC-51164	8289 - 8169
		SUERC-50760	8211 – 7955
		OxA-30549	8238 – 7941
		SUERC-51165	8216 – 7785
		OxA-30506	8021 – 7792
		OxA-30548[2]	8122 – 7962
		OxA-30506[2]	8207 - 8030
		OxA-30547	8012 – 7711
		OxA-30504	8281 - 8166
Post Hole B	HAR–456 (7377 – 6651)	OxA-30503[2]	7232 - 7188
WA 9580	GU-5109 (8259 – 7742)	OxA-30548	8286 – 8163
		SUERC-51164	8289 – 8169
		SUERC-50760	8211 – 7955
		OxA-30549	8238 – 7941
		SUERC-51165	8216 – 7785
		OxA-30506	8021 – 7792
		OxA-30548[2]	8122 – 7962
		OxA-30506[2]	8207 - 8030
		OxA-30547	8012 – 7711
		OxA-30504	8281 - 8166
WA 9580	QxA-4219 (7737 – 7454)	Beta-392850	7944 – 7648
		OxA-30547	8012 - 7711
WA 9580	QxA-4220 (7595 – 7178)	SUERC-51163	7539 – 7308
		OxA-30523	7472 – 7182
		OxA-305031[1]	7485 - 7248

This calculation shows that work started at the Quarry: 8300 BCE and its main use and activity was 8000 BCE, with continuous use (replacing the exhausted Bluestones at Stonehenge) ongoing for at least 1000 years.

English Heritage has invested millions in its new 'money spinner' the Stonehenge Visitors Centre. Within it, you will see many claims and models about the origin and possible function of Stonehenge - this exhibition has cost hundreds of thousands of pounds to design and build. BUT what would happen financially, if their assumptions are proven wrong?

So, is this false history a 'cock-up' or a conspiracy?

12. The Mesolithic post holes can not only date Phase I of Stonehenge - they also prove that a river existed at Stonehenge Bottom at that time and was used to move the Bluestones from the Craig Rhos-Y-Felin quarry.

Moreover, the money within archaeology is sparse, and there are many 'schools' of thought who compete against each other for funding. These schools are the University professors who compete for 'airtime' and media attention to promote their views, which the public perceive as 'expertise'. But science evolves, through new ideas and concepts, yet these 'experts' are firmly cemented in the past with old ideas, publications and credibility - as nobody dares to be found wrong when so much hangs in the balance.

Prehistoric Britain – The Stonehenge Enigma

Chapter 3- Stonehenge Phase II

The Avenue

When the waters started to subside, the builders of Stonehenge had an engineering problem: how to cope with the lower groundwater table, to allow the Stonehenge moat to remain full. Firstly, as we have already illustrated, by lining the Stonehenge moat with a clay waterproofing, so it acted like a dew pond, and in this chapter we shall go into detail of how they built a new earthwork called 'the Avenue' with its own moat which brought the waters closer to the monuments bathing moat.

Processional Walkway

The Avenue was created sometime after the original moated henge, once the original Mesolithic groundwater and shoreline lowered towards the new Neolithic groundwater level. When the water levels fell, the builders faced two problems; firstly, the original mooring could no longer accept boats or cargo, so a new entrance was required. Secondly, the moat would no longer fill as it did in Mesolithic times, as the water table had dropped by about 10 metres.

As we have seen from the excavations by Hawley in the 1920s, the builders had added a liner similar to those found in other Mesolithic period constructions like 'dew ponds' also found in this area. The reason for the liner would have been to retain the water that accumulated by the natural rain and seasonal high tides that would have replenished the moat. It is entirely plausible that insufficient, or infrequently water levels were a common occurrence during the late Mesolithic, therefore if they wished to continue the bluestone treatments, an alternative method to fill the moat needed to be found.

The Avenue is quite curious, and excavations have revealed its ongoing development, as indicated by the post holes dotted down its entire length. This clearly shows that it 'adapted' over a long period to match the retreating shoreline in the Neolithic period, which lasted over two and a half thousand years. Moreover, the physical construction of the Avenue earthwork shows the incorporation of water features. The Southern ditch is much shallower than the Northern ditch of the Avenue. This is because the water lies on the Southern side of the Avenue and does not need extra depth to fill the Southern ditch evenly, while the Northern ditch is further away from the water (and on a gradient). For it to fill evenly to the same depth of water as the Southern ditch, the Northern ditch would therefore need to be 10% deeper. Furthermore, this extra depth to one side of the monument can also be seen in the main ditch of Stonehenge as the main ditch corresponding to the northern avenue ditch is also 10% deeper.

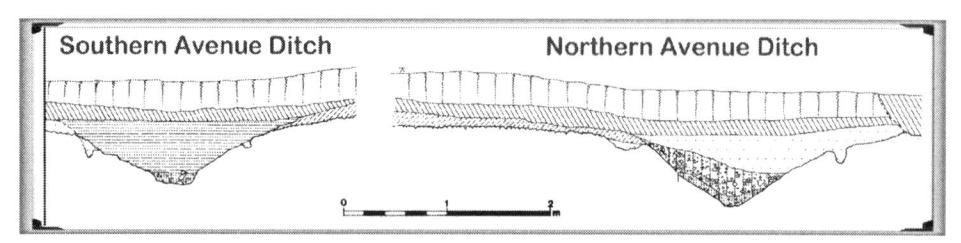

Figure 31- North and South Avenue Ditch comparison

13. The Avenue ditch on the northern side is 10% deeper than the southern side - this variation also happens where the Avenue ditch meets the main Stonehenge moat.

This is proof that the ditches were dug to find the water table at the time of construction.

The wooden poles within the Avenue seem to be somewhat sporadic and impractical at first glance. But if you then add the prehistoric waters to the Avenue, you can see that the poles actually line up in pairs. These pairs of posts seem to appear every ten metres as you proceed down the Avenue, indicating that the Avenue was created in sections. This is a consequence of the periodic need to replacement of the poles as the shoreline retreated. The first main brace of these shoreline poles are seen quite close to the famous North-Eastern entrance by the Heel Stone, extending to the last evidence of the poles at the 'elbow' at the end.

The current 'expert' theories suggest that the path of the Avenue is a processional walkway down to the River Avon. But a careful study of this walkway shows that it makes absolutely no sense in the route it follows - it's not direct, nor logical in its course. What the avenue shows as we see today, is the continuation of its association with the River Avon, after the original Avenue that finished at Stonehenge Bottom had fallen into disuse. This explains the strange haphazard route it now shows. Archaeologists, not finding the valid reason for its course, attempt to justify the route as a 'ceremonial' pathway, which ignores the facts. These 'facts' are compounded as later ancestors constructed Barrows that mimicked their ancestor's constructions and placed burials within them, totally confusing the timeline.

But haven't they put the cart before the horse on this one?

The later attempts to keep a connection to the original builders of Stonehenge can be seen in the Avenue as it moves off to the North East for about 500 metres (the original construction), then suddenly swings off East for another 1,000 metres, then turns again and heads South, like a stretched lower case 'n'. Archaeologists suggest that this is a 'natural route' deliberately passing burial mounds that lay to the East of Stonehenge.

Prehistoric Britain – The Stonehenge Enigma

The facts are; the walkway came first, followed by the introduction of the burial mounds – which is borne out by carbon dating showing that the Avenue was first introduced in Neolithic times, and the burial mounds much later in the Iron Age. Also, archaeologists have identified that the Avenue was built in sections; the first section up to the 'elbow', according to Julian Richards in his book 'The Stonehenge Environs Project', was built during what archaeologists' call 'Period II', including:

- Modification of the original enclosure
- Entrance
- Construction of the first straight stage of the Avenue
- Erection of the Station Stones
- Resetting of the two entrance stones
- Dismantling of the double bluestone circle

> If the Avenue was a processional route, why stop it in the middle of nowhere, only to eventually be joined to the Avon thousands of years later?

Our hypothesis (unlike the current expert views) answers this question fully. The Avenue was built to meet the new shoreline that emerged during the Neolithic period, where (as at the old North West entrance) they received and moored the boats, cargo, and even the stones. Consequently, this then acted as a new entrance to the Stonehenge monument.

Further evidence of this shoreline can be seen in the post holes found in the Avenue. These post holes do not make sense, as they would have blocked the walkway unless they are mooring posts for various phases in the Avenue's construction and water level. A small survey carried out from 1988 to 1990 investigated the last

100m of the Avenue up to the elbow. (Cleal et al., 1995) It found 14 large post holes that could have been used as moorings for boats. These moorings are paired off at 45 degrees to the Avenue, which would match the exact shoreline predicted over several periods.

Recent investigations have revealed that as well as post holes down the Avenue, there is a distinctive man-made mound of 'clay and flint' called Newall's mount (named after it's discoverer) and a second mount, can also

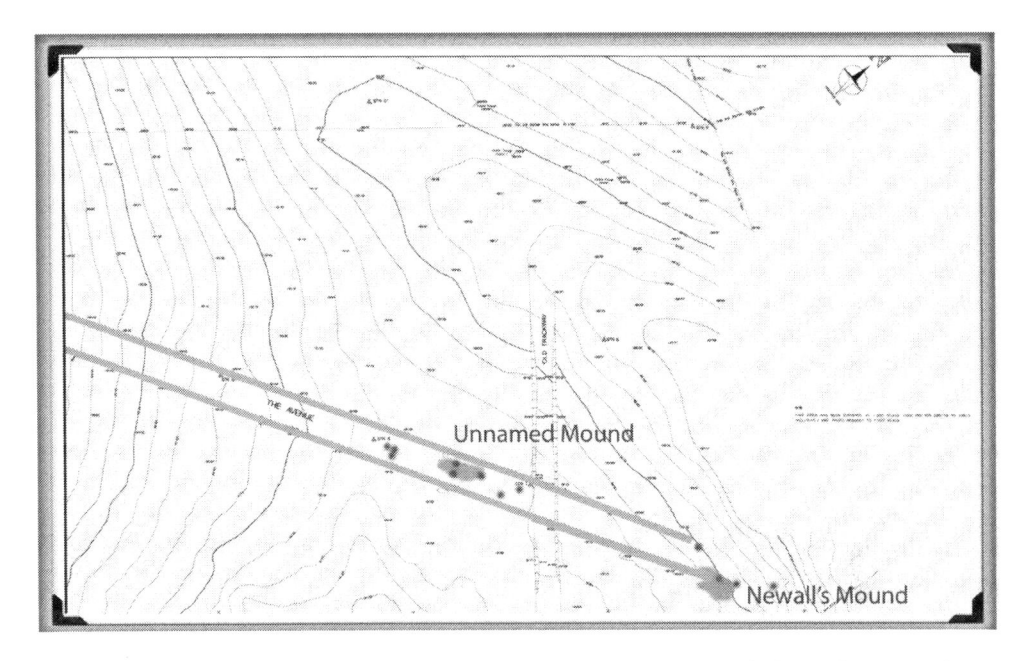

Figure 32- The Avenue showing its termination and the wooden post holes and man-made mounds that were used to unload ships and boats

be found on the contour maps of the avenue (but has yet to be named or excavated), which has the same characteristics and post hole alignment. This indicates that these human-made mounds were used as raised platforms to unload boats as they could not serve any other practical purpose. (Stonehenge - the environment in the Late Neolithic and Early Bronze Age and a Beaker-Age burial, WANHS Magazine, 78, 1984, pp. 7-30)

NB. Such platforms are also found in the nearby site of Avebury, at a location I called Silbury Avenue, (which I discovered in 2014) and leads over Waden

Hill, to a mooring platform called 'Waden Mount' located by photographer Pete Glastonbury in 2004. (Langdon, 2015, 'Avebury's Lost Stone Avenue')

We can also date the extension past the 'elbow', as it no longer has the elaborate moats on either side of the processional walkway. The Avenue beyond the 'elbow' travels over a series of hillocks that could not hold water at any level and therefore made such moats useless and unnecessary. This, again, shows that our ancestors were practical and pragmatic people who included aspects such as ditches for useful purposes, not for religious or aesthetic reasons as current archaeologists believe.

At this stage of the monument's construction, I believe Stonehenge finally turned from being a monument to the moon, for curing the sick for excarnating the dead, to become a shrine to life and the sunrise - which was, in the Bronze Age and after that, taken over by a new civilisation of druids and iron age tribal cultures.

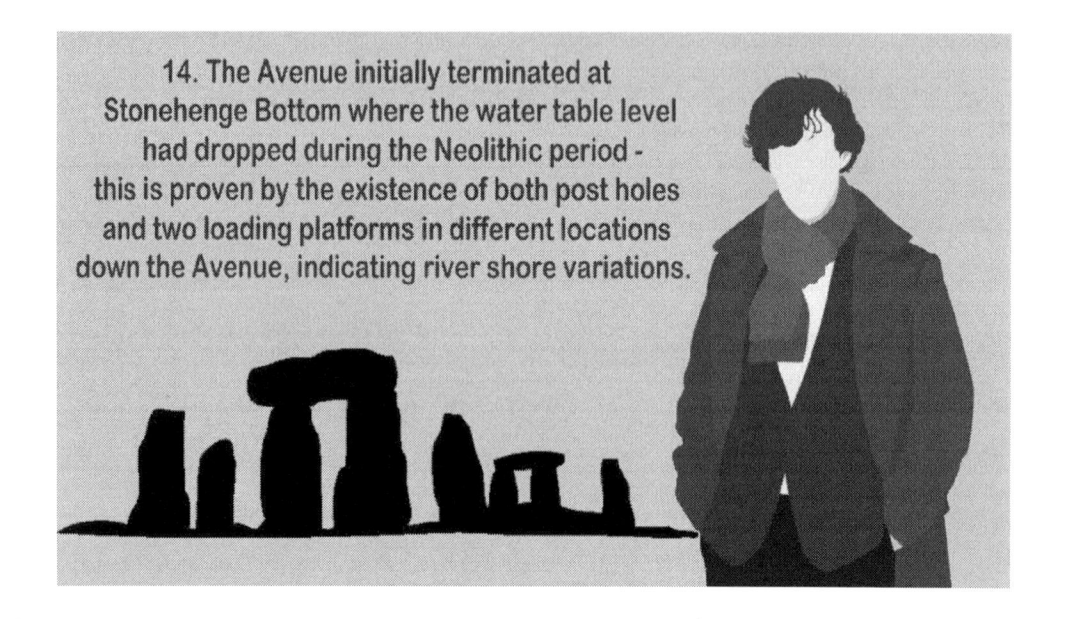

14. The Avenue initially terminated at Stonehenge Bottom where the water table level had dropped during the Neolithic period - this is proven by the existence of both post holes and two loading platforms in different locations down the Avenue, indicating river shore variations.

The Avenue II

An indication of the changes that were introduced in Phase II of Stonehenge can be seen in the development of the Avenue to maintain the ceremonial link between Stonehenge and the river system. Our ancestors started by backfilling the ditch in the North-East sector of the site. Both Hawley and Atkinson observed that the secondary filling was not natural. This backfill extended to a depth of 1 m, at which pottery and bluestone fragments are first seen, clearly indicating that it preceded the arrival of the bluestones.

When the Avenue was first constructed, it could have had a dual purpose: to serve as the new mooring processional way for the dead, and also to help maintain the groundwater levels, because the moat had been reduced to a trickle as a consequence of the lower river levels.

We have seen in the archaeological section of our hypothesis that Hawley had found a liner in the moat. This liner would not have been required when the moat was first constructed, as the groundwater tables were sufficiently high to fill the moat, whether daily or periodically. But a liner would have been necessary once the tidal groundwater no longer reached the base of

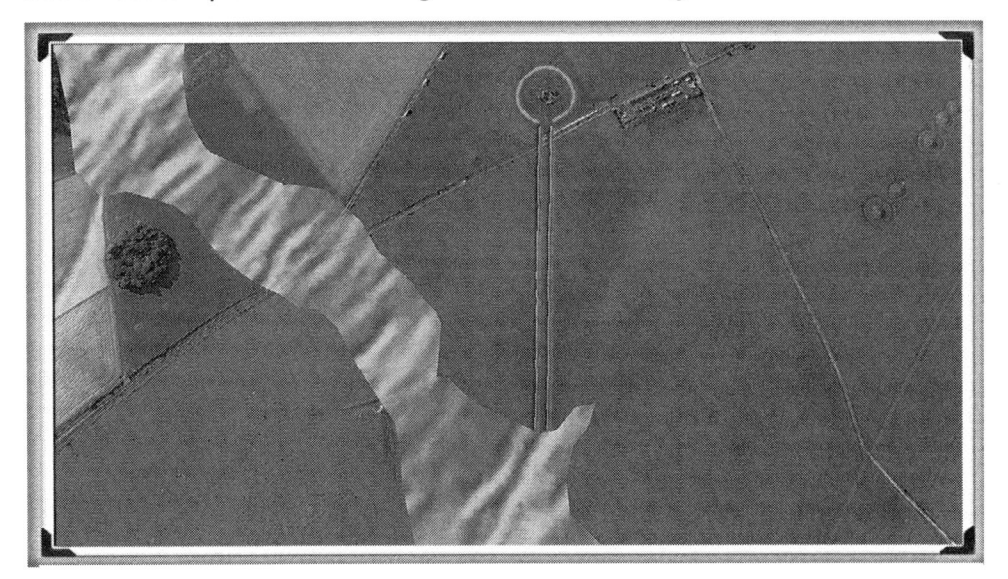

Figure 33- The Avenue terminating at Stonehenge bottom showing the ditches on each side

the pits. To keep the moat waters at a suitable depth, the pits would have needed to be topped up from time to time with either groundwater from the receding rivers around Stonehenge, precipitation like dew ponds or manual transference (or a combination of all three).

The Avenue is a processional causeway that had a deep trench built into both sides (over 1m deep in places). This trench is totally unnecessary unless there is another reason for its use, and that reason was either practical or symbolic.

The ditch allows water to travel along the Avenue all the way up to the existing moat, but there is no evidence that it is directly connected – but it doesn't need to be as we have already illustrated the fact that chalk is a porous material that will allow water to flow through it over short distances.

Sarsen Stones

The Sarsen stones would have been brought to the Stonehenge site before the river disappeared from 'Stonehenge Bottom" to become the River Avon of today. The reason why our ancestors used Sarsen stones is fascinating, as the original structure, which consisted of Welsh bluestones, lasted over 4,000 years as a centre for curing sickness. Clearly, they had a requirement for a very large monument built of a different stone.

From an engineering point of view, the size and structure were significant, and because of the size of these stones, the most effective means of transportation to this site would again be by boat. Even though the deeply forested landscape would have started to thin, the sub-soils would still have been waterlogged and marshy after the groundwater had receded, making it impossible to drag heavy stones across large distances.

The construction of the Sarsen monument is of even greater interest, because if they were building only for aesthetic pleasure, then you would imagine that simply laying one giant stone on top of another would be sufficient, as seen at other megalithic sites. But our ancestors wanted to do something special with these stones, so they carved mortise and tenon joints on their surfaces. The only engineering reason for this method of construction would be that they required this site to last for a considerable time in history and hence it's importance to this civilisation.

The exact date of this process may never be fully known, for we have yet to excavate fully and carbon date the post holes in the Avenue similar to those in the car park at Stonehenge, which would give us an accurate date. But we still have a few clues to provide us with an approximate date, as we know that the river must yet have been present at the end of the Avenue for the unloading of these stones to take place. And it must have been after the groundwater left the North West shoreline, but before the groundwater reached the 'elbow'.

The arranging of the Sarsen stones has left archaeologists without any clues about the dating of Stonehenge. The current theories are based on pottery, and the dating of antler picks found in the ditch; all these items could have been left at a later date. For traditional archaeologists to be correct, then the pottery and the antler picks had to be left 'in situ', the archaeologist's way of saying that something has not moved from the place where it was originally deposited – unfortunately, they were not!

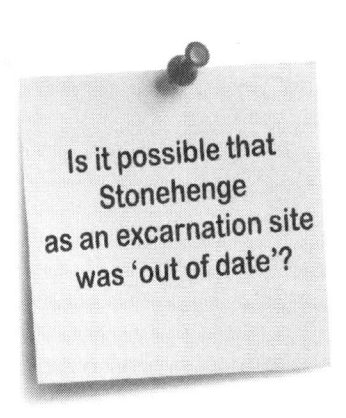

Is it possible that Stonehenge as an excarnation site was 'out of date'?

As an example, the antler picks were found in the ditch. If the moat had been dug and then left untouched for 5,000 years, then you could have an entirely accurate date – but we have proved that the ditch was in fact a moat filled with groundwater. These picks would have floated away. All we can say regarding the picks is that the last time the moat was cleaned out was about 2500 BCE – and that's it! And the same can be said about the pottery.

Let's revisit the Avenue. It clearly follows a path to the river, but the river reached all the way to the East of the site in Neolithic times, and therefore, in theory, the Avenue could have been built anywhere. So why did they build it in that particular direction? The North West entrance is oriented quite deliberately towards the midwinter moonset, perceived as the place of the dead and afterlife. After 4,000 years, is it possible that the monument changed its purpose? Four thousand years is a colossal amount of time – the same period before now, we were in the Bronze Age living in mud huts and dancing to druid music. In the landscape, we see that the monument's use changed, as round barrows started to appear, and burial practices started to change.

If so, perhaps they decided to use the trusted waters of the past still, but change it from curing the sick to celebrating life and rebirth through the sun.

This may explain why the Avenue was oriented to the summer sunrise and, this being the case, give us our third clue to the date the site was built. We are familiar with the masses that welcome the midsummer sunrise over Stonehenge – people wait in expectation, then (if you're lucky) the sun creeps over the Heel Stone to welcome another day; everyone's happy and goes home drunk. When you look at the Heel Stone, it is on the extreme right-hand side of the Avenue, bent over at a silly angle. Our ancestors did not build it that way – the monument was very nearly completely rebuilt at the end of the last century, and stones were moved, and this process happened throughout Stonehenge's history.

The most sensible alignment is straight down the middle of the avenue. This is apparent alignment has only been partially investigated and as a result questions the 'traditional' dating of the site

The sun does not always rise and set in the same place in history as you may expect. The earth 'wobbles' on its axis in a process known as 'procession' - I will not go into detail here, but all you need to understand is that the Sun and moon rises and sets in a different location over a 43,000 year period.

This means that the summer and winter Solstice moves in relation to the horizon a fraction every year. This movement is TINY it's .0002 of a degree every year, but over a long time, say 10,000 years it's a full two degrees. It may not sound much, but when you consider that the moon is half a degree in diameter, then two degrees is the same as four moons (or suns) in a row on the horizon.

We can also 'reverse engineer' this figure to give us a date for the construction of the Avenue. The problem with this measurement is that the point of sunrise is somewhat subjective – as the horizon is obscured with trees at Stonehenge, so the tip of the first sunlight can never be fully seen. What current observers accept is the position of the 'Heel Stone' which obscures the sunrise until a point that it appears to rise above the stones upper part (the peak point).

Figure 34- The Avenue showing the summer solstice sunrise at the time of construction

If we accept, this is the correct point for today's Summer solstice sunrise and plot this point on Google Earth – we obtain a reading of 50.81 degrees. If we now take a reading down the centre of the avenue with the same software, we get a reading of 49.57 degrees. This is a difference of 1.24 degrees since the Avenue was constructed. If each year the sun moves 0.0002 degrees per annum then we will have an approximate date (when the sun is at the centre of the Avenue) this, gives us a construction date of 6200 years ago, or 4180 BCE.

Moreover, to support this dating - there is one antler bone that was found under a Sarsen stone, which does not support the current dating. Now this one can't be explained away like the others, as a 12 ton stone was on top of it for thousands of years, guaranteeing that it could not have been placed there at a later date, or floated there from another part of the site.

It was found in the 'packing' for Sarsen Stone 27 (OxA-4902). This gives us a carbon dating of 4342 – 4039 (IntCal20) or 4191 BCE +/- 152, which is remarkably similar to the Avenue dating method. Therefore, I am happy to conclude that Stonehenge phase two started around 4185 BCE.

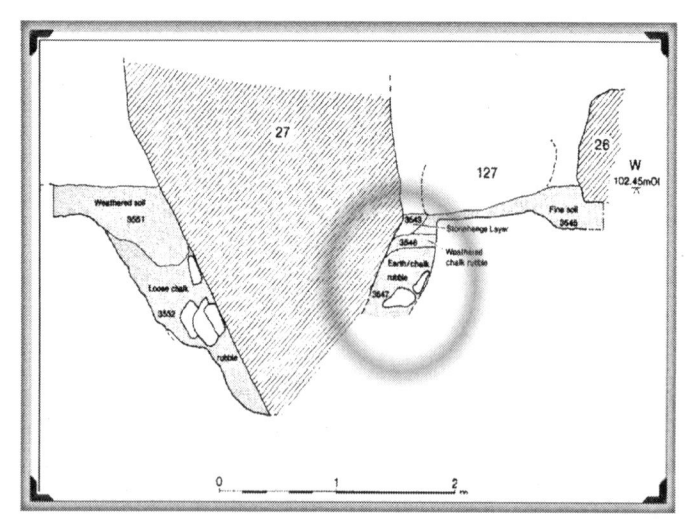

Figure 35- Antler bone found in Stone 27 filling dated 4191 BCE

The experts suggest that the antler bone was placed there by 'accident' and was found in the vicinity of the stone hole when constructed – sadly, this is very improbable as the bone would have been some 1700 years old (if current theory dates are correct) and would have rotted any if found on or near the surface.

Station Stones

The Station Stones seem to have been added during Phase II of the site's development. Aubrey post holes would have been obscured by the introduction of the Station Stones; therefore, they must post-date the original bluestone circle but predate the infilled moat, as they have moats of their own. Whether the knowledge of the tides was no longer necessary, or the station posts held a particular purpose, we currently don't know.

Modern theories use astroarchaeology alignments based on these posts to speculate on the reasons for their existence. Unfortunately, only two of the four Station Stones have a mound and moat, which does not make sense if they are as crucial as these theorists believe. These moats were directly connected to the main moat, as we have proved in the previous chapter. Our ancestors-built barrows as signposts, not burial mounds. These markers are aligned to show not only where to go but, more importantly, how to get home.

If you lived in the countryside or became a fell-walker in the days before GPS and OS maps, you used to have to rely on points on the horizon for guidance. The same simple principle would have been used by prehistoric man to get from A to B without getting lost. Initially, these features would have been on islands, as people used boats to transport themselves and trade. Then, as the groundwater fell, they would have used barrows as markers on the horizon to walk from point to point. We still see milestones today on the side of roads; barrows were the milestones of prehistoric man.

Well, if you follow the line from the centre of the site through the Northern Station Stone, you will go past no less than five long barrows, 15 round barrows, Casterley Camp, Knap Hill Camp, and the White Horse, finally arriving at Avebury. This is not bad, for just 36.4 km of travel. That's one barrow every 500 metres; not even I could get lost with that marker frequency. Mathematically, the chance of this number of barrows being in line over such a small distance is less than half of one per cent (0.05 %), or 2000 to 1 in layman's terms.

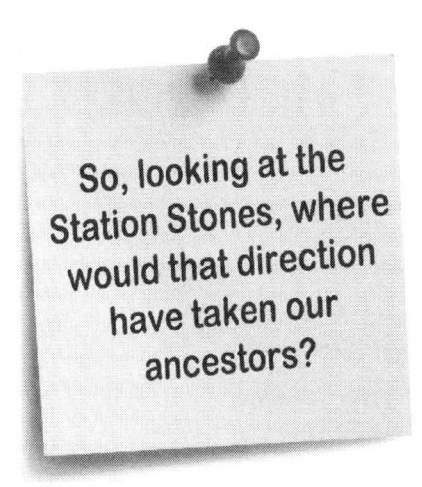

So, looking at the Station Stones, where would that direction have taken our ancestors?

The Southern Station Stone points the way to Old Sarum near Salisbury. Although it is famous for being the site of the original Salisbury Cathedral, archaeologists have also found evidence here of flint tools that date back to 3000 BC. We believe that there is a clear indication that Old Sarum was first used in the Mesolithic Period when it was an island above the raised groundwater level, and that (as in many cases) later sites were built upon the location of this original construction. We look in-depth at this site later in this section.

> 15. The Station Stones (including the Heel Stone) were constructed to point towards Stonehenge's neighbouring sites on the River Avon.
>
> Ditches were dug around the stones to turn them into moats - proof that this was a boat society with their sites on the Mesolithic shorelines.

The most interesting of all the original markers at Stonehenge must be the Heel Stone. The Heel Stone is slightly right of centre in the Avenue and, like two of the Station Stones, it has its own moat. If we line ourselves up with the Heel Stone from the centre of Stonehenge, it aligns with Durrington Walls and Woodhenge. These three places would have been not only essential neighbouring sites to Stonehenge but a gateway to other sites and trading places in the ancient world. Next to each of the moated Station Stones, there was a gap left in the moat to allow people to cross by the stone in the direction it indicated. This no doubt led the walker along a path, now lost to us 5,000 years later, via a system of barrows, to the desired location.

Monument to the Dead

The most popular view of Stonehenge is of a completely round monument with lintel stones completing the circle - but there is a massive problem with this idea, for not all the stones or the stone holes are present. Some people have suggested that the monument is incomplete, but those individuals do not understand its significance and the reason behind the construction.

> Consequently, Stonehenge is aligned with the Winter Solstice Sunset

A monument to the dead as we have previously illustrated, would not face the Summer Solstice Sunrise, it would either face the moon's furthest setting in the night's sky (the northwest and the lost Mesolithic pathway) or it would face Winter Solstice Sunset to mark the shortest day - when light finally overcomes the darkness the symbolism of rebirth (life after death).

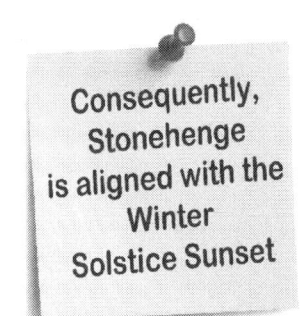

Another reason to ignore the reference to a solar temple, is that the Sun is usually represented as life and a circular symbol as we see in many ancient civilisations in the Middle East and South and Central America – where monuments to the dead are represented by the moon and particularly, a crescent moon.

Figure 36- Stonehenge was 'crescent' shaped not round

Stonehenge was designed to be crescent-shaped, with an alignment to the Winter Solstice Sunset and hence the construction and alignment with a trilithon (two standing stones with a third suspended on top of the two uprights) in the south-west quadrant. Which only one survives and is still upright, which is not surprising as the druids in the Iron Age altered the monuments symbology by pulling the Heel stone to an awkward angle to meet the sunrise of the Summer Solstice, and no doubt pulled down the trilithon in the south-west quadrant.

The 'crescent within the crescent' (the larger horseshoe trilithon standing stones) that faces the Summer solstice sunrise; this is very symbolic as it represents rebirth or reincarnation, it's a poignant message through the ages to us (the descendants of this civilisation), that their homeland may be dead, but the survivors still live on, to begin again.

This can be proven in various ways. In archaeological terms, the fact that the stones are missing is a problem for archaeologists, unless the monument was incomplete.

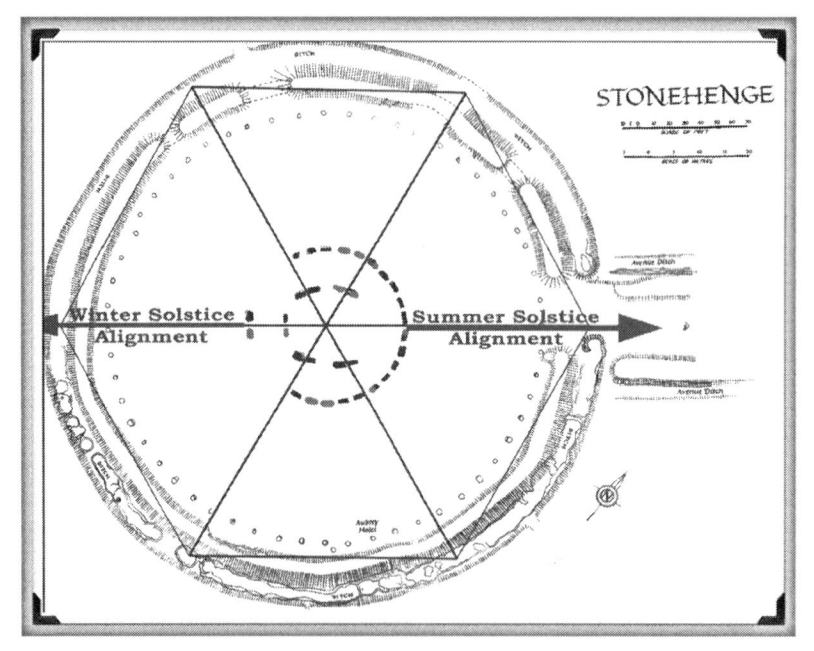

Figure 37 - Stonehenge hexagonal design

All the so-called missing stones of the monument are in the SW quadrant; this area is the furthest away from any roads – if you are going to cart away stones would you not start at a point nearest a road, rather than the stones furthest away.

The second problem with the Solar temple is that some of the existing stones that have not been moved or chipped away are not large enough to take a horizontal lintel stone – such as stone 11. Consequently, the only type of monument that the site could have been designed for is the crescent moon facing the Winters Solstice Sunset.

This is confirmed if you consider how the structure was designed. It would have been based using strings to the centre and the moat forming a Hexagram (the reason this form was used is further discussed in the last book of the trilogy: 'Dawn of the Lost Civilisation').

Slaughter Stone

In the centre of the Sarsen circle lays an extraordinary stone - the Altar stone, the reason it's unique is two-fold. Firstly, it's made of material, unlike the other Sarsen standing stones, called mica. 'Hawkins makes note that while all the other stones were either bluestone or Sarsen, the so-called altar-stone is 'of fine-grained pale green sandstone, containing so many flakes of mica that its surface, wherever freshly exposed, shows the typical mica glitter'. The second reason is that it was positioned to be flat to the landscape; the only other stone that was designed in that fashion is the Slaughter Stone.

Most archaeologists believe that the Slaughter Stone was once a standing stone at the entrance of the monument, these are flawed theories, and a result of a hypothetical drawing by Inigo Jones in 1655. This drawing shows Stonehenge as a perfect circle (Roman Solar Temple) with hexagon-shaped trilithon and three entrances into the site with six erect standing stones as access points, which the slaughter stone was one. This idea was incorporated in John Aubrey's drawing in 1666, which was more accurate, but again had the tendency to place all the fallen stones in upright positions.

This false assumption was further compounded by William Cunning in 1880 when (it was reported) that he suggested his grandfather "saw" the upright slaughter stone in the 17th Century). This mistake was later corrected, yet the myths among archaeologists still remain (Stones of Slaughter, E Herbert Stone, 1924, pp120).

The reality is that the slaughter stone was always (like the Altar Stone) a deliberate recumbent as the excavations of this stone by Hawley and Newall in the 1920s clearly show, as the chalk subsoil was also deliberately flattened before it was placed in its current position. Hawley presumed that the Slaughter Stone was once 'buried', this idea is understandable as the stone

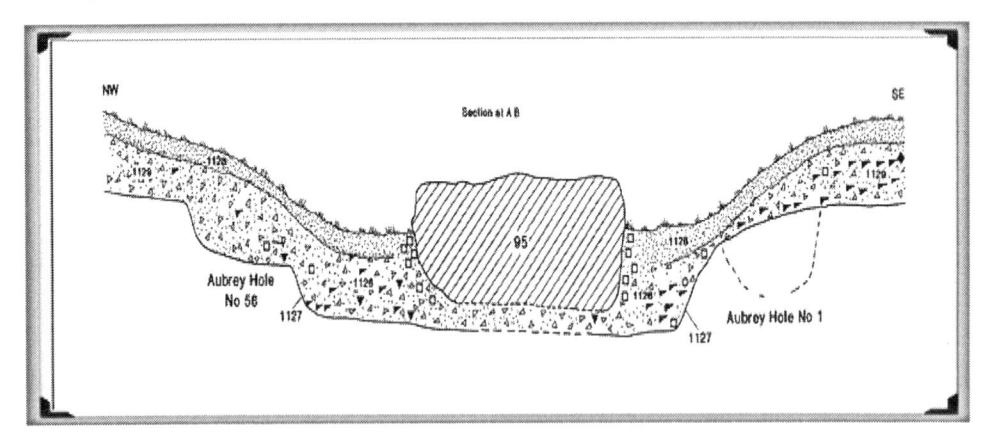

Figure 38- Slaughter stone was deliberately buried below the chalk surface.

does lay below the ground level, but what Hawley never understood is that the reason the stone was in this position was for the same reason the ditch was built around Stonehenge, as it was made to be full of water.

This can be observed by the size of the stone hole called 'E' (WA1165) which lays two metres, North West of the Slaughter stone, but still within the 'hollow' that also contains the stone. Most stone holes at Stonehenge are relatively shallow – less than a metre in-depth, but stone hole 'E' is twice as deep, over 2m. If the Slaughter stone was placed in it (as the experts some have suggested) it would only be 3m high on the surface, compared to 4.57m for the Heel Stone a few yards away.

The only other place in Stonehenge with these more massive pits are within the Ditch section that surrounds the site, which is the same depth allowing access to the groundwater levels In the past when the Slaughter stone was

Prehistoric Britain – The Stonehenge Enigma

placed in this ditch, like the moat, water would have surrounded the stone like an island.

Therefore, what we see today at Stonehenge is a 6,000-year-old relief map of the land the megalithic builders originated from – Doggerland, which now lays below the North Sea.

Not only did they place a 6ft piece of Sarsen stone, flat in a watery ditch, but they also carved out the contours of the island, showing high and low ground, like a contour relief map. Archaeologists have always believed these features were 'weather-worn' by age (although the other recumbent stones have not been weathered in the same fashion), but recent laser technology has confirmed our belief, that this stone was actually carved, as the markings from the tools used, can still be seen at microscopic levels.

Moreover, and more importantly, the stone has been placed in a bizarre position, almost in the way of The Avenue. This shows that this stone and the Avenue have a connection, this type of relationship we see in association with Egyptian Pyramids when 'sight lines' are cut into the sides of the burial chambers to important star constellations to show their associations with the Gods.

16. The Slaughter Stone was deliberately buried into the chalk bedrock and hole WA1165 was dug two metres deep to tap into the ground water and flood the ditch surrounding the stone to create a feature of an island surrounded by water - this proves that groundwater remained even during the Neolithic period around Stonehenge.

Prehistoric Britain – The Stonehenge Enigma

At Stonehenge, the Slaughter Stone and the Avenue are important as they link rebirth with the death of this Great Civilisation, for if we look from the altar stone pasted the slaughter stone they make a sightline, which quite remarkably points directly to Doggerland, as it was located as a small island at the time of the Avenues construction in 4100 BCE. Geologists currently estimate the sinking of Doggerland as two thousand years earlier at 6200 BCE, as they have found a Tsunami that would have hit the island at that point in history.

Yet, as we have seen in the Indian ocean and Japan – when tsunami's hit, they do NOT sink the region, sadly this is just another example of bad science. This is confirmed with a bit of simple maths, as we know that the island is between 15m – 36m (average 25m) (Wikipedia) under the sea as a sandbank (and hence covered in modern-day wind farms). And we know (from satellites) that the sea rises 3.6mm per annum – consequently, by 4100 BCE it was still 6m above sea level, but probably so small it was uninhabitable.

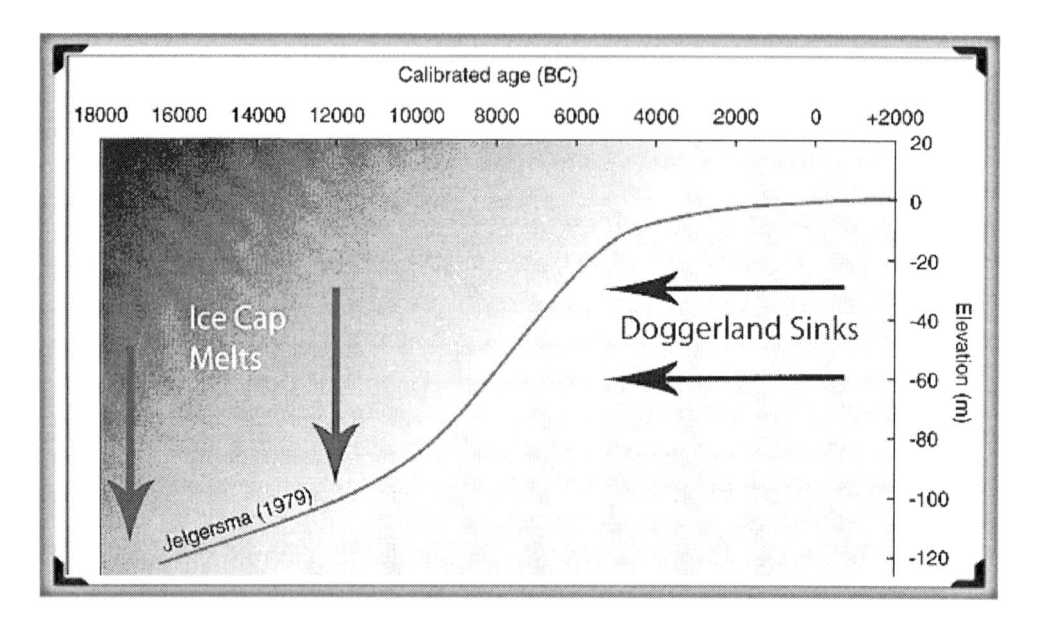

Figure 39 - Sea Level Changes sunk Doggerland

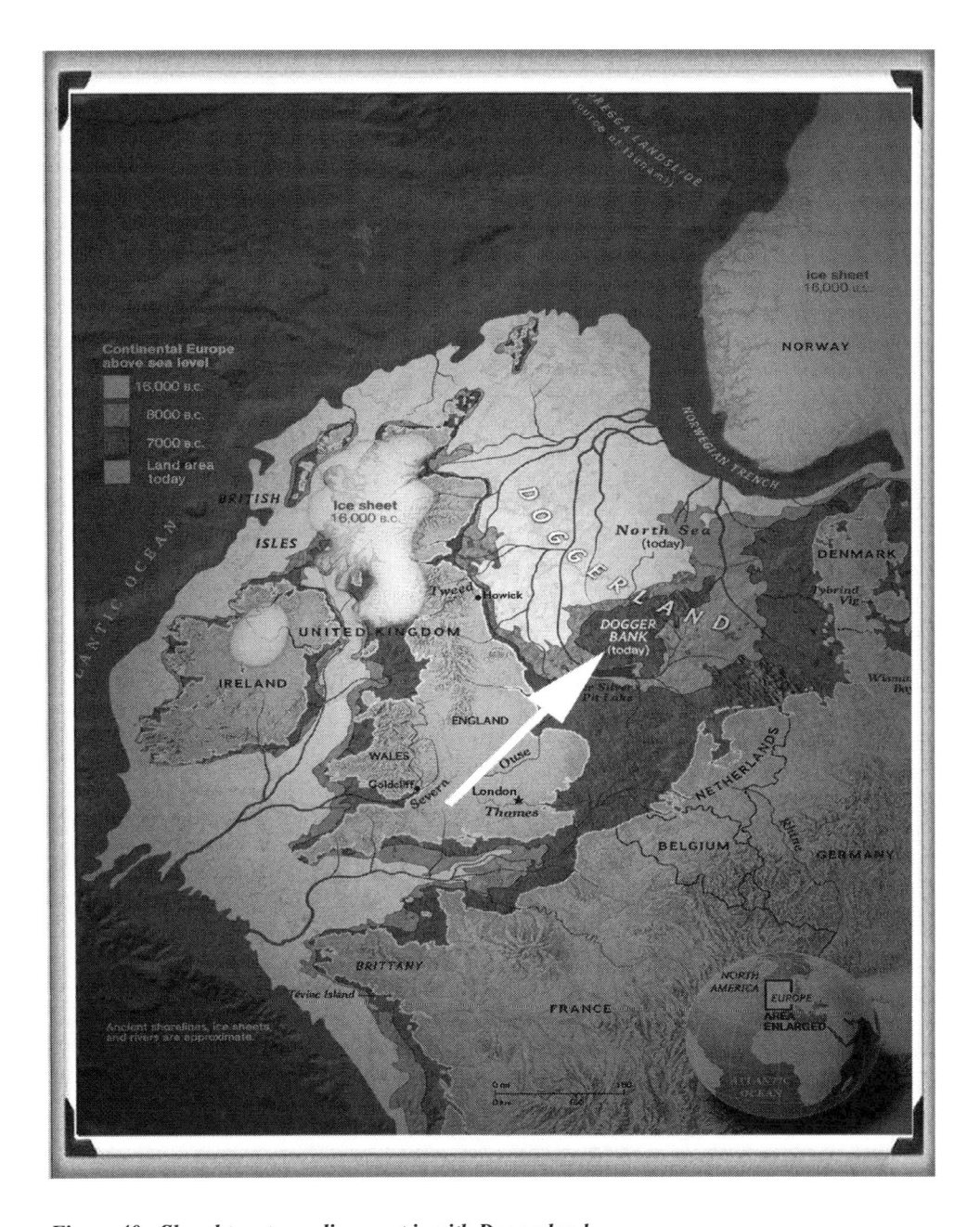

Figure 40 - Slaughter stone alignment is with Doggerland

Snails

Archaeologists use the discovery of small snails in the excavation soils to understand the prehistoric conditions, and possible uses, of the land surrounding archaeological sites. Scientists believe that if we can understand the species and number of these creatures found within the soil samples excavated, we may have a more unambiguous indication of the environment our ancestors inhabited. This methodology can also help us to see if the environment was flooded in the past especially when it comes to excavating ditches to see if they once held water and as a method of dating these moats.

Mollusca

If we look at the site at W58 Amesbury (Coneybury Henge), archaeologists (in this case Roy Entwistle for the 'The Stonehenge Environs Project') traditionally interpret the evidence gained by identifying individual mollusc species, as indicating that taller vegetation must have been present nearby at the time of its construction - as the C. Tridentatum snail inhabits only grasslands. Unfortunately, when you look at the numbers, the assumption just does not 'add up', for only 204 of that breed of snail were found out of a total of 1145 in that sample. Some open-field snails, like C. Tridentatum, also seem to love shaded habitats such as deep forest litter and primeval woodland, according to Dr Roy Anderson's report (Species Inventory of Northern Ireland, 1996). Consequently, the only thing we know for sure is that snails like dark wet places, so they can be found under logs; but if there is a lack of trees, they favour rocks.

This information can be reinterpreted as the tendency for snails to like rocks which is good news for us, as we can now show with a great degree of certainty when the Monolith stones (if any) were erected because there seems to be a massive increase in the total snail numbers in the soil. In this case, at a depth of 1.2m to 1.3m. What needs to be kept in mind is that the Mollusca are aquatic animals and can only survive in wet habitats, with individual plants. The damper, the better for the humble snail; it does not thrive on dry, barren land. I believe that the increase in snail numbers not only shows the type of vegetation in the past but, more importantly, the climate and soil conditions - in particular, the amount of water in the environment.

The snail counts for Coneybury Henge also show that the ditch was at one stage much wetter, at 1.0 m – 1.6 m excavation depth. There are 2,200% more snails present in the ditch than today, which shows either:

- **The flora had overgrown the site**

- **The stones (a snail's perfect home) were present at the site**

- **The ground was wet and boggy, after filling with water and then silting up**

Moreover, it is shown that at 1.8 m to 2.8 m depth there were no snails at all – this could only happen if either the landscape turned into a desert, or the ditch filled with water so that the only soil floating to the bottom of the ditch was watery silt. When you realise that from 1.8 m to 2.2 m the ditch was filled with silt from water, the sequence suddenly makes perfect sense:

W2 Coney Henge Ditch Segment	
Depth (m)	Numbers per Kg
0 - 0.2	130
0.2 - 0.4	103
0.4 - 0.6	228
0.6 - 0.8	455
0.8 - 1.0	2587
1.0 - 1.2	2896
1.2 - 1.4	1206
1.4 - 1.6	1728
1.6 - 1.8	591
1.8 - 2.0	0
2.0 - 2.2	0
2.2 - 2.4	0
2.4 - 2.6	Data Lost
2.6 - 2.8	2
2.8 - 3.0	63

- **A depth of 3 metres or more correlates to the end of the Ice Age, when snails lived in small numbers on tundra (treeless plains) and sparse grassland.**

- **At 2.8 m to 1.8 m, a ditch was built, and water-filled the ditch – a few snails falling into the water would account for the small numbers found.**

- **At 1.8 m to 0.8 m, the ditch dried up and became a marsh surrounded with stones, a perfect environment for our snail to live and breed within.**

- **At 0.8 m to 0.4 m, the stones of the henge were removed and the ditch became a grassy dip in the ground.**

The incredible thing about this site can be seen in the cross-section of Coneybury Henge. It clearly shows why this site was chosen as a henge, and why the ditch filled with water. During the Mesolithic Period, water would have been present on two sides of the site. In fact, the henge sat on a peninsula that overlooked Stonehenge, separated from it by a vast waterway over 100m wide. Moreover, if you look at the Stonehenge site in comparison, you will see that Coneybury Henge is just 3 metres higher.

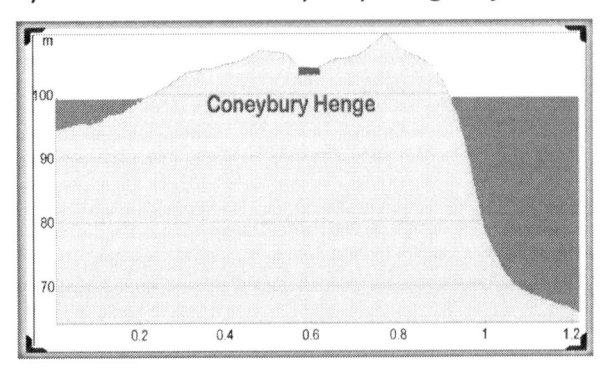

Figure 41- Coneybury Henge Profile

This height difference could be for one of two possible reasons:

• **The groundwater table on this side of the river maybe 2 metres higher, which is quite possible as chalk contains strata that can allow this.**

• **The site was built before Stonehenge when the waters were even higher – which makes it a greater shame that farmers have ploughed it into complete extinction with the possible losses of its history for all time.**

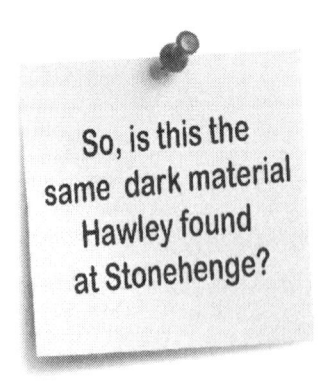

So, is this the same dark material Hawley found at Stonehenge?

This evidence is quite compelling but, interestingly, like the Stonehenge ditch, Coneybury Henge's ditch contained dark material showing that water was present when the ditch was constructed. If we look at a soil report for the same ditch where the snail survey was completed, Helen Keeley found 'a turf line' of soil between 2.58 cm and 2.81 cm composed of humic (organic) materials.

I believe so; in fact, within this layer, Keeley also found the largest deposit of calcium carbonate in the entire sample. Calcium carbonate is a common substance, present in rocks and many other objects all over the world; it is the main ingredient of the shells of aquatic organisms and snails. Calcium

17. The lack of Mollusca (snails) and the finding of calcium carbonate at certain levels in the Coneybury Henge ditch - proves that a moat surrounded the monument was full of water in the Mesolithic period like Stonehenge, due to a higher water table.

carbonate producing creatures such as corals, algae, and microorganisms usually live in shallow water environments; because they need sunlight in order to make calcium carbonate. It was also found throughout the rest of the sample but in much smaller amounts. The most significant quantity was left at the bottom – clear evidence that shortly after the time of its construction, Coneybury Henge ditch was full of water, just like Stonehenge.

In 1988 Pit WA9580 was excavated as we have discussed in the previous chapter, to find a piece of Rhyolite and three carbon-dated layers, that showed that the pit was Mesolithic in date. The excavation also took samples and produced a molluscan table showing a sequence of snails and their frequencies by the depth and therefore, time.

Interestingly, if we compare to another sample on this site taken some 50 metres away in the ditch excavated by Atkinson and Evens in 1978, we see something quite remarkable. The sequence of three species of the rock-loving snails on the Stonehenge site almost match perfectly, indicating a match in environmental conditions at the time of the Phase 1 construction.

Depth (cm)	Carbon Dated Layer BCE	Vitrina pellucida WA 9580	Ditch	Punctum pygmaeum WA 9580	Ditch	Vitea contracta WA 9580	Ditch
0 - 5		n/a	2	n/a	-	n/a	-
5 - 10		n/a	-	n/a	-	n/a	-
10 - 15		n/a	-	n/a	-	n/a	3
15 - 25		-	4	-	4	-	2
25 – 35	7580 – 7090	-	4	1	4	2	-
35 – 45	7700 - 7420	-	10	12	2	9	2
45 – 55		1	17	10	7	7	11
50 – 60	8090 - 7690	12	16	29	23	32	17
60 - 65		-	13	17	15	16	42
65 - 70		3	5	11	15	7	24
70 - 80		6	14	14	20	8	41
80 - 85		8	8	30	11	12	32
85 - 90		2	-	16	11	6	32
90 - 100		2	-	9	1	5	1
100 - 110		1	-	3	-	2	-
110 - 120		1	-	5	-	2	-

These snails also confirm the findings at Coneybury Henge to show that below one metre in the moat ditch no snails existed as it was full of water initially. Atkinson and Evens excavation show only TWO snails were the bottom 106cm of the ditch, as the ditch was 186cm deep and the samples were taken just from the top layer. Moreover, the frequency of these same snails in both the Pit and Ditch shows they are contemporary with each other.

One of these snails - Vitrina pellucida: `Usually in moderately open meadow habitats, in moist or dry habitats in coniferous and deciduous woods, grasslands and waste ground. Occurs also at rocks and walls, in rock rubble of mountain creeks, in the water margin vegetation, on alpine pastures. This snail loves water and rocks – like most snails – is this why we see a peak of snails at most sites at about 50 cm – as it is when the stones were around these moated ditches?

In conclusion, we have now shown that Mollusca data can be beneficial to indicate; if the ditches were moats in the past and the ditches timeline. We can also use this data to compare ditches and pits and by comparing the frequencies of snails over time, correlate their timelines like Dendrology uses tree rings to reflect the environment and consequently dates of construction.

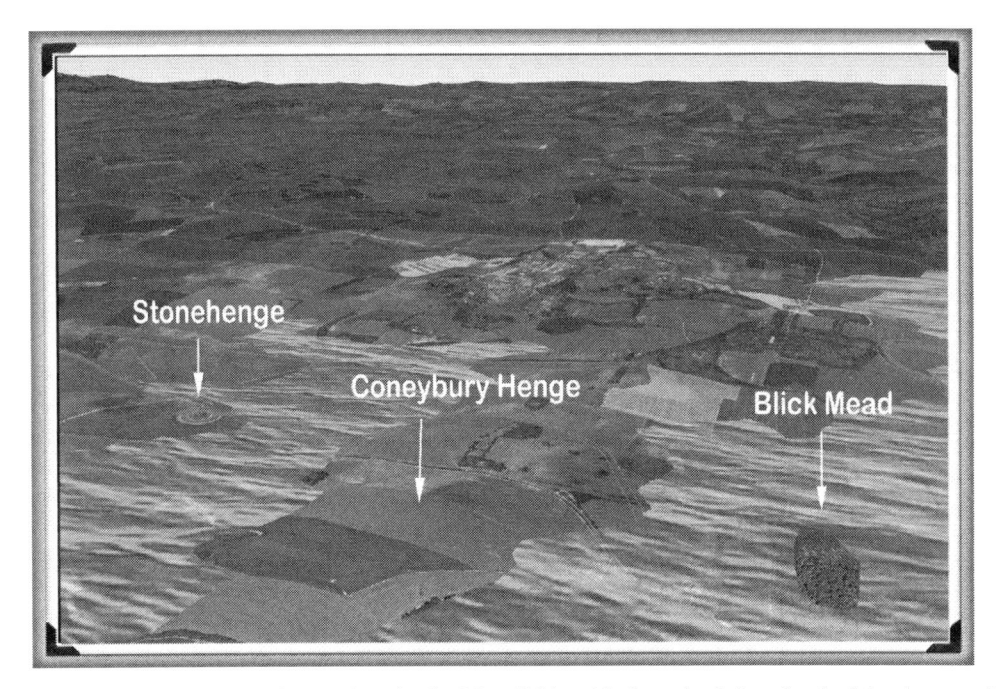

Figure 42 - The Stonehenge Area in the Mesolithic with the raised river level of the Avon and the three sites of Stonehenge, Coneybury Henge and Vespasian Camp (Blick mead)

Construction Phases - Summary

We have split the history of Stonehenge into four separate phases; although most of the construction of Stonehenge happened gradually over the years. We know from the history of old houses that they start as a specific building for a particular function and then change with time to become something entirely different to their original use – hence all the new pub churches!

This was also the case with Stonehenge. This will also give us an opportunity to summarise what we have learnt to date about this site.

PHASE I Construction – 8000 BCE

Ditch Moat

The experts' view of this ditch feature is that it was ceremonial and that it was filled it almost as soon as it was built. This strange 'traditional' view is confirmed from their insistence of taking the antler picks found in the ditch (at the bottom and the infill) and from their carbon dates suggest construction dates for Stonehenge, as if these artefacts were contemporary, rather than positioned their at a much later date (which is my hypothesis), once the moat had fallen into disuse and silt and debris naturally fell in.

> Moreover, why would you dig a ditch over 1m deep just to fill it back in again?

It has been estimated that it took 11,000 working-hours to build the ditch – I don't disagree with this estimation, according to Hawley the ditch is 5ft 6 inches deep (1.7m) and 14ft wide (4.27m) with a flat bottom of 7ft 6 inches (2.3m) with a known circumference of 360ft (Cleal et al., 1995, 67) – with a 60-degree wall.

We are left with excavation 620 cubic metres of solid chalk – this gives us 1500 tonnes of excavated chalk or the equivalent to 277 skips full of chalk. The first question is 'What happened to all that chalk' – if it was placed on one side like Avebury it would be at least 3m tall (as its broken chalk not solid?) if it was placed at the side then it must have eroded over the years – is this another proof of the site being 10,000 years old rather than the 5,000 the experts are suggesting?

Moreover, if you were going to dig a ditch and then just fill it in – why so deep and why would you make a bottom so large and flat – a V-shaped ditch would have saved you 5,000 working-hours of work. It just doesn't make sense!

Figure 43- Antlers found not quite the bottom of the Ditch as claimed - as there is infill under them?

As we have shown in previous sections, the first phase of Stonehenge was the construction of the moat, which was initially built as individual pits or baths with internal walls, rather than a continuous deep ditch around the edge of the site. We imagine that these pits had either a large bluestone on the floor of the pit, or chips of bluestone added like bath salts, to obtain the full benefit of the waters.

The moat would have flowed in and out of the pits, as they were below the Mesolithic groundwater table. This flow of water in and out of the baths was dictated by the moon and was understood by prehistoric man. No doubt this would have added to their sense of wonderment and made the site even more magical than it appears today. As a testament to the power of the moon, and to help them predict its movements and, therefore, the daily and seasonal tides, the builders dug 56 holes, which we now call Aubrey Holes in honour of their discoverer. They also sent to the Preseli Mountains in Wales for a supply of Bluestone megaliths.

Bluestones – Aubrey Holes

Bluestones were brought by wooden barges the short distance (just 82 miles) from the Preseli Hills in Southern Wales. The higher groundwater levels would have allowed the transportation of the bluestones via a more direct route compared to the current theories that the bluestones were brought by boats sailing around South West Britain, or were dragged overland for hundreds of miles through forest (which would have been impossible, requiring levels of manpower greater than the estimated population of Britain at that time).

Moreover, both these sites would have been on the shorelines of an aquatic forest that covered Britain, and therefore wood for transportation by boat/floater would be plentiful. Prof. Richard Atkinson in his book Stonehenge (Penguin Books, 1956.) Provides an example of how the 7-ton unfinished Altar Stone could be floated on a log boat made of pine with a density in the region of 35 lb/ft^3 (560 kg/m^3). He calculates that a raft of some 700 cubic feet (20 cubic metres) could carry the stone along with a crew of 12 average men.

Such boats do not tend to survive the ravages of time, although an example of this type of boat was found in Derbyshire in 1998, which was dated to circa 1300 BC. It was 11 m (36 ft) long, capable of carrying 4 tons (the weight of a Stonehenge bluestone). If you lashed two or more boats together, you could carry much heavier stones.

An even easier option is to strap sufficient wood to the stone that it becomes buoyant. The same Altar Stone could be floated with just ten cubic metres of pine – half as much as the boat – if the wood was simply lashed to the stone. This could then be dragged behind two smaller crewed boats for guidance. The stones, when cut, would be brought down to the shore via a 'log rail' that used levers to move the stones. Once the stones were deposited at the shore at low tide, logs would be attached to the top and bottom of each stone. As the tide came in, the stone would float on its wooden raft. Men could then stand and punt the stone downriver, avoiding rocks and sandbanks.

At Stonehenge, the raft would be guided to the shallow North West side of the peninsula, where the groundwater was shallowest, and the mooring posts had cross posts attached. The lifting system for getting the stones out of the water would have needed only a minimal number of men, as it used the tide to lift the blocks in the air. The stone was brought to the mooring at high tide and lashed to the cross bar with large ropes. When the tide retreated, the stone would be left hanging above the water, allowing the removal of the flotation logs. A track could then be laid so that the stone could be levered to the site, or a sledge could be brought under the stone to slide it the short distance to the monument.

Figure 44- Atkinson showing that four small boys could have easily taken these 4-tonne stones to Stonehenge by boat

Either system would require a minimal number of workers: 10 to 20, far less than a conventional estimate of 200+ men lugging rocks across Salisbury Plain. This lever system would be second nature to a water-based civilisation. Using trees as their main source of materials, they would quickly have adapted to use wooden levers to manoeuvre their boats, either through punting or by adding a couple of upright sticks to the side of the boat to create oars that could propel their boats much faster than punting or canoeing.

Palisade and Excarnation

This was the conclusion of Phase I at Stonehenge – a facility that had a dual purpose. Firstly, it was a place of healing; we have seen in previous sections that the stones, when used in water, could heal the sick. But it would have been clear that not all the people who came to Stonehenge to be cured could be successful.

The monument would also have been used as a place for the dead and the journey to the afterlife. Indeed, we still use the same custom and practice today in our modern hospitals. These are our centres for the sick, but hospitals are also the place where we keep the dead in a mortuary prior to their burial. Our Mesolithic ancestors had the same philosophy of sickness and death and kept them close to each other at Stonehenge.

To understand the construction of Stonehenge, you must be able to interpret our ancestors' beliefs and motives. The dead had to return to the land in the sky, and the only way that could happen was through giving the body to the only creatures that shared the sky with the ancestors – the birds.

Figure 45- Excarnation Platform - these are called Dolmans by archaeologists who are at a loss for their true purpose

Archaeologists have found evidence of these excarnation practices at other sites in Britain. One similarity of these sites lies in the presence of a palisade to protect the bodies from animals other than the birds who fed on the corpses. Such a palisade was found at Stonehenge in the early 1990s, during excavations in the new visitor's entrance. The palisade successfully cuts the natural peninsula off from the heavily wooded mainland to which it's attached.

As there are several main burial mounds on higher ground overlooking Stonehenge, we can only imagine that the entire site was sacred, and may have been completely cleared of woodland so that it appeared much as it does today, laid bare of trees and bushes. One of the remaining 15 barrows overlooking Stonehenge was constructed at the same time, to take the excarnated bones from the site; this area is known as Normanton Long Barrow. Unfortunately, not much of the barrow still exists, but it would have had a distinctive boat shape, surrounded by a moat. This design was a representation of an object and concept the Mesolithic people knew well, as it was their symbol for survival and everyday life.

Archaeologists know of the palisade and its possible use as a type of shield for the site (in fact, some recently suggested it was a snow barrier)!

But without the groundwater river, it doesn't make sense, as you could just walk around the thing to gain access. The only possible reason for the palisade is to join the two areas of river, isolating the peninsula as a sacred place and preventing anything without a boat accessing the site, allowing the dead to go to their maker without being eaten by land animals.

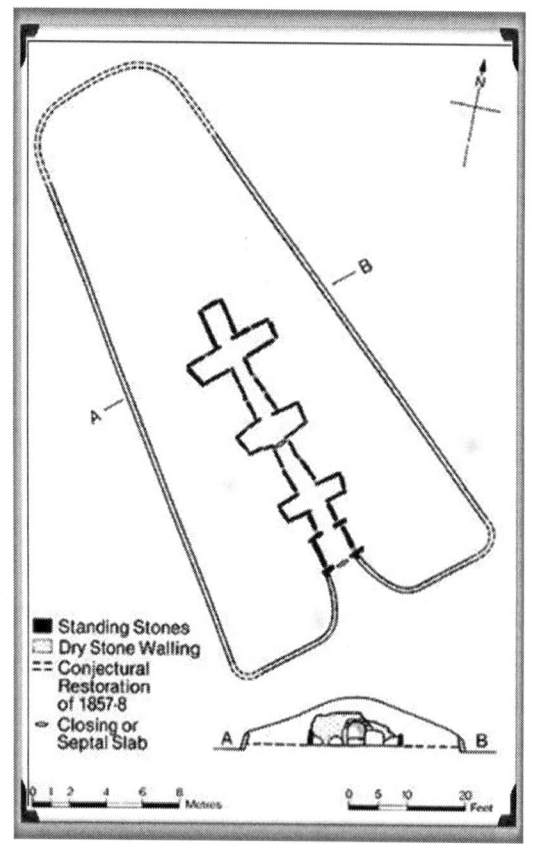

Figure 46- Typical layout of a Long Barrow showing the distinctive boat shape - where the bones would be placed ready for the journey to the afterlife.

Prehistoric Britain – The Stonehenge Enigma

PHASE II Construction – 4100 BCE

As the groundwater of Britain slowly started to subside and separate into what would become the Irish Sea, North Sea and English Channel, the landscape of Britain altered significantly. The earlier immense waterways were reduced to lakes and smaller rivers. At Stonehenge, the mooring station at what is now the old car park had dried up by the end of the Mesolithic Period, and the site needed to change if it was to survive as it had over the last 4,000 years.

The Heel Stone and the two Station Stones.

The two Station Stone features found on the Stonehenge site are situated on the North West and South East side of the main monument within the ditched circle - both have individual moats surrounding them. This can be seen clearly in the Station Stone situated on the North West, also known as WA3595 (North Mount), was discovered in 1956 (Atkinson et al.,1956). Where Atkinson observed that 'a small gully running East-West appears to lie beneath the rubble and earth bank'.

This is an indication that the gully was a connecting strip, linking the main henge moat to a smaller moat surrounding the North West Station Stone. It wouldn't be an unrealistic suggestion to then the southern Station Stone was also connected to the main moat. If we are to believe traditional archaeologist's commonly held view that the moat surrounding the main monument at Stonehenge was constructed purely as a landscape feature, why would our ancestors connect the two smaller ditches to the main one?

The heel stone also has a ditch indicating its significance. This ditch is almost bisecting the avenue ditch, which would have also been full of water. These ditches are invisible today as they were filled in long ago when the water left the site - but if the moat and channels were not for water but symbolic purposes, why were they left to fill with soil and disappear from view – it makes no sense unless they are water features that have dried up over the years as the water table has now fallen by 30 metres?

Figure 47- Southern Station Stone Ditch

Hawley and Atkinson, both suggested that they were built at the same time "The ditches of the North and South Barrows are suggested as belonging to this phase (Phase 3b) purely on their resemblance to the Heel stone ditch, an observation made by Professor Atkinson(1978,78)." (Cleal et al., 1995,274).

Both the North and South Station stones and the Heel stone ditches are of considerable depth 1 – 1.2m deep. Symbolic ditches needed only to cut the surface to meet their requirements. In all cases, these ditches are full of 'silt' or 'marl'. Moreover, it is possible that the same clay liner was added to these features as the excavation reports various anomalies that are unexplained and what I see as evidence of water in the ditches. "There were about 18 inches of dirty chalk upon the bottom... between this, and the humus is a layer of humus with flint single... apart of a decayed horn pick and some flint chips were found on the bottom silt" Hawley (Cleal et al.,1995,278).

This water deposit was also found by Pitts in his 1979 - 80 (C91) excavation where he observed "chalk intermixed with periglacial marl which covers all of the bottom and moat of the sides…. Natural silting of the greater part of the ditch is acceptable" – this indicates that this was left to silt over time and only filled when the Avenue fell into disuse, and the original stones were moved.

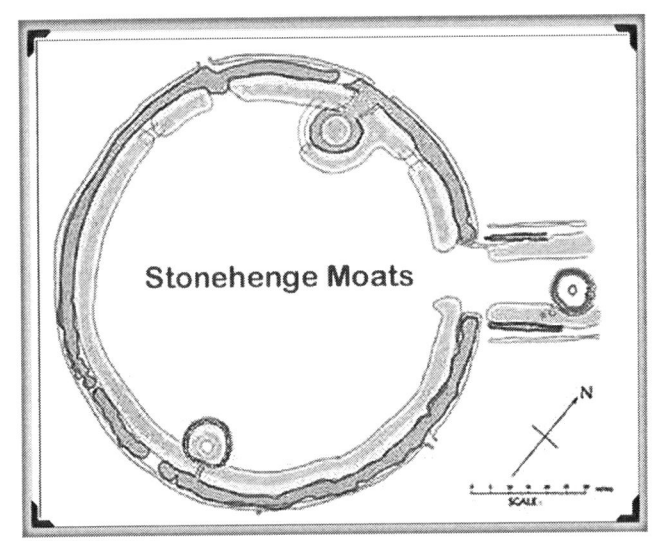

Figure 48- Stonehenge Moats - including the North, South and Heel Stones and moats

Palisade

We should not forget that Stonehenge is incredibly old, and some of its features would have been changed to adapt to the new landscape. Therefore, when the groundwater table dropped at the area of the site that is now the car park, the palisade would have failed in its function as a barrier against animals. There is clear evidence that the palisade was extended to the elbow of the Avenue to preserve the integrity of the peninsula once the

18. The moats that surround the Northern, Southern and Heel Station stones have been found to contain silt and marl within these ditches - proving the presence of water due to higher water table levels at their time of construction

Prehistoric Britain – The Stonehenge Enigma

Neolithic waters fell. Finally, constructing a new palisade barrier inside the Stonehenge Moat known as the Y & Z post holes, to allow the excarnations to continue.

PHASE III Construction – 3500 BC to 2500 BC

At the end of the Neolithic Period, the groundwater had subsided to almost their present levels. The large river that had existed at Stonehenge bottom for 5,000 years, since the great Ice Age melt, was gone. The groundwater that once covered the land had moved to the surrounding seas and channels, flooding the island once called Doggerland and leaving it 30 metres under the sea. At Stonehenge, the moat had dried up and was dug out for the last time probably for ceremonial purposes. Consequently, the tools used to clean out the moat (antler picks) were left where they broke in the ditch. Sadly, archaeologists currently take these tools, as the basis for their incorrect dating of the site, not to when the monument was at the height of its power, but to the time when it was last used as a monument to the dead.

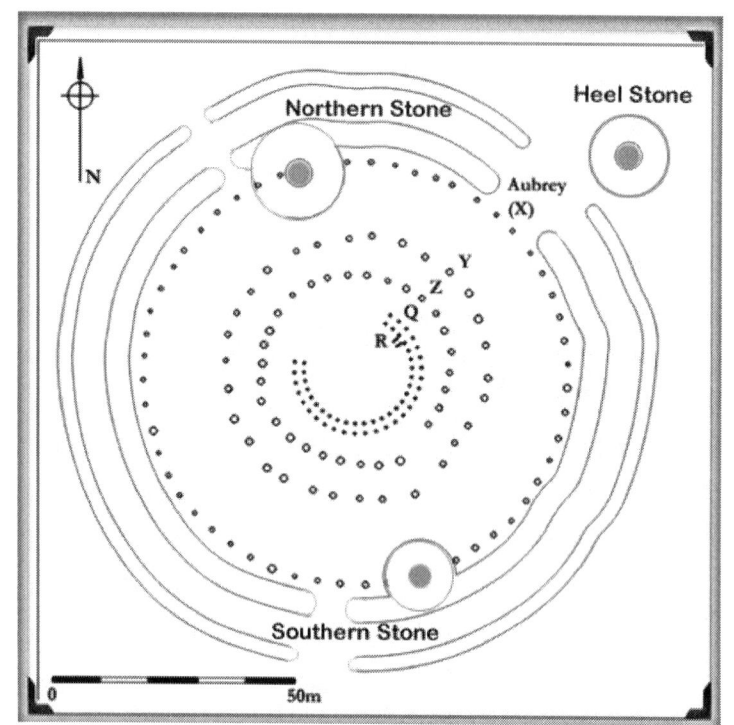

Figure 49 - Palisade Y & Z Holes surrounding the Excarnation Holes Q & R

The Avenue

The loss of the river Avon at Stonehenge Bottom meant that the road (The Avenue) had become a path to nowhere. The site continued to have immense significance and would have had continued to have visitors and pilgrimages and hence a natural approach to and from the river Avon developed from a comfortable landing spot to the Stonehenge site. This indicates that boat travel still dominated how this civilisation, as a foot only path would have gone straight over the hill to Durrington Walls, or perhaps they had founded another site for their bluestones which had a direct source of clean water.

Bluehenge

Professor Mike Parker-Pearson found, in 2008, the outline of a stone circle by the banks of the Avon next to the extended Avenue causeway. It was reported in the Daily Mail that:

"The monument has been tentatively dated to between about 3000 and 2400 BC."

Excavation revealed several stone settings that are thought to have been erected around 3000 BC. It is estimated that there may have been as many as 27 stones in a circle 33 feet (10 m) wide. The name "Bluestone henge" is derived from the discovery of small stone chips in some of the stone settings. These bluestones are also found in Stonehenge and consist of a wide range of rock types originally from Pembrokeshire West Wales, some 150 miles (240 km) away. Archaeologists suspect that bluestones in the circle may have been removed around 2500 BC and incorporated into Stonehenge, which underwent significant rebuilding work at about this time.

The stone circle settings were surrounded by a henge, comprising 82 feet (25 m) wide ditch and outer bank which appears to date from approximately 2400 BC. Unlike Stonehenge, there do not appear to be any significant solar or lunar orientations within the monument." There are two very relevant and interesting points about this find. Firstly, it proves our hypothesis about the use of the bluestones with water, and consequently the necessity of locating them next to the Avon. Moreover, using our hypothesis, we can date this sequence more accurately, as we know that at the time of the construction of Phase I and II of Stonehenge, the Bluehenge location was under about 30 metres of groundwater. The Bluehenge circle must, therefore, be later than Stonehenge Phase II in date. What Bluehenge indicates is that the Stonehenge area continued to be used as a centre for

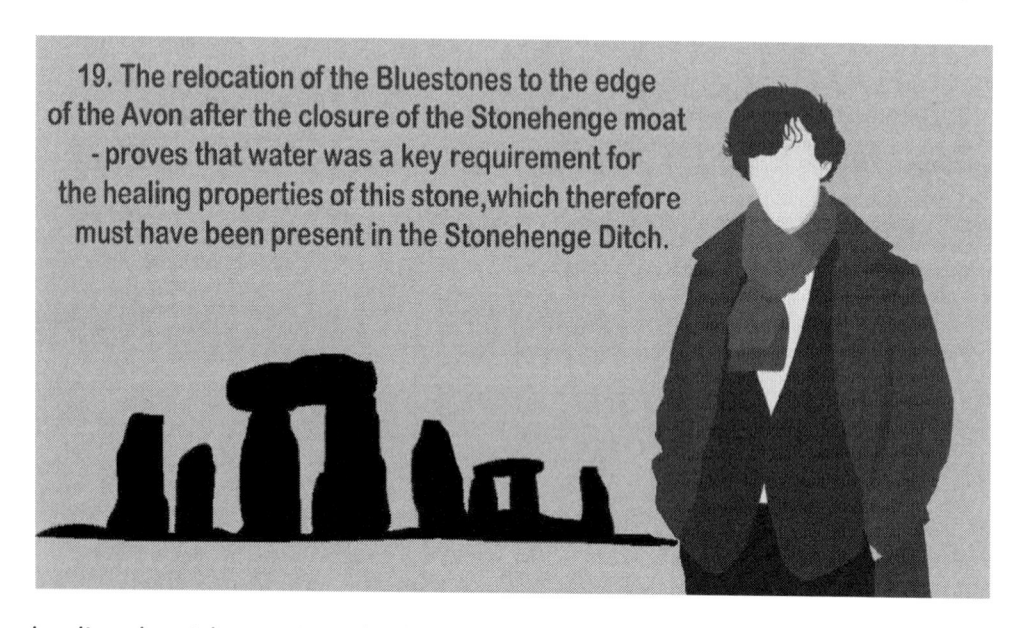

19. The relocation of the Bluestones to the edge of the Avon after the closure of the Stonehenge moat - proves that water was a key requirement for the healing properties of this stone, which therefore must have been present in the Stonehenge Ditch.

healing the sick even into the bronze Age until it was relocated closer to the main water source at the end of the 'extended' Avenue.

Round Barrow Alignments

We have noticed that Stonehenge's three moated stones are aligned to three of the most important sites in the area: Avebury, Old Sarum, and Durrington Walls and Woodhenge. Further investigation has led us to believe that more alignments occur with round barrows over land. This would have been the only sensible way for prehistoric man to navigate over land, as maps had yet to be invented, and we know that all ancient civilisations used points on the horizon as location references.

This would also explain why not all barrows contain skeletal remains.

PHASE IV Construction – 2500 BC to 1500 BC

Bluehenge

Even after moving the bluestones down the valley to the Avon, it seems that Bluehenge was abandoned not long after its construction. Perhaps the waters at Craig Rhos-Y-Felin fell too low to load the boats or that the rivers that once connected the Avon to the Welsh rivers become too low and impassable, or the knowledge of how to use the stones to cure the sick was lost or superseded. It is likely that the stones were either returned to Stonehenge or broken up and used for building during the Roman or Medieval period.

Heel Stone Alignment

During the latter part of Stonehenge's prehistory, it lost its initial function as a mortuary, as our ancestors' beliefs changed, and burial practices altered from excarnation to cremation as seen in the pits of the Aubrey Holes. They still, however, needed a monument to reflect the voyage to the afterlife. At some time in the Iron Age, or after the groundwater had dried up, the Heel stone that once indicated the passage to Woodhenge was moved to align with the sunrise. It was deliberately tilted slightly as it was not a perfect alignment so that the midsummer sun rose from behind the stone.

Chapter 4- Durrington Walls (Woodhenge)

If you go to the original North East path break in the Stonehenge ditch, you find the Heel Stone, which was moated during the Mesolithic Period. You will also find a direct alignment to Stonehenge's nearest neighbours, Woodhenge and Durrington Walls.

The fact that the Avenue is wider than the break in the ditch around Stonehenge has always been a mystery to archaeologists. This mystery is compounded by the Heel Stone's position to the right of the Avenue, rather than in the centre. The Avenue was built after the Mesolithic ditch was created; therefore, these individual moated stones start to make some sense as alignment points.

The Heel Stone was positioned before the Avenue's construction; the moated stone points to Stonehenge's sister site Woodhenge and not, as is currently believed, to the midsummer sunrise.

In 2016 Durrington Walls hit the headlines with *"Remarkable new archaeological discoveries are beginning to suggest that Stonehenge was built at a time of particularly intense religious and political rivalry.*

Just two miles north-east of the World Heritage site, at an important archaeological complex known as Durrington Walls, archaeologists have just discovered what appears to have been a vast 500-metre diameter circle of giant timber posts. The find is of international significance.

Originally archaeologists, using geophysics rather than excavation, had thought that they had found buried standing stones, so the discovery has totally changed their understanding of the site – the largest ancient monument of its type in Britain.

However, the most significant revelation is the discovery that the newly identified timber circle complex was probably never fully completed – and that, just a few months or years after construction had started, there was a dramatic change in religious – and therefore almost certainly also political – direction. Work on the circle was stopped abruptly by around 2460BC –

despite the fact that it was nearing completion. The 200-300 giant 6-7 metre long, 60-70 centimetre diameter timber posts were lifted vertically out of their 1.5 metre deep post holes – and were probably used to construct or expand other parts of the complex.

Figure 50- Durrington Walls showing the post holes surrounding the ditches.

What's more, within a few months or years, the post holes themselves were then deliberately filled with blocks of chalk and were covered up for most of the circuit by a bank made of similar chalk rubble. Two of the post holes have just been fully excavated – and, at the bottom of one, the prehistoric people who decommissioned and buried the site, formerly occupied by the giant timber circle, had placed one of their tools (a spade made of a cow's shoulder blade) at the bottom of the post hole before it was filled in. It certainly hints at the ritual nature of how the change of religious direction was implemented.

It was as if the religious "revolutionaries" were trying, quite literally, to bury the past. The question archaeologists will now seek to answer is whether it was the revolutionaries' own past they were seeking to bury – or whether it was another group or cultural tradition's past that was being consigned to the dustbin of prehistory".

In 2015 Sky News reported:

Sadly, most of this article is pure fiction and what I call archaeological 'mumbo jumbo'!!

"Scientists have found a larger version of Stonehenge just one mile from the site of the famous Wiltshire stone monument. The Durrington Walls 'superhenge' is larger than Stonehenge and may include as many as 90 large stones. Built about 4,500 years ago, the stones lined an arena that was probably used for religious ceremonies or solstice rituals.

Using ground-penetrating radar on Salisbury Plain, scientists found the stones lying on their sides and buried under three feet of earth. Some of the stones are nearly 15ft and were originally placed along the southeastern edge of the circular enclosure that measured nearly a mile wide - making it the largest earthwork of its kind in the country.

The stones may not always have been part of the henge, possibly being toppled over before being incorporated into it - not an act of vandalism but an attempt to save whatever was thought to have been important about the stone, experts think".

In 2015 the ground survey found "90 large stones, lying on their sides and measuring nearly 15ft" under the ground – then in 2016 we have "200 - 300 giant posts 6-7 metres long" - So, was there

The Story over 12-months has changed dramatically!!

Prehistoric Britain – The Stonehenge Enigma

another ground radar survey between the two claims or were the 'experts' caught guessing.

> **Never Fully Completed??**

Sadly, the misinterpretation of the evidence doesn't end the nonsense and gives us a clue to this deception - "However, the most significant revelation is the discovery that the newly identified timber circle complex was probably never fully completed".

You could say that about the entire site – if you believe what the archaeologists tell you. Durrington Walls is a classic 'half-moon shape, which is evident as the bank is missing towards the River Avon in the East and there is no bank to the South where they found these anomalies. Now the bank is no small matter like Stonehenge, as it is 30m – 40m wide and 3m high in the North-western sector of the site.

Archaeologist to date have yet suggested why the banks are missing – if it was a 'Henge' it would have had banks and ditches surrounding its entirety.

The first thing that strikes you when you look at Durrington Walls is that it seems incomplete; it looks like a half-circle from aerial photographs, and from the ground, you get a sense of it only being half finished. But most illustrations include the eastern section because magnetometer surveys of 2006 show that under the surface there are more ditches although you might question their purpose, as it is not apparent. The eastern side of the site was clearly built much later than the original westside. The east bank is smaller and does not match the specifications of the original ditch and moat, which was roughly 5.5 m deep, 7 m wide at its bottom, and 18 m wide at the top.

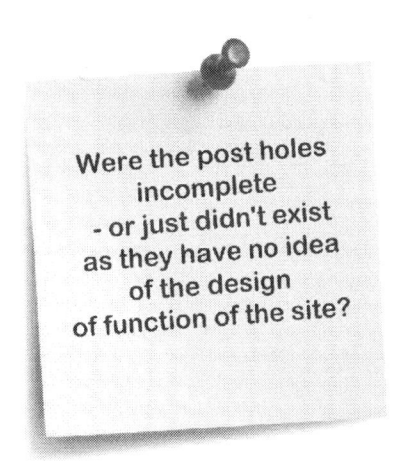

> **Were the post holes incomplete - or just didn't exist as they have no idea of the design of function of the site?**

Prehistoric Britain – The Stonehenge Enigma

The bank was 30 m wide in some areas. The bank and ditch indicated by the magnetometer surveys are less than half that depth; the bank is only about a third of the size of that on the northern side. The current theory and plan of Durrington Walls simply does not stand up to investigation, for it is clear that the Eastern side of the camp was added at a later date when the prehistoric groundwater had started to recede. This would include the Southern circle found in the 1960s.

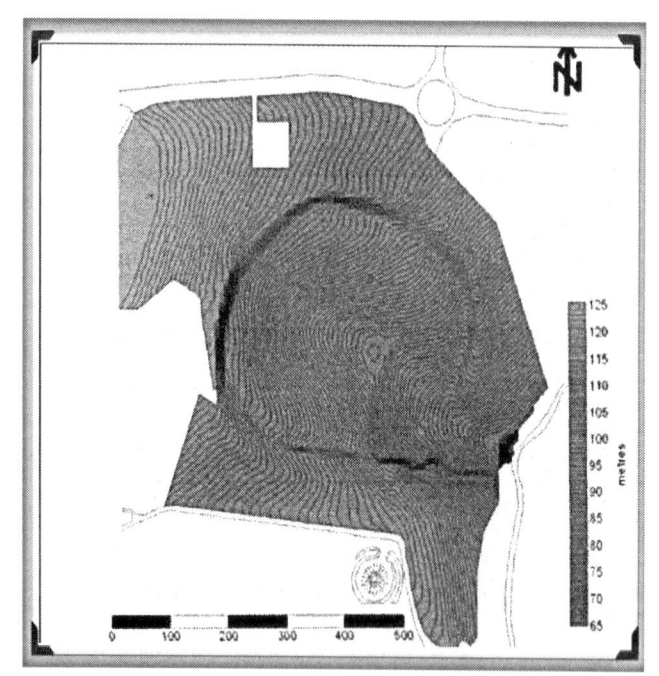

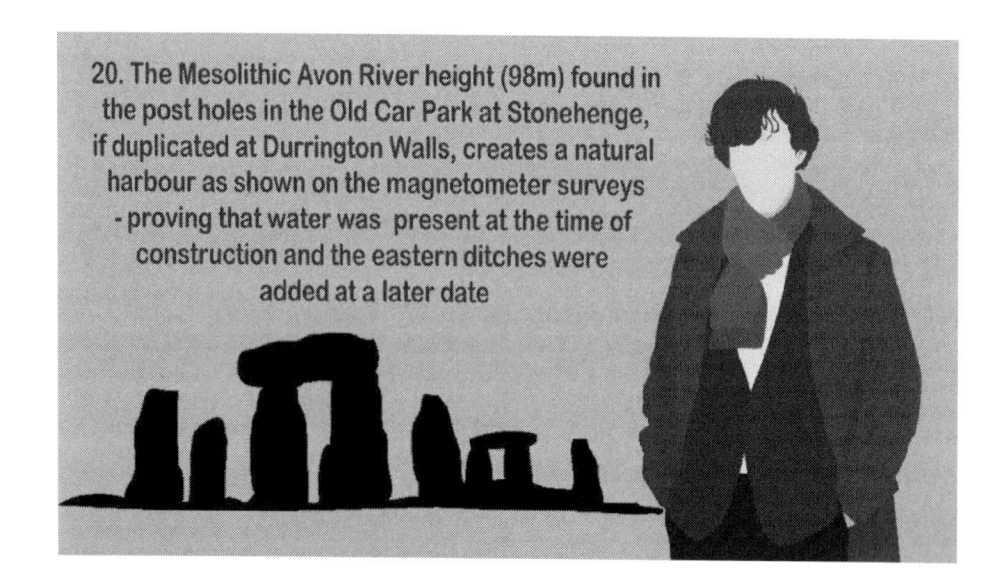

Figure 51- 2004 magnetometer survey by Payne and martin – indicating water minerals from the Avon.

20. The Mesolithic Avon River height (98m) found in the post holes in the Old Car Park at Stonehenge, if duplicated at Durrington Walls, creates a natural harbour as shown on the magnetometer surveys - proving that water was present at the time of construction and the eastern ditches were added at a later date

Prehistoric Britain – The Stonehenge Enigma

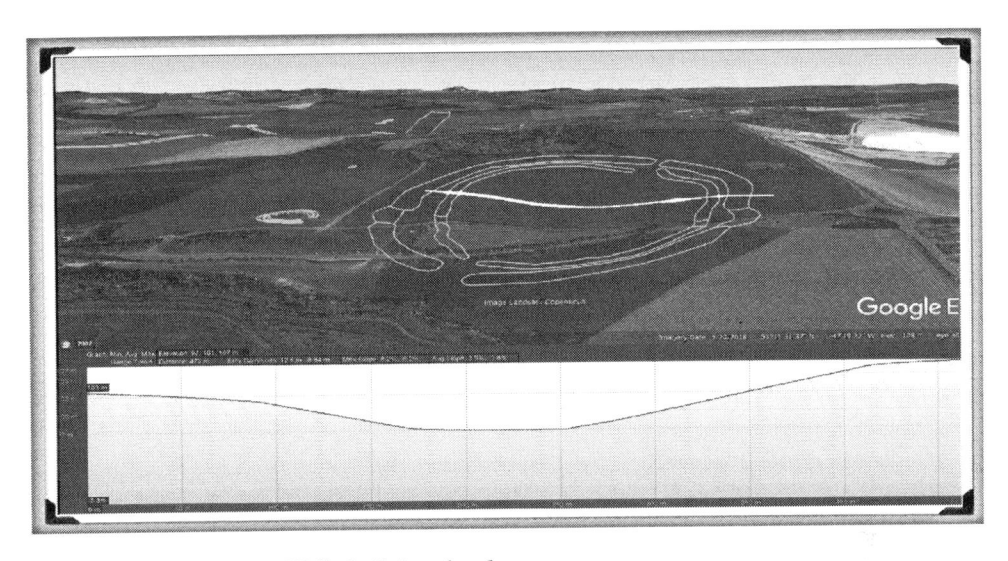

Figure 52- Durrington Walls built in a bowl

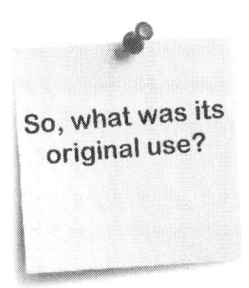

So, what was its original use?

To answer that question, you must look at the site's terrain, position and layout. The first thing that hits you is that the site is not flat - in fact, it's a huge bowl. Archaeologists say that it is a settlement, but anyone who goes camping will tell you not to pitch your tent on a slope, and for a very good reason: you will wake up one morning covered in water, as when it rains the water runs downhill.

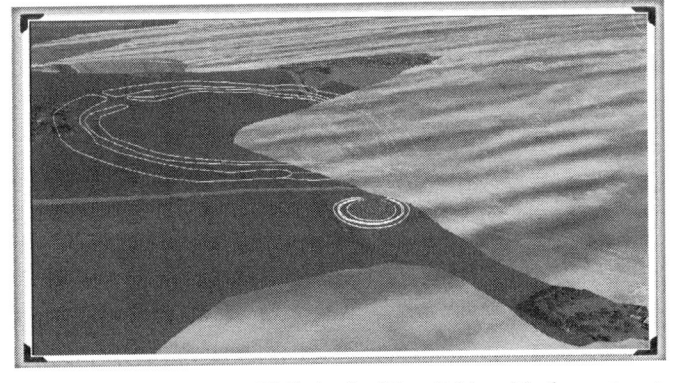

Figure 53- Durrington Walls in the Mesolithic with the water at the same height as we saw in Stonehenge (98m)

Archaeologists will insist that, because they have found a few postholes that they believe are the foundations of a couple of roundhouses, the site must unquestionably be a settlement – this is because they are

Prehistoric Britain – The Stonehenge Enigma

dumbfounded by its position and shape. If we now add the higher Mesolithic groundwater tables as presented in our hypothesis, as we have shown at the Stonehenge site when the river Avon was 30m higher in the Early Mesolithic period. This site (which is less than three river miles down the road from Stonehenge) becomes a perfect natural harbour, with shallow sides for pulling boats ashore and 4-metre deep ravine in the centre of the harbour. Moreover, with a northern and western bank that would have provided shelter from gales.

Woodhenge (which lays to the South of Durrington Walls) has two entrances: one directed towards Durrington Walls' harbour and, more importantly, a mysterious second entrance that trails to our Mesolithic shoreline. This is a clear indication that groundwater was present at Woodhenge during Mesolithic times. Not only would it explain the strange shape of the camp, but also the magnetometer survey (Parker-Pearson, 2006) showing the continuation ditches to the east were dug after the groundwater had fallen in Neolithic times.

Even more impressive is how the landscape reflected the receding shoreline during the Neolithic when the waters receded (as we saw at Stonehenge and The Avenue). The present-day minor road runs along the course of the Neolithic shoreline circa 4000 BCE.

Figure 54- Durrington Walls Neolithic Shoreline post holes - moorings

Unbelievably, the answer is yes!

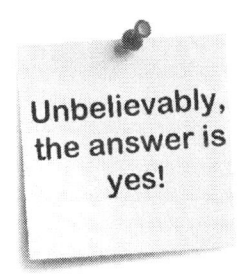

We should not be too surprised by this, as lakeshores and coastlines still have paths along them today so that we can fully enjoy them. There is no reason to believe that prehistoric man did any different 5,000 years ago, and such a path would also have a practical purpose as the shorelines were used as a mooring site. If we are correct about the road and the mooring points, is it possible to find the same type of post holes here as we saw in the old car park at Stonehenge?

Wainwright, in his excavations of Durrington Walls, discovered lots of them. These postholes would make a natural landing area for boats, mooring up for Woodhenge, when the waters fell in the Neolithic period.

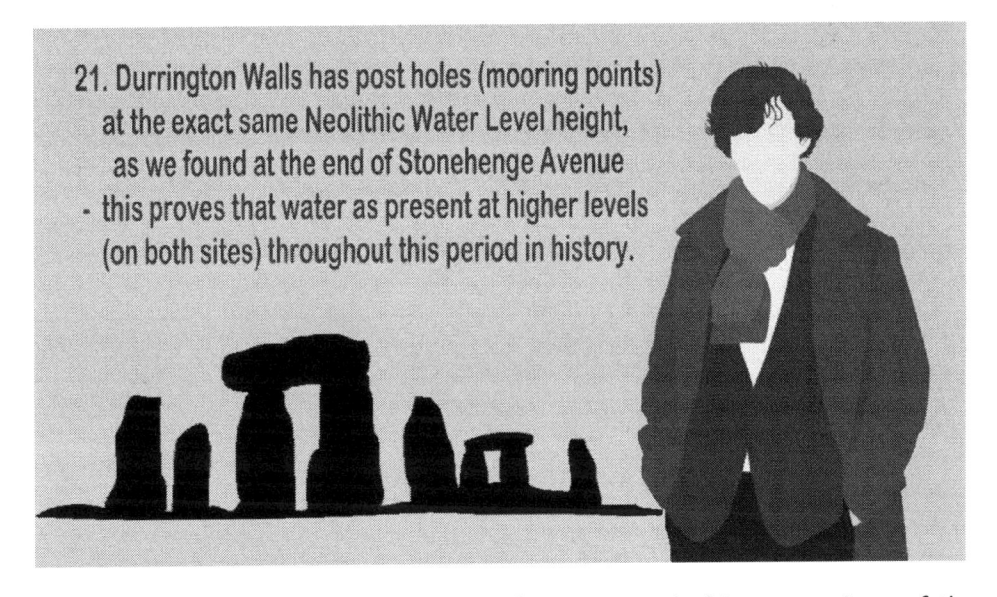

21. Durrington Walls has post holes (mooring points) at the exact same Neolithic Water Level height, as we found at the end of Stonehenge Avenue - this proves that water as present at higher levels (on both sites) throughout this period in history.

Water was also reported my Mike Parker-Pearson in his excavations of the site in 2009 when they located ancient springs that were in the centre of Durrington. A strange place to put a settlement, where you are building houses - unless like Much Farm these houses were in fact on stilts and the waters were underneath the house. These 'crannogs' are found throughout Britain and are dated from the Bronze Age – but there is no reason not to

Prehistoric Britain – The Stonehenge Enigma

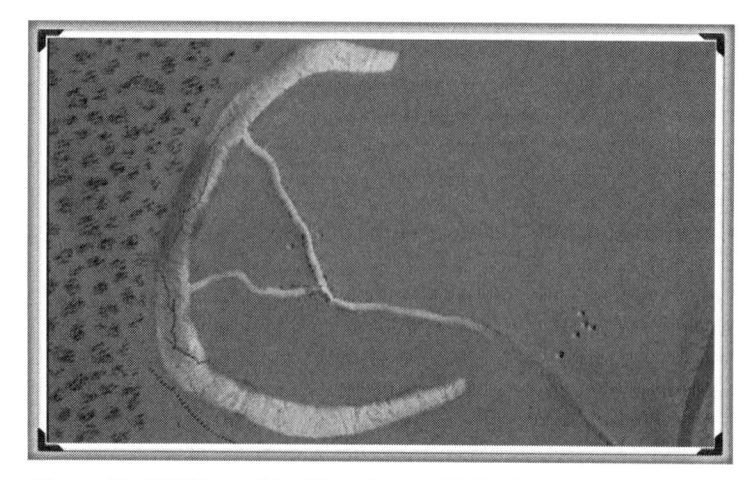

Figure 55- MPP's model of Durrington Walls showing the internal ditches and springs within

believe that this boat society would have been first to use these aquatic houses as the perfect mooring platform for their boats.

Furthermore, the authors of these press releases and reports failed to understand why these posts were eventually removed and backfilled. It doesn't make sense to complete (as they suggest) a third to half the site, then stop and removed all the post you planted, if it's for 'ceremonial' reasons. Unless of course, the post were there for a more practical purpose, like a windbreak for the harbour. This would logically result in them 'slowly' disappearing over a few decades through rot and removal.

We should also remember that a considerable number of posts were also found to the south of this site and at Woodhenge next door. So, the idea that they didn't have enough posts to finish off (as suggested in their report) is merely archaeological guesswork and therefore nonsense.

Figure 56- Crannogs have the same post hole outline as round houses

Prehistoric Britain – The Stonehenge Enigma

Another survey by this group reported in 2020 some findings and dates, which accidentally supported my post-glacial hypothesis. They carbon tested pits in the landscape and came up with yet another ludicrous theory about a 'late Neolithic pit structure', as they have found clusters of pit features (of the same size and depth as we saw in the Stonehenge ditch), which they imagine was a giant ring 1.2miles in diameter surrounding Durrington Walls – which the authors suggested is a 'marker' to strangers not to approach!

What they found is a 'Dyke' from the river Avon to a 'Causewayed enclosure' and a selection of pits on the shorelines of the river Avon in Palaeochannels (like Stonehenge Bottom) that was part of the expanded river Avon during the Mesolithic period. The nature of Dykes we will detail in depth later in the book under the 'Environmental Evidence Section' – where such pits dug in the dyke, would reach groundwater keeping the waterway flooded, as we saw at Stonehenge.

Figure 57 - Neolithic Ditches North Section - part of a Palaeochannel dyke – connecting it to the Avon

The Palaeochannel ditches are of most interest as we can get (like the old car park pits) accurate dates to the levels of the river Avon for future dating of other sites – like we have achieved at Durrington, knowing that the three Mesolithic pits at the old car park were dated around 8100 BCE for a recorded height of the river Avon of 98m. We can now add Borehole 9A BH 1 (SUERC-92464) at 7179 BP +/- 28 and 8A BH2 (SUERC-92465) at 5788 BP +/- 28 to this catalogue.

And this type of a Dyke was not the only one found at Durrington Walls, for the most obvious evidence of water and the heightened water table can be seen on the southern side of the site as a massive ditch. This massive earthwork is currently either totally ignored or is dismissed as a 'lynchet' feature.

This 'elephant in the room' is a clear indication of the use at Durrington Walls in the past and like the avenue at Stonehenge an indication of how this civilisation attempted to keep the monument working as the waters of the Neolithic retreated from the site.

If you look again at the magnetometer survey (Fig.51) closely and remove the incorrectly perceived continuation of the existing moat around the North and West sides of the site, you find a Dyke. This feature is not concave as they would tell you, it is like all Dykes, completely straight and runs all the way from the end of the western moat all the way to the River Avon, which is impossible for a natural lynchet, which only run parallel to hill contours.

This Dyke would have been added (and then extended) once the original moats failed, as the shoreline and water table dropped throughout the Neolithic period to follow the river Avon, so boats could access the site.

Figure 58- Dyke that is the western ditch of Durrington Walls

Prehistoric Britain – The Stonehenge Enigma

Case Study- Woodhenge

This monument has a series of 'massive' wooden post holes - at this point, I need to explain that archaeologists don't seem to understand the difference between a 'Post Hole' and a 'Stake Hole'. You use stake holes for posts such as fences as they can be easily buried in the ground as they have a sharp point – this point naturally compresses the surroundings (due to the shape and hammering from above) so they don't move or wobble!

A 'Post Hole' is totally different as it has a flat bottom and needs rubble to stop it rocking from side to side. Stake holes are easy as they are 'self-burying' while post holes are more work as you need to dig a hole for it. The only reason you would do all the extra work of digging a flat bottomed hole (especially in chalk) is if the wooden pole is to take some kind of weight from above, for a stake hole is useless for this type of structure as it would sink (overtime) under the weight pushing down on the point and probably fall over.

Therefore, if you have a round wooden single-storey building with a simple roof as current archaeologists suggested for some of these post hole structures, why use these massive posts as it is 'over-engineering' and time consuming – especially with simple tools?

Cunnington excavations at Woodhenge in 1929, suggested that some posts are up to 60 inches in diameter:

"clear evidence was obtained in excavation that the six centric rings of holes once held posts or tree trunks varying from 1ft to 3ft in diameter according to the size of the hole...... the size and depth and distance varies in each circle.... In the outer circle holes are 6ft apart from centre to centre, from 1 1/2 ft to 2ft in depth and from 2ft to 3ft in diameter. In the second circle the holes are larger and further apart, averaging about 4ft in depth and 3 ½ to 4ft in diameter. The largest of all were those were those of the third circle, being about 6ft deep with a diameter at the top from 4ft to 5ft " (Cunnington. M.E., 'Prehistoric Timer Circles', Antiquity A Quarterly Review Of Archaeology Vol.1, 1927)

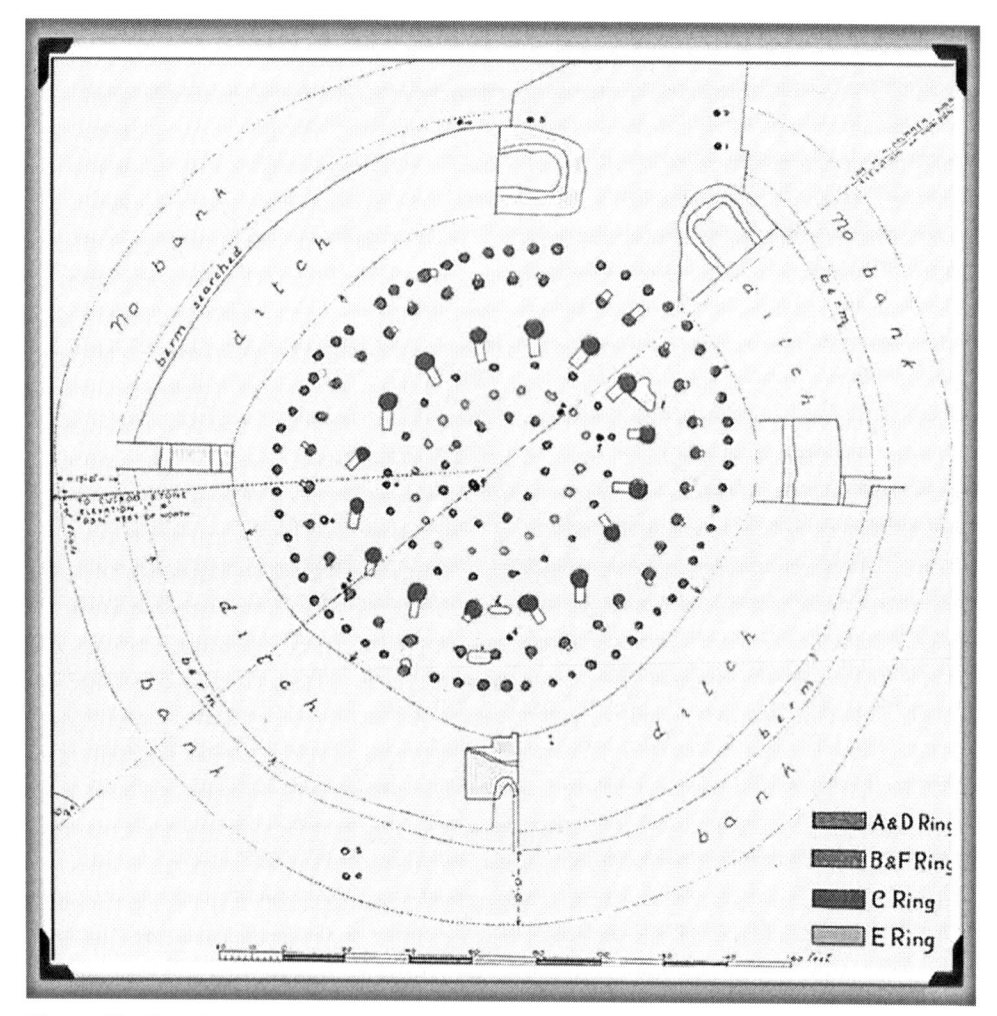

Figure 59- Cunnington Excavation plan 1929

Sadly, Woodhenge shows us yet another illustration of flawed science in archaeology. Even with a 'second rate' excavation report from the 1920's the conclusion of modern archaeologists is that this structure was a single-story house – a slightly grander feature to the traditional 'iron age' house. This is simply nonsense. If we look closely at the evidence presented here, we obtain a totally different and more accurate conclusion to the nature of this structure.

Firstly, if we look at the layout of the site (which lacks much detail), we can see from these original excavation plans the scale of this understatement, as the existing 'concrete' posts, on the site, are far too small. The most recent photo was from the excavation by Pollard in 2007, indicates that these posts are at least five times larger than the current representations.

The next fact that goes unanswered is the reason for the large ramps by the post holes. You don't take time to put 32 ramps into the soil unless it is essential as you just added at least another month to the building work for the site and 500 working-hours. What archaeologists have missed (or failed to mention) is in which direction these ramps were cut – as it tells us more than the entire excavation report by Cunnington.

The massive 4 – 5 ft pine posts of the 16 postholes (known as the C Ring) would weigh 214kg per foot of length. Therefore, a sizeable healthy person (we will go into detail who these megalithic people are and where they came from in the next book of the series – 'Dawn of the Lost Civilisation') could pick up one foot of pine and place it in a hole without assistance or a need for a ramp.

Consequently, an eight-foot pine tree trunk could easily be placed on the shoulders of 8 people and put straight into the hole, which is the current estimations by archaeologists for a single storey structure. Therefore, the empirical evidence suggests they are wrong, and the pole was much more significant.

Figure 60 - Woodhenge post holes much larger than the concrete posts on the site!

Prehistoric Britain – The Stonehenge Enigma

What we have seen at Stonehenge is similar ramps not by the 4-tonne bluestones but by the Sarsen stones that weighed an average of 25-tonnes (the trilithons are 35-tonnes) but half the size of these ramps.

So, how large is a 25-tonne pine post?

A 25-tonne, pine post of width between 4 – 5 ft would be 39m long or 128ft, and a 35-tonne pine tree is some 177ft long. But do Pine trees grow that tall? Just down the road from Durrington Walls is Longleat Forest, within this forest there are pine trees called Giant Sequoia. These trees grow to nearly 200ft tall.

Moreover, the site plan does also give us another clue to the length of these poles. If to look carefully at the angle of the ramps into the giant postholes, you will notice that they are not all facing the same direction. The only logical reason for that to happen is if you erect the pine poles in a set order so that they would not hit or interfere with each other when attempting to erect the posts.

This allows us to come to some remarkable conclusions about the construction and the process of how it was built:

1. **Holes were filled in an anti-clockwise direction starting at hole 1 (at four o'clock to the site)**

2. **Poles must have been more than 100' long as otherwise, you could erect them in any order and direction.**

3. **The ditch that is current at the site was added at a later date, as you would need to bring the poles through the ditch and in some cases be in the ditch to erect it.**

4. **The 4 to 5ft diameter posts all entered the site from the south, as it has the minimal distance to travel – as these poles were either rolled or dragged on a sledge and therefore probably the direction of where the pine trees have initially been growing or unloaded, after being floated down the river.**

But that's not all?

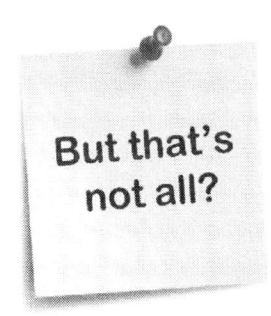

Now the slopes for 'Ring C' (the largest posts) are 5 to 8ft long, which are even longer than the Stone ramps (3 to 4ft) at Stonehenge (Fig.58). This probably shows the large (Sarsens are only 13ft tall) leverage factor required to be pulled upright with an A-frame, which then allows the posts to slide into position and then into the hole.

Ring B – the 3.5 to 4ft diameter trees, also have ramps, but much smaller (3 to 4ft), indicating less leverage and therefore half the weight/height? Moreover, they were placed into position after the C Ring, as their ramps point away from the centre with no common direction.

The last row of postholes (A), 1 to 3ft in diameter, do not have ramps and are sporadic in nature and size – which leads me to believe they have no structural significance and was probably more like a palisade covering, to either enclose the structure or allow mud or reed covering (wattle & daub) and protection from the elements.

Figure 61- Broch which was a later version of Woodhenge - made of Stone

The internal posts (D to F) are superficial and probably were there to support the first-floor structure, as we see in their successors in British history the 'broch' – a stone version-built thousands of years later for the same purpose.

But my money would be on the tower being of a lower ratio of 1 to 1, with the base, making it 135ft high and the same height as Silbury Hill, a little further up the river Avon and its design I would suggest, would have been the same 'layer cake' design as we will see in the chapter on Avebury.

Therefore, what would you build next to a harbour to attract and direct boats – obvious isn't it, a fire beacon (with a stone base) as we know from written history and the Pharos of Alexandria (280 – 247 BCE).

Figure 62- What Woodhenge probably looked like during phase I of its construction – with a spiral staircase.

Furthermore, this link with the harbour is illustrated by the construction of the Moat, Bank and then a Dyke. As we have suggested, the Woodhenge ditch would not have existed at the original time (Phase I) of the construction of the C and then the B rings. It seems that it was added at the end of Phase I when the structure was complete and before Ring A was established, as it points to the shoreline of the Neolithic Avon River. This alignment disproves the current 'expert' theory about being an astronomical alignment with the Solstice Sunrise.

Evidence for the construction of the postholes (with gaps in the circle which were later filled with smaller posts) indicate that the ditch had filled from age, or by design. The main opening (in the A circle) to the northeast is not in line with the gap in the ditch, and the two other spaces in the circle, would track across the ditch in the southeast and northwest.

As for the dating of Woodhenge (and Durrington Walls), like Stonehenge, unrelated antler and bone fragments have dated it to about 2400 BCE, which is very convenient. The problem is that most of the post hole samples at Woodhenge were either lost or have been stored away and not tested since the excavations between 1926 to 29, for reasons known best to the experts.

22. Woodhenge is a wooden tower next to a harbour which suggests that it was a fire beacon (Lighthouse) - proving that the River Avon was much larger (and higher) in the past than today which was utilised by this civilisation.

Moreover, like the samples taken from the old car park in 1966, pine charcoal were reported to be found "similar to the charcoal found at Woodhenge" was the quote from the labs at the time, who failed to carbon date the samples as the experts had declared them Neolithic, supporting the antler pick dates. Although now, once this gross error was exposed, we know these pine charcoal wood dates to be in fact Mesolithic 8100 BCE - which 'begs-the-question' so are the pine charcoal dates found at Woodhenge also Mesolithic?

Less than a mile down the river is 'Blick mead', (Vespasian's Camp),which has also been found dates ranging from 7900 BCE, (remember our bluestone estimation for Stonehenge is 8000 BCE), to 4050 BCE, with multiple RC dates from the 8th to the 5th BCE. Sadly, until someone finds these samples and carbon tests them, to get an accurate date for Woodhenge and Durrington Walls, this unscientific archaeological ad hoc dating methodology will continue.

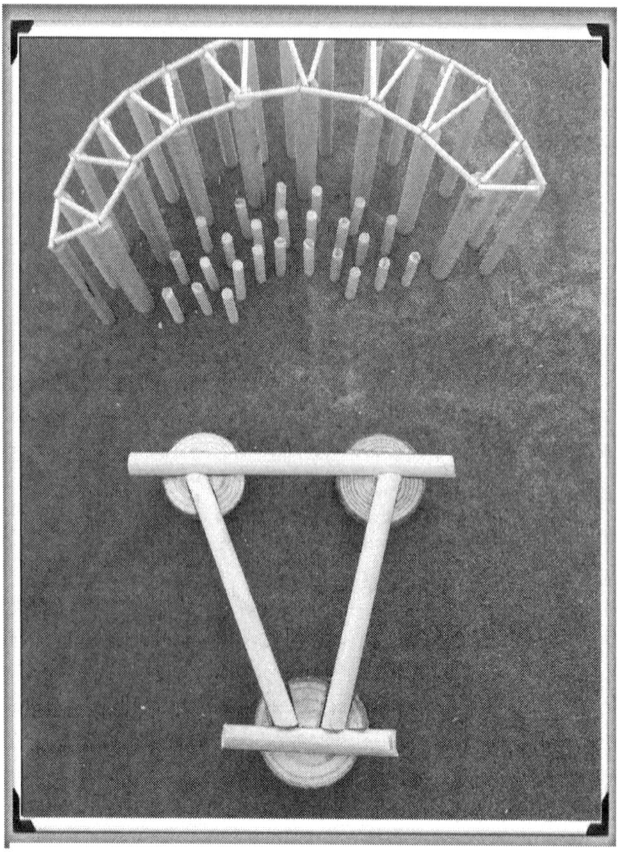

Furthermore, the engineering structure created by this civilisation – like the design at Stonehenge, has been overlooked by archaeologists looking for a more simplistic 'hunter gatherer' solution for this superstructure, which has ended up with a single storey roof, that is clearly well over engineered for that purpose. What we can see at Woodhenge (and also at The Sanctuary at Avebury) is the 'triangulation' of wood joints using the mortice and tenon techniques we have seen on the Sarsen stones at Stonehenge - this structural technique (which are incorporated in modern towers today) allows to construction of extremely high wooden towers, which is what we see at Woodhenge.

Figure 63- Woodhenge Unique construction technique for building towers - still used today

Chapter 5- Old Sarum

If we use the Southern Station Stone as a direction marker from Stonehenge, it points South by South East. If we then follow the line on a map of our Mesolithic landscape, showing the raised river levels of the past, we find that it points to a fantastic site just 10 km away from Stonehenge: an island in the middle of an extensive waterway. This island would be located quite easily by boat. But even so, we have found that barrows and other sites serve as markers on the shoreline, to allow boats to navigate to this island from Stonehenge even at night or in bad weather.

The positioning of this site is most interesting, as it lies very close to the English Channel which would have taken boats off to the continent. It is quite possible that this was Britain's first seaport, as it seems to be the last known occupied Mesolithic island. If so, it would have been one of the most critical sites not only in Britain but in what we call Europe, as it would have been involved in nearly all Mesolithic imports and exports to and from France, Spain and the Mediterranean countries.

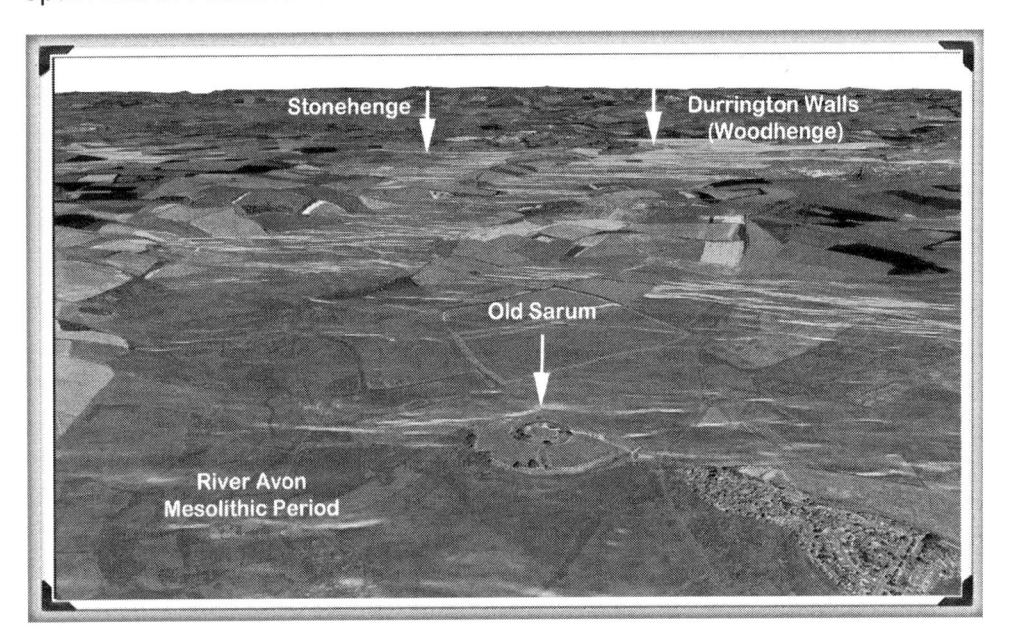

Figure 64- The Island of Old Sarum in the Mesolithic Period

Prehistoric Britain – The Stonehenge Enigma

The island of Sarum would have been a magnificent sight, sitting in a vast river as wide as the eye could see. At the time of Phase I of Stonehenge's construction, the groundwater around Sarum would have reached higher than the outer ditches we see at Old Sarum today. This gives us our first clue as to when the ditches were constructed, as it would be an impossible task to dig ditches if the area flooded twice daily. It also explains one of the anomalies at Old Sarum, a large deep ditch in the South of the site that serves no defensive purpose and was originally believed to be an old landslide.

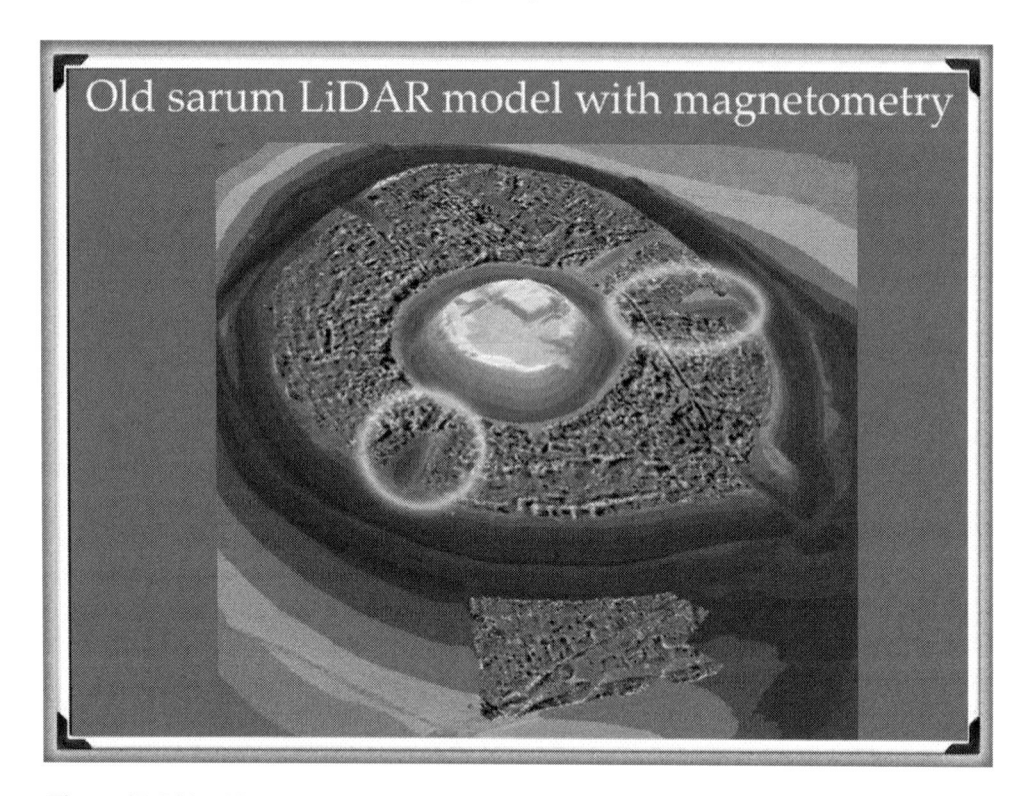

Figure 65- Lidar Magnetometry Survey showing two Dykes

When we look at the only survey of the site, we notice that there are two deep ditches that lead from the outer to the inner ditch, both of which, have been partially filled. During the Mesolithic, the groundwater would have flooded both, the outer, and because of the dykes (canal) cut in between the moats also the inner. Current theories on this site speculate that the central

Prehistoric Britain – The Stonehenge Enigma

moat was dug for the motte-and-bailey castle that stands there today, but without firm evidence, this is just speculation – although as the centre of the site is now raised, it would be probable that both the Romans and then the Normans, cleaned out the prehistoric ditch and then extended further down to the new water table, to keep the inner ditch as a defensive moat, placing the excess spoil in the inner area of the site.

23. The two dykes (canals) within Old Sarum that connect the inner and outer ditches - proves that these features are moats and therefore a higher water table was present during the Mesolithic and Neolithic periods.

Looking at this island in Mesolithic times, the raised groundwater tables would have filled the original inner ditch, which is some 7 metres deep, in the same way as the moat that surrounded Stonehenge in Phase I of its construction. We, therefore, suggest that the moat was first dug in the Mesolithic Period. The Romans, and then the Normans, would have used the existing moat or enhanced it for their requirements. The current archaeological belief that the Romans or the Normans dug the ditch does not stand up to scrutiny, as the outer ditch already existed at the site during their occupation, and it would have been simpler and cheaper for them to use the existing structure than to ignore it and make another.

The site at Old Sarum is much bigger than Stonehenge and is of a similar size to Avebury. One can only guess at what would have been in the centre of the

Mesolithic island. From the amount of reused Sarsen stone found in the remains of the Norman castle and the original cathedral, we can infer that a megalithic structure like Stonehenge or Avebury stood at Sarum during prehistoric times. If you extend a line from the centre of the motte-and-bailey at Old Sarum through the centre of the church (the original Salisbury Cathedral), it points to Stonehenge.

Churches built on prehistoric sites are not uncommon. There are many instances of pagan religions crushed by Christianity taking over their sacred sites and using the stone circles as a building material for their churches. So, we believe that in prehistory three stone circles existed at Sarum: one large outer circle and two smaller inner circles, indicating the way to Stonehenge. Later, as the groundwater fell, our ancestors built Sarum's outer banks to keep their sacred site an island. At Avebury, a similar configuration can be seen, with two smaller stone rings inside the large ring that borders the outer moat.

In the Neolithic Period, the groundwater table dropped by about 10 m, and the island of Sarum was joined to the mainland by a peninsula. Our ancestors, therefore, built giant ditches 12 m deep, to keep the site surrounded by groundwater. The Southern and Northern mooring-points could no longer be used, as the groundwater had receded too far, so the Neolithic people created a new landing point to the West. They left a gap in the considerable ditch, so that people and goods could enter the island; this would have looked very much like a bridge across the water.

At the end of this footpath, they built another mooring station that protruded from the edge of the moat-like a peninsula, so that boats could be moored safely around the feature. For some bizarre reason known only to early archaeologists, the platform is shown on some maps as a Roman road connected to a road some 200 metres away on the West side of the island. Unfortunately, for that theory to be correct would take a leap of faith and nature.

The landing platform, which is shown as a lumpy protrusion on maps, has a 1:2 slope, with a vertical drop of over 30 metres. I would suggest that a

Roman horse and cart would not be an advisable means of transport for this terrain unless they were equipped with ABS brakes and a parachute.

The historical record does give us some clues to Old Sarum's deeper past and the ways in which the groundwater that surrounded the island dictated its history. The original Salisbury Cathedral was built here, only to be moved down to the valley a few hundred years later. Can you guess the reason for the move? That's right, the lack of water! It seems that even over the cathedral's brief history at Old Sarum, the groundwater continued to subside. As this story is well known, why did no-one wonder how deep the rivers might have been thousands of years ago?

Figure 66 - Neolithic Loading position with a pathway cut over the outer moat to the interior

The Maths

Currently, the groundwater table around Old Sarum is 56.5 m above sea level. The well in the Norman fort is 70 m deep from an altitude of 130 m, which shows that the groundwater is today 3.5 m below the Norman well. Therefore, the groundwater table in 1000 AD - when the well was first constructed - must have been at least 60 m, so in 1,000 years the groundwater has fallen 3.5 m. If we multiply this thousand-year drop in groundwater table by 9, then add 56.5 m to account for the existing groundwater table, we can estimate the groundwater table 9,000 years ago, i.e. in 7000 BC. That would make the groundwater table (9 x 3.5 m) + 56.5 m = 88 m.

The outer banks of Old Sarum are 89 m above sea level – close enough, I think?

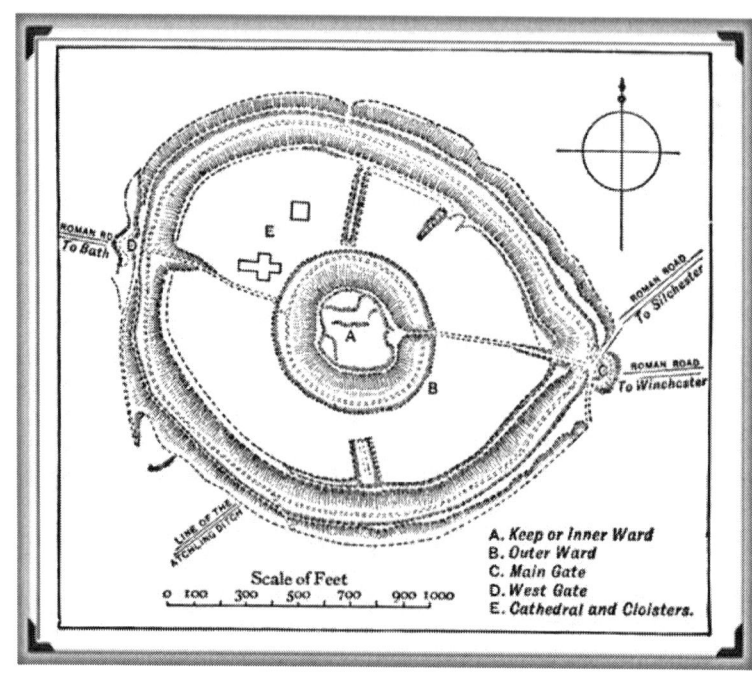

24. The pathway cut through the outer moat connecting to a raised platform for unloading boats - proves a high river height in the Neolithic period.

25. The Well dug in the Norman period which is now Dry - is a proof of the changes in ground water levels over time.

Figure 67 - Plan of Old Sarum - with 'impossible' Roman road to Bath with a 1:1 vertical drop

Chapter 6 - Avebury

The Northern Station Stone of Stonehenge is in direct alignment between the centre of the Circle and Avebury.

Avebury lies in an area of chalkland in the Upper Kennet Valley, at the Western end of the Berkshire Downs, which forms the catchment for the River Kennet and supports local springs and seasonal watercourses. The monument stands slightly above the local landscape, sitting on a low chalk ridge 160 m (520 ft) above sea level; to the East are the Marlborough Downs, an area of lowland hills. Archaeologists freely admit that the history of Avebury before the construction of the henge is uncertain because little datable evidence has emerged from modern excavations. But stray finds of flints at Avebury, dated between 7000 and 4000 BC, indicate that the site was visited in the late Mesolithic period.

If we now apply the same groundwater table adjustments demonstrated in our hypothesis, we are left with a landscape rendered unrecognisable by groundwater, as the Avebury Circle becomes an island. The most remarkable

Figure 68- Long Barrows around Avebury used as beacons for direction hence orientation

Prehistoric Britain – The Stonehenge Enigma

thing is that Avebury now looks like a sister site to Old Sarum: both are perfectly round islands surrounded by groundwater; both have two inner circles and are aligned to Stonehenge via its moated Station Stones.

The next item of interest is the orientation of the long barrows. If you look at a map of Avebury (Fig. 63), you can see that the barrows are not all oriented in the same direction. Archaeologists would have you believe that these monuments were only made for the dead but, if that was the case, why don't they point to a particular direction, such as the sunrise or sunset, or something equally symbolic? From our Mesolithic groundwater map, we can show that East Kennet Long Barrow was the first hill marker you would see if approaching Avebury from the Eastern inlet. Although West Kennet Long Barrow is seen side-on, it would still be visible as a smaller marker, as it had large white stones added to its Eastern entrance to give it greater visibility.

When the groundwater started to recede, as we saw at Old Sarum, our ancestors tried to keep their monument an island by adding ditches. These ditches would have been shallow at first, becoming deeper over the centuries until they were finally abandoned, leaving what we see today.

This gradual process explains more clearly how and why such a task was undertaken, as the logistical requirements of building the Avebury ditches 'in one go' would have been beyond a prehistoric civilisation whose only tools were antler picks and stone axes. Current estimates suggest that it took 1.5 million working-hours to build the Avebury monument. In simple terms, that's 200 people working full-time for 3 to 4 years. This is clearly not plausible. As you will be able to imagine if you have ever visited the site or you understand the requirements of manual labour, it would take a lot more to construct such a large area with such basic tools. The nearby human-made Silbury Hill contains 248,000 cubic metres of chalk and would have taken 18

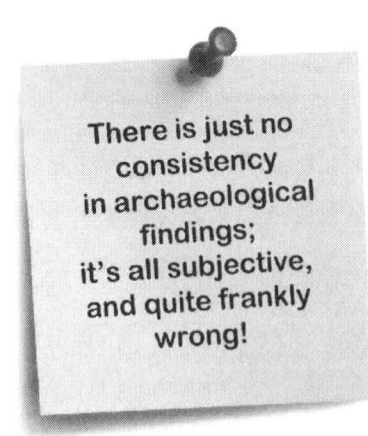

> There is just no consistency in archaeological findings; it's all subjective, and quite frankly wrong!

million working-hours to complete (Atkinson 1974:128). That's equivalent to 500 people working full-time for 15 years. Yet we are expected to believe that Avebury's 125,000 cubic metres of chalk took just 1.5 million working hours to move.

> This gradual process would explain another archaeological mystery that the 'experts' avoid - with what tools were they built?

It's more likely that these monuments grew over centuries, slowly but surely, the ditches starting at just two metres (like Stonehenge) getting deeper over hundreds of years as the moat was regularly cleaned out until they reached the final dimensions of 11 metres deep and 22 metres wide.

Now everyone knows that Stonehenge, Avebury and Old Sarum were cut out of the hard chalk with antler picks - or do we? For if the archaeologists are right, the entire site must be littered with the broken

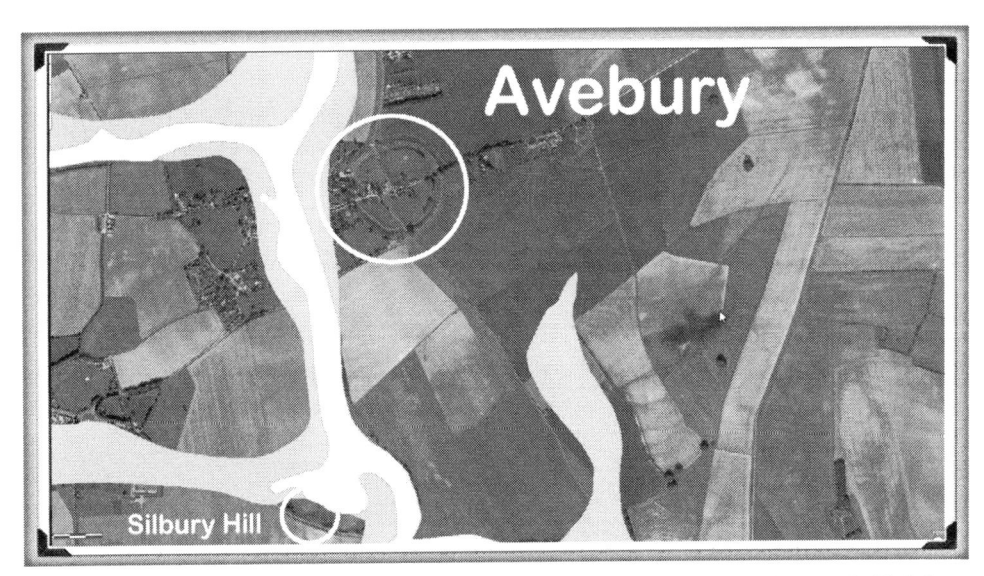

Figure 69- British Geological Society Map of Avebury showing 'Superficial Deposits' left by the remains of the Kennet in the Mesolithic Period

Prehistoric Britain – The Stonehenge Enigma

remains of these objects - but there not! Half of Stonehenge has been fully excavated and found just 82 pieces probably from about 50 full antlers.

> So if antler picks didn't dig the ditches, what did?

At Avebury even less have been found - either antlers are the most formidable natural tools in the world or what we see are the remnants of tools used after the construction for alterations or to clean out (not cut) the ditches. Mike Parker-Pearson found strange cut marks in the bottom of a ditch at Durrington in 2008. These cut marks were so thin that they could only be made by a metal blade, like a bronze or copper axe. The only problem is that according to traditional archaeology - Bronze technology is not available during this period history - unless, of course, the accepted Victorian dating periods are fundamentally wrong, and metals were used long ago.

More recent discoveries now indicate that the peoples of Europe had Bronze as early as 4600 BCE in Bulgaria found in a Gold and Bronze grave - so there is no good reason to believe that the builders of Stonehenge did not have Bronze or copper axes to cut the chalk, towards the end of the Mesolithic period as they would be trading with these places in Europe using their boats.

Moreover, the cross-section drawing of Avebury drawn in 1914 by St George Grey shows that our ancestors took great care to make sure the bottom was flat - the question is why?

If it's a ceremonial ditch (as some archaeologists suggest) why flat and so deep, indeed would not a small easy to cut v- ditch would suffice and be less time-consuming?

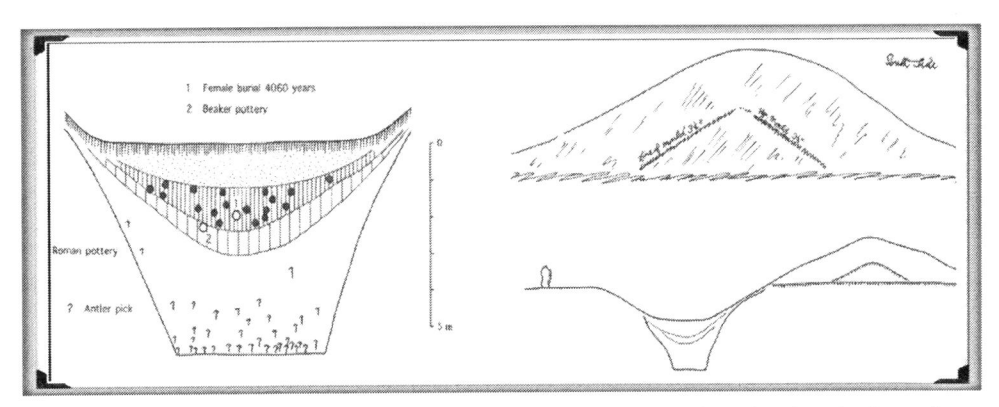

Figure 70- Harold St. George Grey, with his sketch of the excavation showing the large flat bottom and his evidence on the bank that it was built in stages

Moreover, the excavation serves us with the 'smoking gun' of evidence we have been seeking. Because as St. George Grey's men dug, following the ancient ditches cut deep in the soil they had to stop working, as the workman had hit the water table level and the ditch started to flood.

BUT! is there any evidence that these ditches were once full of water?

Now, this is in Summer 1914, and they have reached the water table level. We know in winter the water table would be higher and more importantly, we have shown in previous chapters that the water tables were higher in the past than today. This proves that when this ditch was originally dug, it filled with water turning it into a moat.

Figure 71- The 'Smoking gun' water found at the bottom of the ditch - even today

Prehistoric Britain – The Stonehenge Enigma

> **26. THE SMOKING GUN!!**
> The excavation in 1914 by St.George Grey had to be halted as the ground water had been reached and the Ditch started to flood becoming a moat once more - this proves beyond all doubt that the higher river levels (as indicated in the BGS superficial deposit map) would have flooded the Avebury ditch with water.

Furthermore, the question that needs to be answered is 'why a flat bottom moat' as you are not going to see it when it is full of water. The simple answer is the same reason that we today dredge rivers and boat canals – to remove the silting.

Natural silting over time will create a round bottom to the moat. If you make the bottom flat, it will take longer to silt up than if it was round, prolonging its use or for the need to remove the silt. Is this what we are finding in the 'fill' of these ditches, and the tools used to keep the moat clean and free from weeds, would be the Antler picks and cow shoulder blades found in excavations in small quantities.

Eventually, when Avebury lost all of its groundwater, our ancestors built Silbury Hill as the new landing site to the complex. Silbury Hill is the largest human-made island in Europe and was set at the end of the Neolithic waterway. Composed mainly of chalk and clay excavated from the surrounding area, the mound stands 40 metres (130 ft) high and covers about 5 acres. As we have already seen, it would have taken 18 million-man hours to deposit and shape this vast pile of chalk and earth on top of the natural hill that forms Silbury's foundation. The base of the hill is circular, 167 metres (548 ft) in diameter. The summit is most importantly, flat-topped and 30m (98ft) in diameter.

Avebury Construction Sequence

Phase I – 8000 BCE
After the Post Glacial Flooding - waters subsided and Windmill Hill became an Island which was the first Trading Post in this area. As the waters from the flooding subsided the site had to cut ditches for boats into the side of the hill - we now call these early trading sites with round canal cuttings, Causewayed Enclosures.

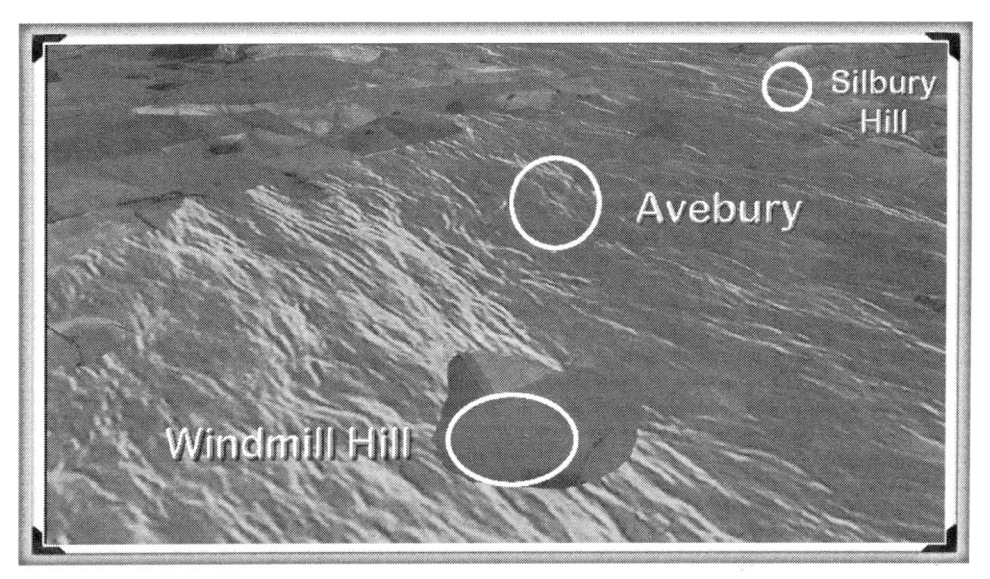

Figure 72- Windmill Hill is a 'Causewayed Enclosure' that was the first trading place at Avebury

Phase II – 4000 BCE
When the waters no longer reached the canal/moats of Windmill Hill they looked south of the site for a new home and chose Avebury. They then dug ditches bigger than ever to take larger boats and ships with a wall to protect them from the weather/storms.

Phase III – 2500 BCE

When the water fell so far that they could not get the ships to Avebury they created a landing site on the Kennet with a stone walkway to Avebury we call

'Silbury Avenue' which attracted ships and boats via a gigantic beacon built on a human-made hill known as Silbury Hill.

Silbury Avenue

In 2014 a remarkable new Stone Avenue was located at the UNESCO World Heritage Site of Avebury in Wiltshire. Previously, two other Stone Avenues called the 'West Kennet', and the 'Beckhampton' are known to archaeologists as they have some of the massive Sarsen stones that line these Avenues still present, but this newly discovered pathway was never thought to exist.

As the discoverer, I have named the pathway 'Silbury Avenue' as it is merely the path directly to Silbury Hill over Waden Hill. The discovery was made by digital photographic pictures that show a series of green 'patches' that measures over 470 metres in length towards the apex of the hill. We can

Figure 73- Waden Hill showing the patch marks of stone holes under the soil

therefore estimate if it ran down the far side of the hill towards Silbury Hill, it would have been approximately 1470 metres in total length.

From these measurements and by counting the discolourations of this new Avenue, we can estimate that 'Silbury Avenue' had at least 19 pairs of stones to the apex with an average of 25m between each pair. We can also estimate the width of this avenue at about 15m to 20m. In comparison, the West Kennet Avenue (calculated from Google Earth) has a pairing at a distance of about 22 – 24 metres, and a width of the Avenue is approximately 15m to 17m – so a very close match.

Figure 74 - Waden Hill in contrast with stone markers added

Excavations and restoration work carried out by Keiller and Piggot in 1936 on the West Kennet Avenue showed that this part of the Avenue was built in series of ten straight sections and not the smooth serpentine shape as suggested by the eighteenth-century antiquarian Stukeley.

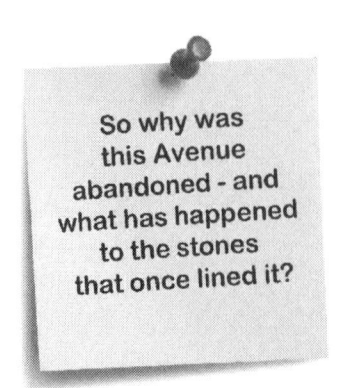

> So why was this Avenue abandoned - and what has happened to the stones that once lined it?

Where stones were missing, they placed concrete markers above the excavated stone holes where they had formally stood, so providing a record of the northern section of the Avenue. Paradoxically, Keiller's plan survey of this section of the West Kennet Avenue shows it heading away from the southern entrance of the henge, while 'other' pairs seem to repair this 'error' with an awkward zig-zag route to connect with the southern entrance.

Recent archaeological commentary on the Avenue has suggested two interpretations for this convoluted approach route. Burl claimed that this was a mistake, of the prehistoric builders in starting the Avenue at both ends but failing to anticipate an accurate direction for each section to join up (Burl 2002). But Gillings & Pollard argued that Keiller's excavation plan is a mistake, and re-excavation will establish a more direct route for this section of the Avenue (Gillings and Pollard 2004, p. 78).

Yet quite rightly (Sims 2009) suggested that if it were a mistake, then it cannot explain why elsewhere in the Avebury monument there are more complex highly accurate pre-planned features.

The reality is that Burl, Gillings and Pollard are all wrong, as the discovery of my new avenue shows why such a strange 'zig-zag' shape was formed – as the original stones were aligned with 'Silbury Avenue' from an earlier date than the West Kennet Avenue. This Avenue led directly to Silbury Hill but was then abandoned for a path leading SE around the base of the hill to 'The Sanctuary', at a later date.

Moreover, an earlier antiquarian of the seventeenth-century, John Aubrey, recorded how the other end of the Avenue connected to the western entrance of the Sanctuary with the exact same dog-leg design. Showing the two ends of West Kennet Avenue were additions.

The change of direction on the Southern section of West Kennet Avenue shows that this Avenue was used at a very late date in Avebury's history and after the Sanctuary's construction. This would explain why the Sanctuary was altered so many times in its past. The likelihood is that The Sanctuary was the termination point of the 'Ridgeway' over an adjacent hill.

Silbury Avenue doesn't go in the shortest line to Silbury Hill, but to the highest point, where we find a series of nine Barrows directly to the east side of the new Avenue. Archaeologists have dated these features as Bronze Age, although no excavations have ever been attempted as the barrows (or other features on top of the hill) were destroyed even before Stukeley visited the site in the 18th century.

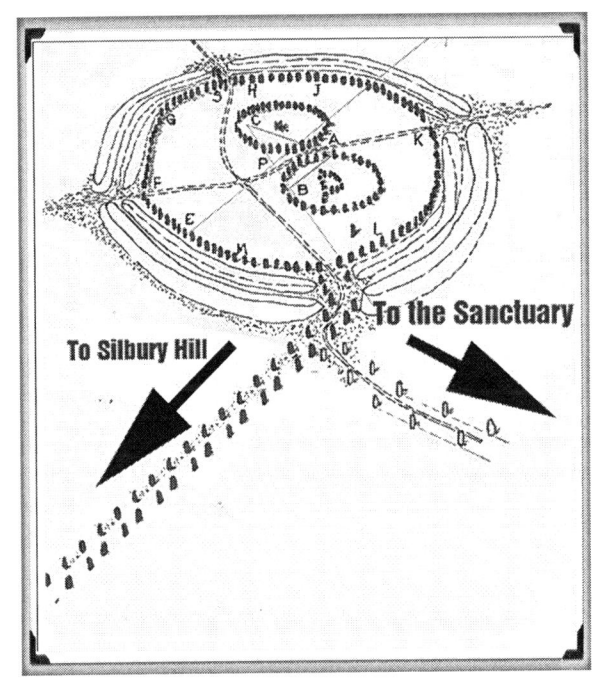

Figure 75 - the 'Zig Zag' Avenue currently seen is simply explained

The only significant findings made in this area was in "An oval-shaped pit", three feet deep, and discovered by workmen in 1913 while digging a trench for water pipes on Waden Hill. The pit, situated 105m NE of the pond on the hill, contained Windmill Hill sherds, sarsen muller, two flint scrapers, charcoal and burnt flints, together with broken bones of sheep, pig and ox, some of them burnt."

The barrows on the left of Silbury Avenue indicate that these features were built after the Avenue was constructed and not because of them, as the path passes the barrows to one side without termination. Although the new

Figure 76- Waden Hill showing the pathway stones and the Round Barrows at the Apex to the left only

Avenue would have led towards Silbury Hill, it did not terminate at the monument as it was inaccessible due to it being surrounded by deep water, which can still be seen today during the winter seasons.

The topology shows that Silbury Hill would have been built as part of the River Kennet, on a natural peninsula. This high groundwater table which causes this flooding is due to springs that have recently been located. (Whitehead, P. and M. Edmunds. 2012. Palaeohydrology of the Kennet, Swallowhead Springs and the Sitting of Silbury Hill, English Heritage, Research Report Series 12-2012.

After the 'great melt' of the last ice age, this area would have been almost completely flooded at the start of the Mesolithic period. The only part of Avebury above this 'initial water level' would have been Windmill Hill – which is NW of the current Avebury site. This site shows evidence of occupation as it is what archaeologists call a 'Causewayed Enclosure', as they (incorrectly) imagine, that the moats built to accommodate boats were, in fact, dry ditches in an attempt to contain cattle - although a fence would have been quicker and more effective.

Prehistoric Britain – The Stonehenge Enigma

Windmill Hill

The use of this site for this purpose of storing cattle is nonsense, as the time and effort required to dig a ditch rather than build a fence is immeasurable. Although, I have no doubt that after their original use, many thousands of years later, they did serve the purpose of farmers who could not afford nor had the time to build fences.

I have renamed these monuments 'Concentric Circle' sites, as they are a product of the same civilisation as the 'megalithic builders' and have this very distinctive design feature, of which Greek philosophers and writers have left a written history and used that term to describe their trading sites.

Once the waters of the Mesolithic subsided, a couple of thousand years later, Windmill Hill would have not been accessible by boat and therefore another site closer to the new water's edge would have been required – this is the Avebury we know today. Consequently, the ditches were built to accommodate (like Windmill Hill) the ships and boats of this trading civilisation.

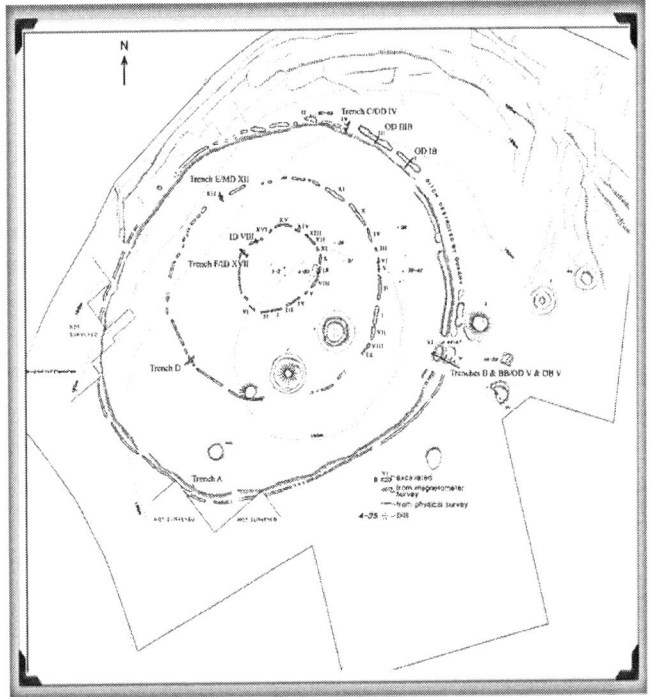

Unfortunately for our ancestors, the groundwater levels continued to recede, as they have done consistently since the end of the last ice age. When the waters failed to reach the moats of Avebury, and they faced the same option

Figure 77 - Windmill Hill

as they had two thousand years earlier to either – to abandon or replace?

Again, they decided to replace, our ancestors, therefore, moved the boats to a natural harbour slightly downriver from Avebury at a place we call Silbury Hill. The River Kennet would have been much smaller in the Neolithic Period, but still three to four times larger than today.

Silbury Hill

If you understand how the landscape looked and was used in the past, then such beacons can be easily found all over Britain, even ones built, to a similar design to Silbury hill To find this unique design we can look at the most recent re-excavation and detailed examination of Silbury Hill, by English Heritage. For only a few years ago it needed to be 'shored up' because of the reckless archaeologists of the past, cutting vast tunnels and shafts into the hill, looking for tombs and treasure making it totally unstable. This investigation showed for the first time that the hill was built like the pyramids of Egypt and South America in steps. This is from The Daily Mail in 2010:

Silbury Hill - one of the most mysterious and striking monuments in Britain - was a prehistoric 'cathedral', built layer by layer over 100 years, a new study suggests. The 4,000 year-old earth mound, which towers over the Wiltshire

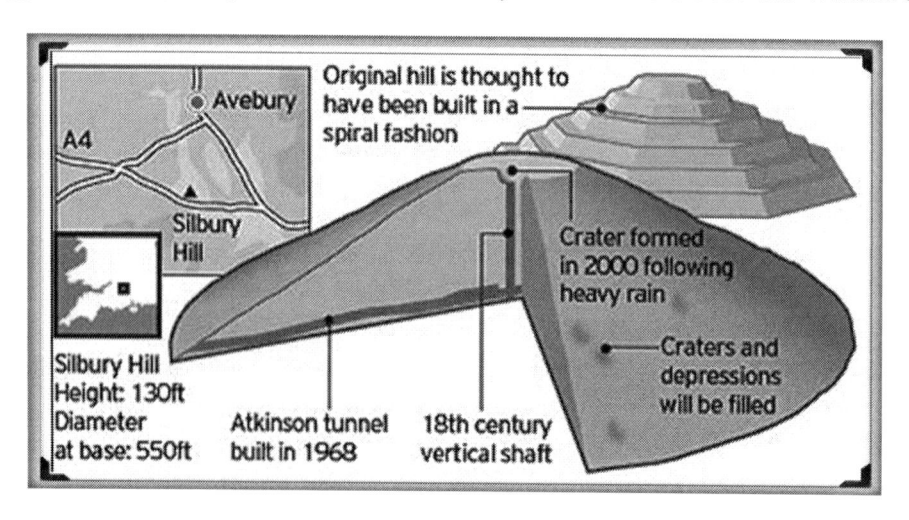

Figure 78 - Silbury Hill made like a 'layer cake'

countryside, was the tallest human-made structure in Europe until the Middle Ages.

However, despite its size, and repeated attempts to tunnel into the heart of the mound, archaeologists have long been puzzled about how and why it was created.

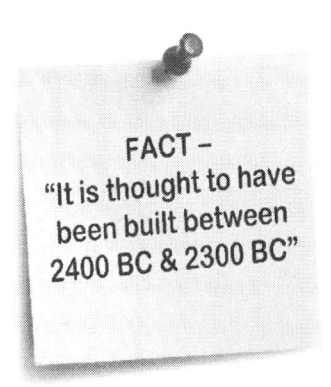

> **FACT –**
> "It is thought to have been built between 2400 BC & 2300 BC"

Now a new book published by English Heritage suggests that the 120 ft high hill was not built to a grand blueprint but was assembled by at least three generations of Bronze Age Britons between 2400 and 2300 BC. A study of soil, rocks, gravel and tools inside the hill shows that it went through 15 distinct stages of development.

Dr Jim Leary, English Heritage archaeologist, said the creators were building the mound as part of a 'continuous storytelling ritual' - and that the final shape of the mound may have been unimportant. He argues that the familiar outline of stepped sides and the flat top visible today is primarily the result of Anglo-Saxons and later alterations.

"Most interpretations of Silbury Hill have, up to now, concentrated on its monumental size and its final shape,' he said. 'It has generally been thought to be a concerted effort of generations of people building something out of a common vision and spiritual zeal akin to that spurred the creation of soaring medieval cathedrals.

'The flat top, especially, was often seen to be a "platform" deliberately built to bring people closer to the skies. 'But new evidence is increasing telling us that our Neolithic ancestors display an almost obsessive desire to constantly change the monument – to rearrange, tweak and adjust it. It's as if the final form of the Hill did not matter – it was the construction process that was important."

Silbury Hill lies close to the stone circles of Avebury and a few miles from Stonehenge. Archaeologists estimate that it would have taken 700 men working for ten years to build out of soil and chalk. It started as a low gravel mound before it was transformed into a pile of soil and rock surrounded by a ditch.

Dr Leary added: *"The most intriguing discovery is the repeated occurrence of antler picks, gravel, chalk and stones in different kinds of layering, in ways that suggest that these materials and their different combinations had symbolic meanings. We don't know what myths they were representing but they must have meant something quite compelling and personal.*

What we do know is that by the time work on the hill had started in the later Neolithic period, the surrounding area was already saturated with evidence of past use; it was a place that was heavily inscribed with folk memories that recalled ancestors and their origins. What is emerging is a picture of Neolithic people having the same need to anchor and share ideas and stories as we do now, and that built structures like Silbury Hill may not be conceived as grand monuments of worship but intimate gestures of communication."

The hill was damaged in the 18th century when archaeologists sank a vertical shaft from the top. In the 1840s, a tunnel was dug into the mound from the edge, while in 1968 BBC2 filmed a new attempt to tunnel into the centre of the mound.

After parts of the mound began to sink in 2002, English Heritage reopened the BBC tunnel, took samples of soil and rock, filled in the gaps and sealed the mound for good.

Dr Leary now believes the mound went through 15 stages of construction - and up to 100 different phases within four or five generations. It would make sense that a monument was a round-based hill made in layers (similar to Marlborough Mound – sometimes known as Merlin's Barrow, also excavated by Dr Leary, hence his idea!). The question not answered by archaeologists is - why build this monument in stages?

Fortunately, the answer is simple – to make it higher, for Silbury was a beacon to attract ships to its harbour. Over time the height of the mound was raised to increase the beacon's visibility.

Figure 79 - Marlborough Mount - Built like Silbury Hill

'The flat top, especially, was often seen to be a "platform" deliberately built to bring people closer to the skies.

Unfortunately, the article is also full of nonsense like this quotation. So, the ancestors built a hill at the bottom of a valley to get closer to the skies – is it me, or can anyone see the error in this statement? You may therefore respond to my criticism by asking – wouldn't a beacon on top of a hill have greater visibility? Yet the reason the beacon is located in the watery harbour and not on top of a hill is that the light shows the exact location of mooring places, in bad weather and at night, when visibility is poor.

This type of device can be seen throughout our recent nautical history as illustrated at the Spurn Point Lighthouse. The earliest reference to a lighthouse on Spurn Point is 1427, which was a coal-fired lighthouse at the ground level. There were several lighthouses of various designs until in 1767; John Smeaton was commissioned to build a new pair of lighthouses (one a 90ft tower). The 1895 lighthouse is a round brick tower, 128ft tall, painted black and white. It was designed by Thomas Matthews. Its main light had a range of 17 nautical miles.

Silbury Hill also started at ground level and was built up (like Spurn Point) over hundreds of years until it reached the 120ft height seen today.

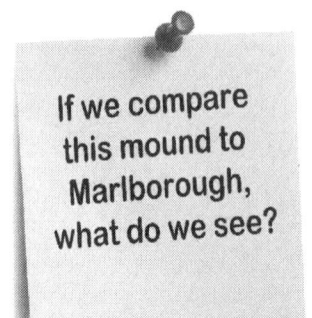

If we compare this mound to Marlborough, what do we see?

From the Guardian 31st May 2011

For generations, it has been scrambled up with pride by students at Marlborough College. But the mysterious, pudding-shaped mound in the grounds of the Wiltshire public school now looks set to gain far wider acclaim as scientists have revealed it is a prehistoric monument of international importance.

After thorough excavations, the Marlborough mound is now thought to be around 4,400 years old, making it roughly contemporary with the nearby, and far more renowned, Silbury Hill.

The new evidence was described by one archaeologist, an expert on ancient ritual sites in the area, as "an astonishing discovery". Both Neolithic structures are likely to have been constructed over many generations.

The Marlborough mound had been thought to date back to Norman times. It was believed to be the base of a castle built 50 years after the Norman invasion and later landscaped as a 17th-century garden feature. But it has now been dated to around 2400BC from four samples of charcoal taken from the core of the 19-metre-high hill.

The Marlborough mound has been called "Silbury's little sister", after the more famous artificial hill on the outskirts of Avebury, which is the largest manmade prehistoric hill in Europe.

Marlborough, at two-thirds the height of Silbury, now becomes the second largest prehistoric mound in Britain; it may yet be confirmed as the second largest in Europe.

Prehistoric Britain – The Stonehenge Enigma

Jim Leary, the English Heritage archaeologist who led a recent excavation of Silbury, said: "This is an astonishing discovery. The Marlborough mound has been one of the biggest mysteries in the Wessex landscape. For centuries, people have wondered whether it is Silbury's little sister, and now we have an answer. This is a very exciting time for British prehistory."

The dating was carried out as part of major conservation work amid concerns that tree roots could be destabilising the structure.

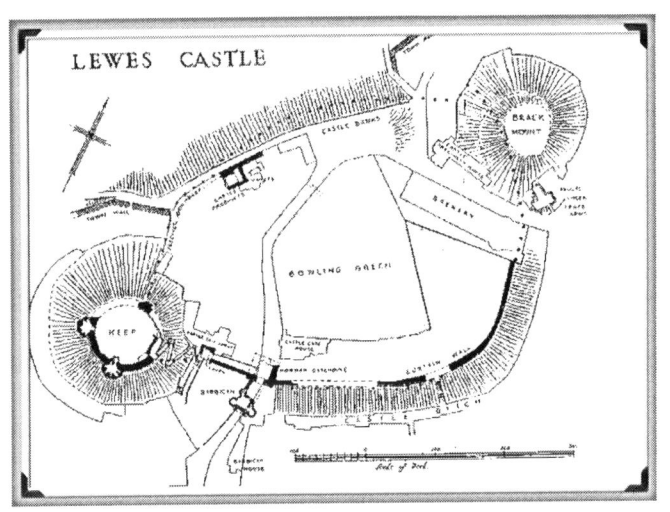

Figure 80 - Lewes Castle with a 'second mount' - which predates the Norman fortifications

We find these beacons throughout Britain, but they remain undiscovered by archaeologists as they are believed to be Norman in origin. Sadly, this is the simplistic nature of archaeology - if it's a mound - it must be a Norman Motte and Bailey - if it has a ditch and on top of a hill – it must be an Iron Age fort?

In Lewes, on the South Downs, there are two beacons in this small Sussex village, both had the same function - to attract shipping. The first is prehistoric and called the 'Brack Mount', historians here believe it was part of the old Norman Castle and show pictures of a wall connecting the traditional Motte and Bailey with this 'additional feature'.

Recent excavations have shown that this beacon has a Norman well installed at the top of the mount (probably for the castle?), the problem for archaeologists and historians dating the mound is - why on earth would you build a 50 foot high earth mound, and then dig a 60ft well, unless it predates the Norman Castle?

Lewes in Prehistoric times was one of the largest inland harbours in Britain, and this mound would have had a fire on top to attract shipping. If that was not interesting enough and an excellent example of a beacon for ships and boats, a second one was built some four thousand years later, when the groundwaters of Lewes (like Avebury) were much lower. This was built for the Monks of the French Cluny Monastery that obtained supplies and people from France and needed to show their location along the English Channel just after the Norman conquest when maps were – not very accurate!

Figure 81- Lewes Tump - used by the 'Cluny' monks to attract ships from the English Channel

The Harbour

Silbury Hill was built as a beacon for Avebury within a deep natural port, that now surrounds the Hill which still floods in wet winters. However, they had a problem as the trading centre Avebury was just under a kilometre from this new port and therefore, a trackway was needed to be constructed to the old site.

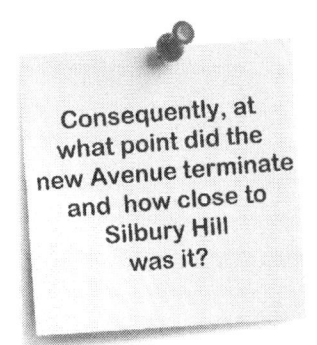

> Consequently, at what point did the new Avenue terminate and how close to Silbury Hill was it?

Silbury Stone Avenue was this new pathway. It goes from Silbury Hill harbour to Avebury over Waden Hill; this trackway was lined with the same gigantic sarsen stones we now see currently in West Kennet Stone Avenue and also believed to have existed in Beckhampton Avenue.

Photographic evidence shows that the Silbury Stone Avenue went to the apex of Waden Hill beside the ploughed-out barrows located to the eastern side of this new Avenue. The most direct route from the peak would have been an SSW direction towards the base of Silbury Hill, but the gradient down this slope is large and would be an improbable route for ladened carts.

The best route for travellers would have been a longer, but with a far easier gradient to walk and carry goods, so not surprisingly, this path (which is still in existence today) and also used as a boundary marker between fields, can be found down the centre of the hill.

Figure 82- Silbury Avenue - at the start of the Trackway looking up Waden hill from Avebury

We have found at sites like Old Sarum and the Avenue at Stonehenge, loading platforms placed on the ends of tracks and edges of the ditches, where boats used to dock and load. So, therefore, did Silbury Avenue have something similar?

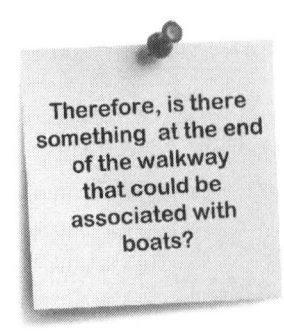

> Therefore, is there something at the end of the walkway that could be associated with boats?

The answer was found on a 'LiDAR' map of the area which showed a large mound at the end of the suspected avenue.

In 2004, Pete Glastonbury (photographer) rediscovered what he termed 'Silbaby' mound. This mound appears in early archaeological maps of Avebury but was lost through the introduction of the A4 on Ordinance Survey maps. After six years of campaigning and requesting an investigation, soil samples were finally taken to date the mound (which had always been presumed to be a modern dumping ground from the A4's construction).

So, the archaeologists thanked Pete for all his hard work, diligence and years of campaigning, but as he was not an 'archaeological professional', or a member of the elite 'academia club', they renamed his Silbaby - 'Waden Mount' - now that's what I call archaeological politics for you.

Midway between Silbury Hill and the road that runs from West Kennet to the henge is what appears to be the remains of a mound that has a resemblance to the profile of Silbury. It lies just to the south of the main A4 road that runs alongside Silbury itself and, though partly obscured by vegetation, is quite visible to visitors going to the West Kennet Long Barrow. It is relatively large when compared to most of the round-barrows in the area and must contain a substantial amount of material.

For want of something more formal, its similarity in shape to Silbury Hill has generated the nickname of "Silbaby" although the text of William Stukeley's book mentions "Weedon Hill" which might be a reference to it.

Curiously, though being a prominent feature in such an important landscape, very little appears to be known about it despite much research by local

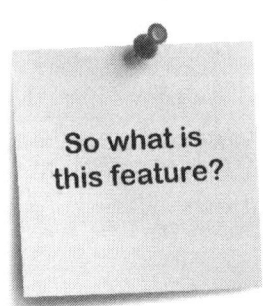

> So what is this feature?

Prehistoric Britain – The Stonehenge Enigma

Figure 83- Waden Mount

photographer Pete Glastonbury who has now brought it to the attention of archaeologists in the hope that it will soon receive some serious investigation. If it does prove to be contemporary with Avebury's other ancient monuments its unusual position on the flood-plain of the river (as opposed to the usual hill-top position of Bronze Age round barrows) and closeness to the enclosures will make it a fascinating site for theorists.

William Stukeley appears to have recorded a feature at the same position and some old illustrations and maps also show it though others seem to ignore it. Of significance must be the fact that it is connected to the river by a small and probably artificially enhanced spur that carries the water of Waden Spring on which the mound appears to sit. The proximity of the road makes it difficult to judge quite what the original profile of the mound may have been if it does precede the Roman period. With the recent discovery of a substantial Roman settlement in the area, there is the possibility that it may be a legacy of our continental visitors.

The evidence of some more recent earthmoving may ultimately be found to be responsible, or its artificial appearance might just be the chance result of natural forces at work, but until an explanation for its existence is found it will surely remain another enigma amongst the many others that already exist at Avebury. Perhaps the central mystery about it currently is why, when this landscape has been crawled over by numerous archaeologists and researchers during the past century or more, has it apparently been ignored?

Core samples were taken in 2010, and we await the official findings - but preliminary reports from Pete suggest it is human-made and has a similar composition and therefore date to Silbury Hill.

Waden Mound (Silbaby) was built at the end of Silbury Stone Avenue for a reason. We know that it was surrounded by water as the Waden Spring is found even today at its base, and the external view of the mound is round like Silbury Hill. From its height and size protruding into what would have been the raised water levels of the Kennet, it was more likely made specifically for the Silbury Stone Avenue, as a stable earth platform to load

Figure 84- Waden Hill showing the two possible pathways from the apex of the hill

boats as seen at other sites like Old Sarum and Stonehenge

The research into Silbury Hill's use is still ongoing and even today as I write this paragraph; I have new LiDAR scans of this area, which indicate that the path over the centre of Waden Hill may have been 20m West of the current track. The scan shows a deep indent which may be the original footpath which leads from the apex even more directly to Waden Mount. Only real excavation work will answer this question in time, and that is unlikely as archaeology is grossly underfunded at present, even for such a significant discovery.

The waters around Silbury Hill eventually dried up as the groundwater receded even further over the next thousand or so years - therefore, a new mooring point was needed to maintain Avebury's trading status. At this time, there doesn't seem to be another typical harbour on the River Kennet available, so they created the final loading point on the River allowing traders to unload their ships and probably smaller boats, and this new loading quay is called 'The Sanctuary' which was once the natural termination point of the Ridgeway path (supposedly Britain's oldest pathway) which led to the 'Uffington White Horse'.

So, what happened once Silbury Hill dried up?

It's entirely possible that the use of the Sanctuary was a sign of Avebury's concluding days as a trading centre. As the mooring point was on the River, this would limit the number of boats that could moor daily. It is quite feasible that Silbury Hill beacon could still have been used as a lighthouse, as shipping would need to pass the Sanctuary before reaching Silbury Hill.

Moreover, it's also possible that technology was by this time more advanced, and as we saw from the example of 'Spurn point lighthouse' a new type of lighthouse structure was developed. If we look for a description of The Sanctuary, we find it's both peculiar and familiar at the same time.

Situated beside the A4 road on Overton Hill the Sanctuary is the site of a stone circle that once formed the terminal point of the West Kennet Avenue. Large enough to contain the outer ring of stones at Stonehenge, its earliest parts are dated to around 3000 BC, which is about the same period the cove in the northern inner circle of the henge was erected. Unless any evidence to the contrary is found it is believed to have only become linked to the distant henge when the avenue was built about 2400 BC.

Figure 85- Silbury Hill was a lighthouse/Fire beacon for the Harbour below

Now destroyed and only consisting of small concrete markers where the various elements once stood, the Sanctuary must have played an important part in the function of the henge. When Aubrey saw it he recorded it as a double ring of stones. Although Stukeley also recorded quite a number of stones on his drawing of it he was to witness much of its destruction during the period of his visits. The destruction was so complete that the site was to become lost and forgotten until Mrs. Maud Cunnington was able to locate it once more in 1930 prior to her excavation of it.

It is a confusing site from an archaeological point of view. Despite a number of excavations (one as recent as 1999), it continues to be a challenge to researchers. It appears to have started as a series of small circles comprising of wooden posts, some of which have now been established as being quite massive. Whether these were evidence of a roofed building or just remained as standing posts is the subject of debate. Eventually, after many modifications, it was to evolve into a stone circle about 130 feet in diameter which has now disappeared. Whatever its purpose it remains an essential and fascinating part of the Avebury complex.

Consequently, when Silbury harbour dried up, this was the only logical landing site on the River Kennet near Avebury. So, they built a wooden lighthouse-like Woodhenge with the same external diameter of 138ft but with a smaller inner timber circle and posts just up to 24 inches wide (not 60 as at Woodhenge) and hence probably half the size high.

Moreover, Silbury Avenue was now redundant, and so they moved the large avenue sarsen stones from on top of the hill down to the east side and created West Kennet Avenue as we see today – with the 'zig-zag' kink and path correction as you enter Avebury.

27. The remarkable discovery of Silbury Avenue based on just a few crop marks and the Post-Glacial Flooding Hypothesis - proves that not only is the theory correct and rivers were much higher in the past than today, but moreover, this technique can be used to find and date the lost monuments of Britain.

Section Three – The Landscape Evidence

The most compelling evidence for my hypothesis - that prehistoric monuments were built around a flooded environment – can be seen within a detailed topological inspection of most ancient sites. The landscape layout of these monuments shows that their entrances and mooring areas oriented to the Mesolithic shorelines seen by the contours of their surroundings.

However, like jigsaw puzzles, once you have assembled the end pieces and the borders, the picture becomes much easier to understand, and this is the case with our most ancient monuments. The most effective method we have found for locating this evidence is to look at the profiles of these sites, and then their position relative to their topology. By doing so, ghosts of the original landscape can be found in the contours that have changed little in the last 10,000 years.

Our research has shown that Stonehenge was not the only monument in this area of the landscape to be affected by the rise in groundwater tables. Other sites in the general vicinity were similarly affected, all of which indicates that these sites were socially connected by the waterways that once flowed through the area.

Consequently, in this section we shall concentrate in detail on the archaeological evidence in the form of ditches and monuments, to allow us to get the best picture on how this civilisation organised itself and the advanced engineering skills they possessed that has left the 'experts' bewildered at these achievements and function, as they resort to unscientific theories and religious beliefs, in an abortive attempt to explain the obvious.

Chapter 7 - Antler Picks that built Monuments

A type of tool found widely among the sites of Neolithic communities in North Western Europe. They are formed from a red-deer antler from which all, but the brow tine has been removed; the beam forms the handle and the brow tine the 'pick'. They were used for excavating soil and quarrying out stone and bedrock. The marks left by their use have been detected on the sides of ditches, pits, and shafts. Experiments suggest that they were used rather more like levers than the kind of pickaxe that is swung from over the shoulder. (Oxford Dictionary of Archaeology)

If you read any book or watch a program about archaeology and the construction of their monuments and sites, you will hear the experts talk about the findings of antler picks in the general vicinity and link the structure with these objects. As the description above indicates, these 'tools' are from red deer, which shed these natural growths on an annual basis.

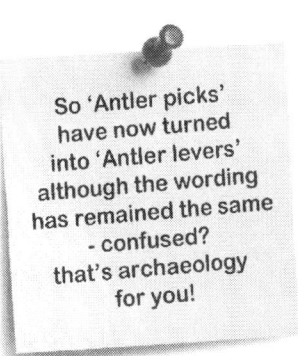

> So 'Antler picks' have now turned into 'Antler levers' although the wording has remained the same - confused? that's archaeology for you!

According to archaeologists, this was the main tool of prehistoric man - a natural resource that became a handy tool in excavating the ditches and digging holes in the chalk bedrock that surrounded most of their sites. This is where the Victorian term 'antler picks' originates and still exists today, but for an unknown reason, this tool has now changed its use (but not its name), as archaeologists have now realised that if these 'antlers' were used to cut into hard bedrock chalk, they would leave blunt ends and scars from flint re-sharpening, which there is no evidence.

Yet, if you look at any prehistoric report about the construction of the monument, you find that there is a degree of 'acceptance' that antlers were used as the main source of digging out the chalk downlands. Here is a typical report from English Heritage's 'bible' (Stonehenge in its landscape, 1995, Cleal et al.) and the use of Antler picks.

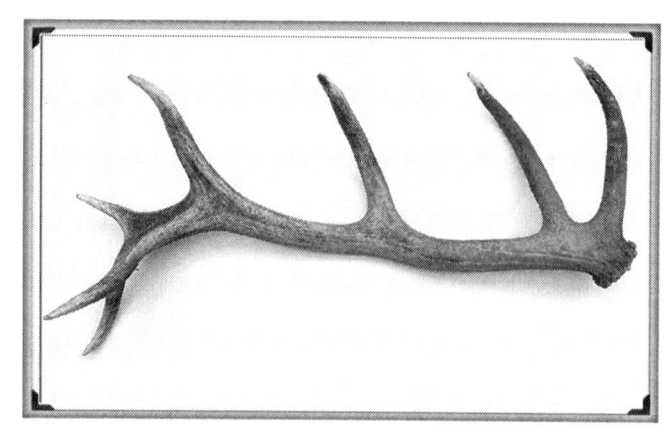

Figure 86- Typical Antler

"Over 130 antler implements are known to survive from excavations by Gowland, Hawley and Atkinson et al. Antler implements have frequently been associated with Neolithic and Early Bronze Age monuments in Britain located on chalk or limestone, and it is generally assumed that they were the principal implements used in the digging of ditches, postholes and stone holes.

In a paper on the Neolithic, engineer Atkinson (1961) wrote "the tools used - antler picks, bone wedges and occasionally stone axes - are well-known and require no further discussion. However, some of the generalisations made in the literature about antler implements require modification in the light of the finds from Stonehenge."

The Victorian Archaeologists found antlers all over Stonehenge and in the ditches that had filled up over the years. So, the conclusion 'was that no other tools' – apart from antlers and bone parts had been used as this was the only remains found. However, the only part of the antler that could successfully break the solid chalk is the harder 'tines'.

The problem with the tines is that they all grow the same way, and so they would not naturally allow a clean strike at the chalk bedrock if used like a 'pickaxe', unless you removed two of the three tines. And hence the 'gobbledygook' sorry line in the Atkinson's report which says that 'methods of modification and the forms of the picks are more varied than has been hitherto appreciated'.

If we are seeing systematic use and preparation of these tools as has been suggested by archaeologists in the past, we should first see two clean cuts with a stone axe or cutter to 'prune' the antler and then secondly blunt and reshaped tines with compression strikes from a stone or another blunt instrument on the antler stem behind the tine spike - but we don't!

Of the 118 antler picks found at Stonehenge, 82 antlers had the harder tines attached. Of the 82 with tines - only 25 had the other two smaller tines removed; this is only 21% of the antler finds. Moreover, of the 25 picks that could be used – none had compression marks or had signs of sharpening.

Remembering, these 25 picks was the entire finds within the Stonehenge area, which archaeologists have suggested was constructed in three phases over a 700-year period.

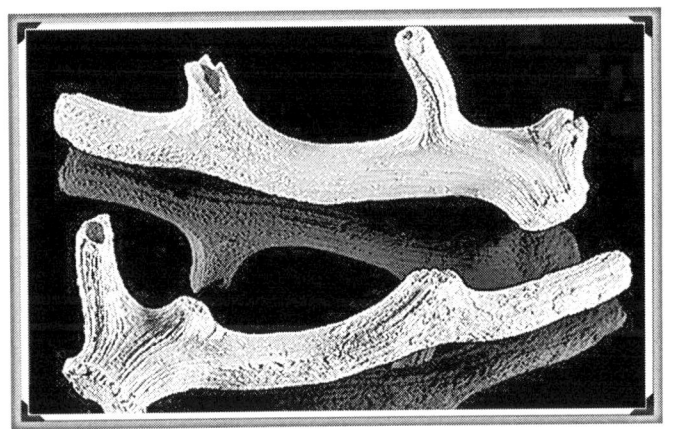

Figure 87 - English Heritage Display of Finds from Stonehenge showing Antlers with broken and not blunt tines

Moreover, in Phase I of the Ditch; Bank and Aubrey hole construction (which would have contained the Bluestones from Wales). It has been estimated that these tools need to remove 87,000 cubic feet of chalk, taking 30,000 working-hours. Yet, according to the location were the discarded antlers were found, there were only seven suitable antlers available with the correct tines, this would mean that each whole antler had removed 12,429 cubic feet, without damage.

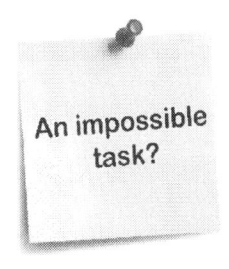

An impossible task?

Sadly, even more, implausible as this massive figure suggests, is that we have not taken into consideration the size of the antler. Obviously, the bigger, the better, for the more extended the antler, the better the levering motion to remove the chalk blocks. This being the case, they must have used the most massive antlers possible, especially when you consider that the number of Deer in Britain in prehistoric times is far greater than today and 'bucks' shed their antlers on an annual basis. At present, there are 1.5 million Red Deer in Britain – but even with the same size of the population in prehistoric times the builders of Stonehenge could have chosen from at least half a million antlers.

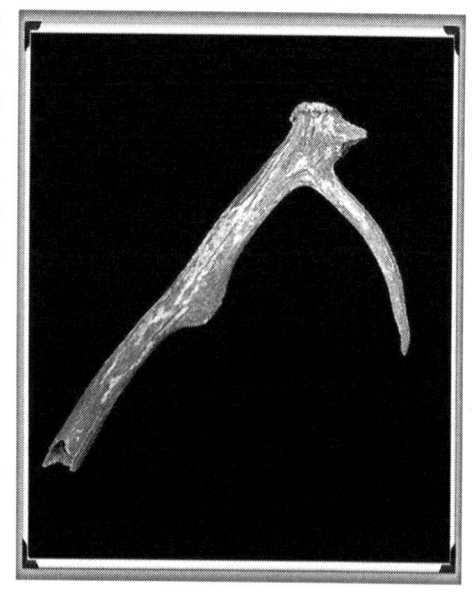

Consequently, only the largest and best antlers should have been available to this highly organised society' who could muster a group of people not only dig out 87,000 cubic ft of chalk but also plan to obtain 56, 4-tonne Bluestones from 200 miles away in the mountains of Wales.

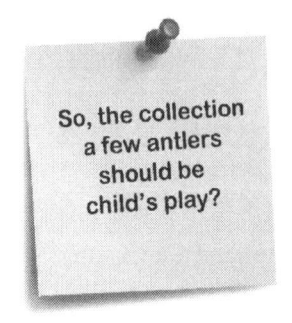

Figure 88- Antler Pick found by Hawley

> So, the collection a few antlers should be child's play?

However, the evidence shows that this was far from the truth. The distribution analysis shows that of the total number of antlers found, their sizes varied greatly. The Average length of a typical antler found at Stonehenge is just 210mm (8.5"), and some antlers are as small as 150mm (6 inches) in size compared to the largest found which was 299mm (12 inches) in length, and only one of this size was found. Antlers typically measure 710mm (28 in) in total length, although large ones can grow to 1150 mm (45 in).

The statistics from English Heritage 'could be much better' and more accurate as they only measure the distance between the bur (the thickest part that is attached to the head) and the trez which is the third tine up from the base bur. The Trez is not the strongest tine on the antler - that is the brow. However, there are so few antlers cut to this correct and more effective way that EH decided this strange method to compare sizes - even so, we can see how these antlers were not clearly selected for their size. The Average size (distance from Bur to Trez) was 190mm (7.5") some as small as 110mm (4") - compared to the largest again available of 410mm (16").

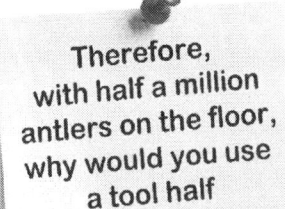

> Therefore, with half a million antlers on the floor, why would you use a tool half as effective than available?

This strange lack of evidence can also be seen in other monuments where even greater numbers of 'antler picks' would be required but have to date not been found, such as Avebury, which has one of the largest for a monument in Britain as it contains three stone circles within. Current archaeological estimates suggest that it took 1.5 million working-hours to build the Avebury monument which includes digging out 3.4 million cubic feet of chalk, that's forty times larger than Stonehenge.

Excavation at Avebury has been limited. In 1894, Sir Henry Meux put a trench through the bank, which gave the first indication that the earthwork was built in two phases. The site was surveyed and excavated intermittently between 1908 and 1922 by a team of workmen under the direction of Harold St George Gray. He could demonstrate that the Avebury builders had dug down 11 metres (36 ft) into the natural chalk using 'red deer antlers' as

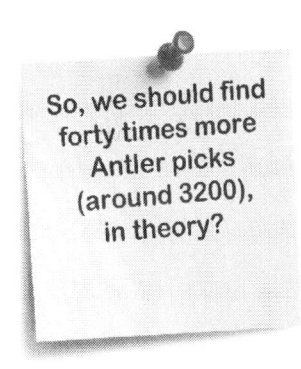

> So, we should find forty times more Antler picks (around 3200), in theory?

their primary digging tool, producing a henge ditch with a 9-metre (30 ft) high bank around its perimeter. Gray recorded the base of the ditch as being four metres (13 ft) wide and flat, but later archaeologists have questioned his use of untrained labour to excavate the ditch and suggested that its form may have been different. Gray found few artefacts in the ditch-fill, but he did recover scattered human bones, among which jawbones were particularly well represented. At a depth of about two metres (7 ft), Gray found the complete skeleton of a 1.5-metre (5 ft) tall woman. (Wikipedia)

Grey cut through the ditch and suggests the tools that built this structure, but the expected vast amounts of abandoned antler picks from their labour are minimal to non-existent. The reality is that he found more human bones than antlers.

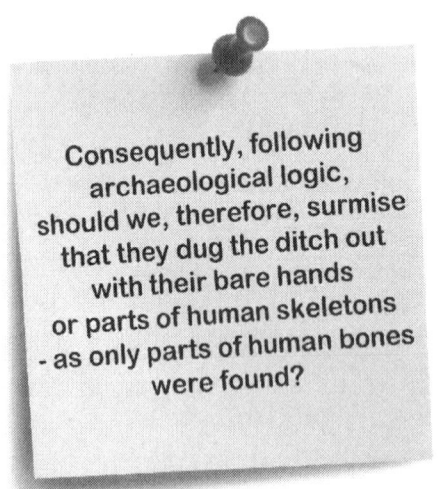

> Consequently, following archaeological logic, should we, therefore, surmise that they dug the ditch out with their bare hands or parts of human skeletons - as only parts of human bones were found?

To highlight the absurdity of this antler myth, we need not look any further than English Heritage's publication called 'Radiocarbon Dates, from samples funded by English heritage from 1981 - 1988' - one would imagine that if we scratch below the surface of these monuments, the broken remains of the tools used to build these magnificent constructions would be obvious. However, the book tells another story.

Of all the samples found; 'Antler' was the second smallest behind Animal Bone, Human Bone, Wood and Charcoal by a large margin. In fact, Animal Bone was three times larger than antler. However, human bones were five times the largest find - the reality is they found only three pieces of antler (one from the bank of Avebury in 1937, one from West Kennet Avenue and one from the Avebury ditch in 1909), and even then, we are not sure what parts of the antler were found.

> So, we found just one antler bone tool from Avebury – the largest prehistoric human-made ditches in Britain.

Therefore, how can a scientific discipline claim that these features were made from antler picks and shoulder blade shovels when there is just one fragment of antler ever carbon-dated at Avebury?

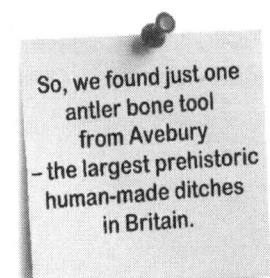

Prehistoric Britain – The Stonehenge Enigma

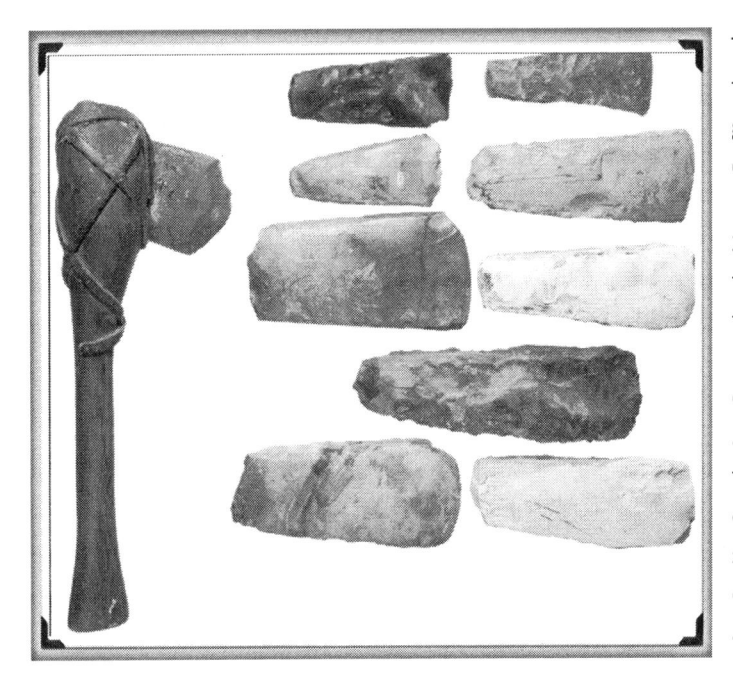

Figure 89- Used Neolithic Stone Axes found in Central Europe – a far more intelligent choice than an Antler?

The truth is that this myth has grown around the excavations in the last century at Stonehenge when the archaeologists found antler picks in the ditches. Carbon dating was a new science in the 1950s, and only organic samples could be dated – therefore, antler picks were perfect for testing out this new dating process, and the site had just been 'revamped' by the ministry of works in 1958, to become a new tourist attraction – adding paths, concreting prehistoric sarsen stones and rehanging lintels.

Therefore, a new date in the distant past was excellent news for the media and consequently, the archaeological circus started and, it has never finished – with a constant need for publicity rather than sound science.

The reality is that rather than using antler picks to build these monuments, the workers used a much hardier and more practical tool which we know that does not break as often and was abundant at the time of the construction of these sites – the stone axe.

This is the ONLY tool that could have possibly been used to cut down the trees for these monuments – yet they put it away to use an inefficient antler tool when it came to dig out either pits or ditches? Such an idea is so absurd that it does question the expertise of those who continually suggest that the antler pick were used for such tasks and the construction dates based on these tools are accurate.

Moreover, some have broken ranks in recent years and offered tantalising clues on a more rational explanation of our history and the deception game being played by academia Mike Parker-Pearson in his book 'Stonehenge' revealed that they found 'cut marks' in the chalk in an excavation at Durrington Walls (Woodhenge) that looked like it was made from a 'metal' instrument.

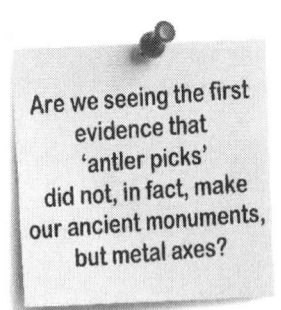

Are we seeing the first evidence that 'antler picks' did not, in fact, make our ancient monuments, but metal axes?

This would make a lot more sense than current archaeological theories - but what is the big deal if this was true. Why not just accept the evidence and go forward with these more practical metal tools being available?

Well this then 'digs' archaeology into a larger theoretical hole for metals (such as Bronze) was supposedly not invented until about 2500 BCE in Britain - hence the Victorian term of the 'Bronze Age' (2500BCE - 70BCE), which would need to be adjusted in most text books as it is inaccurate. Moreover, we now know that bronze and copper axes were available elsewhere in Central Europe and the Mediterranean, thousands of years earlier. And it is quite feasible they therefore had such tools (as we have already illustrated in previous chapters) for this was a trading civilisation with boats, that sailed to the four corners of the ancient world – which is also not written in our history books

Figure 90- Copper Axes also available at the time of these monuments' construction

Chapter 8 – Barrows

*A tumulus (plural tumuli) the word tumulus is Latin for 'mound' or 'small hill', from the PIE root *teuh- with extended zero grade *tum-, 'to bulge, swell' also found in tumor, thumb, thigh and thousand - A mound of earth and stones raised over a grave or graves. Tumuli are also known as barrows, burial mounds, Hügelgrab or kurgans, and can be found throughout much of the world. A tumulus composed largely or entirely of stones is usually referred to as a cairn. A long barrow is a long tumulus, usually for numbers of burials. The method of inhumation may involve a dolmen, a cyst, a mortuary enclosure, a mortuary house or a chamber tomb.*

Not overly precise is it!

It's a grave, although the Latin word does not mean the grave, but a 'small hill'. That's a big difference; they also can be long or round, stone or earth, etc. When we look at the traditional archaeological definition of tumuli, we are offered:

- Bank barrow

- Bell barrow

- Bowl barrow

- D-shaped barrow - round barrow with a purposely flat edge at one side often defined by stone slabs

- Fancy barrow - a generic term for any Bronze Age barrows more elaborate than a simple hemispherical shape.

- Long barrow

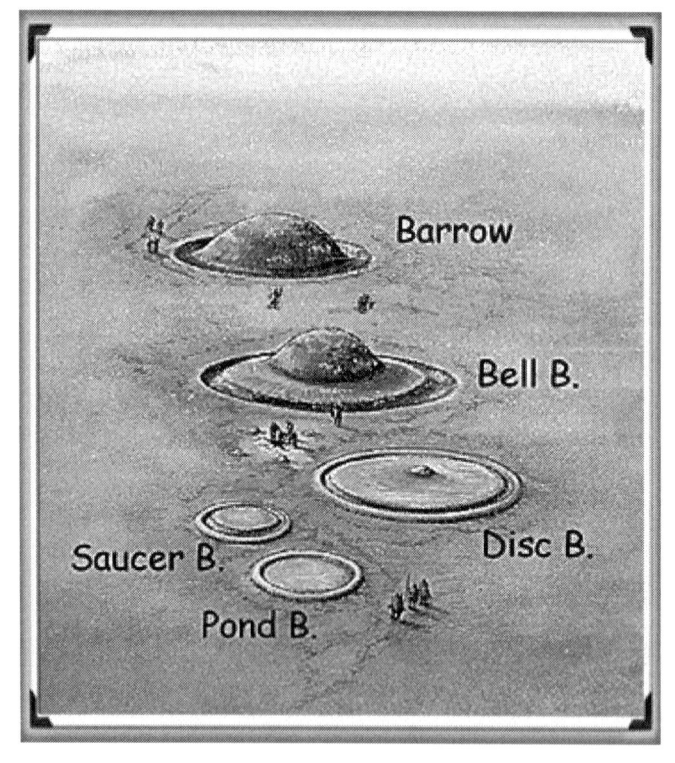

[Figure: Illustration showing types of barrows labelled Barrow, Bell B., Saucer B., Pond B., Disc B.]

- Oval barrow - a Neolithic long barrow consisting of an elliptical, rather than rectangular or trapezoidal mound.

- Platform barrow - the least common of the recognised types of round barrow, consisting of a flat, wide circular mound, which may be surrounded by a ditch. They occur widely across southern England with a marked concentration in East and West Sussex.

- Pond barrow - a barrow consisting of a shallow circular depression, surrounded by a bank running around the rim of the depression.

- Ring barrow - a bank which encircles several burials.

- Round barrow - a circular feature created by the Bronze Age peoples of Britain and also the later Romans, Vikings, and Saxons. Divided into subclasses such as saucer and bell barrow.

- Saucer barrow - circular Bronze Age barrow featuring a low, wide mound surrounded by a ditch, which may be accompanied by an external bank.

- Square barrow - burial site, usually of Iron Age date, consisting of a small, square, ditched enclosure surrounding a central burial, which may also have been covered by a mound

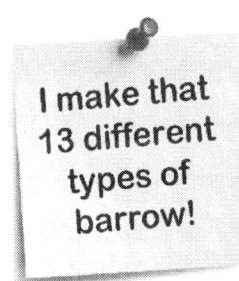

If the archaeologists are right, and barrows are just grave plots, they could be any shape. But do we believe each had a different function or the same purpose in various forms? The truth is that there are (in my view) just five categories of barrow:

> *I make that 13 different types of barrow!*

- **Long Barrow** - the most significant and earliest form used for burials

- **Round Barrows** – big and round used as markers

- **Pond Barrows** – wells for water extraction

- **Disturbed barrows** – Round/Long/Pond Barrows that have degraded over 5,000 years by the elements and man's attempts to destroy or excavate them

- **Copy barrows** – imitation Barrows from a later date, mimicking their ancestors.

Barrow Altitude

We have surveyed a sample of 50 prehistoric sites and monuments within the Stonehenge area, to look at their topology, in connection to the landscape. Our findings show that the traditional belief, that prehistoric man, located his burials, ceremonial sites and structures on top of hills are wholly inaccurate - in fact, in our survey shows that only 8% of sites are on top of a hill.

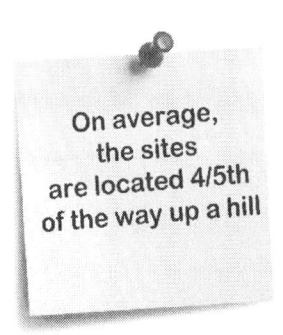

> *On average, the sites are located 4/5th of the way up a hill*

This includes our most ancient site, Stonehenge. Consequently, we are led to believe by archaeologists that our ancestors brought the bluestones all the way from Wales (some 250 miles) only to stop 50 metres short of the top of the hill because they were….. tired, or some other obscure unknown ceremonial or astronomical reason.

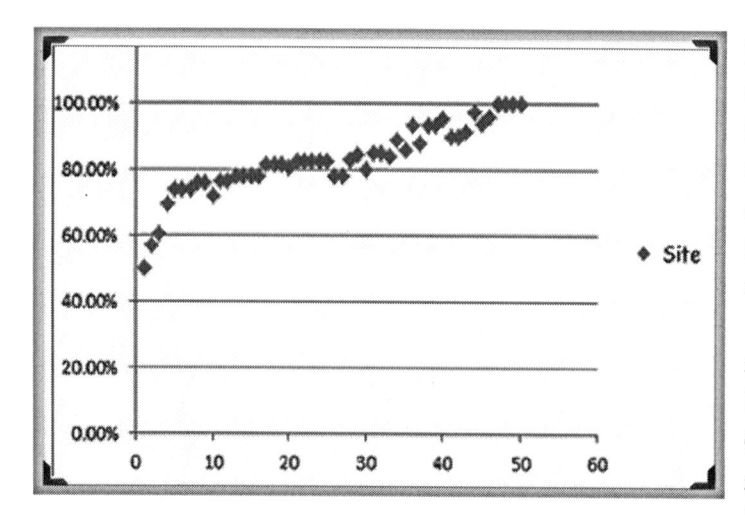

Figure 91 - Fifty ancient site locations around the Stonehenge Area

Moreover, our survey also shows that these barrows were not constructed at random heights either. In the Stonehenge sample, the lowest burial was at 89m OD (above current sea level), the highest at 115m OD. The only logical reason you would construct your barrow at the mid-point or two-thirds up a hillside would be that there was another overriding factor to consider. This reason can only be that you can't build a barrow below this level as it would be underwater.

The variations shown in these sites is due to the groundwater tables falling from the Mesolithic (high) to the Neolithic (low), after which barrows were no longer built for their original purpose as the Bronze, Iron Age, Vikings and even Saxons civilisations copied their ancestral rituals and barrows for burial purposes only, and these are the only barrows built are below the old prehistoric water table. This empirical evidence I call 'archaeology of the landscape' – where we can date the ancient sites by the location of their shorelines.

Long Barrows

The first thing we should note about Long Barrows is that they are unique to Northern Europe, unlike Round Barrows, which are found all over the world. Archaeologists agree that the Long Barrow is the oldest monument to exist in our landscape. As shown by the carbon dating from Carnac in France of St Michael's tumuli (a Long Barrow) dated to 6850 BCE. Prior to this confirmation archaeologists have always believed these enormous and elaborate structures which include giant megaliths at their entrances clearly belonged to a civilisation that lived long ago. Moreover, they are also aware that the bones from many dead people were collected together inside the chambers, rather than in individual graves, or cremations that were seen at a later date.

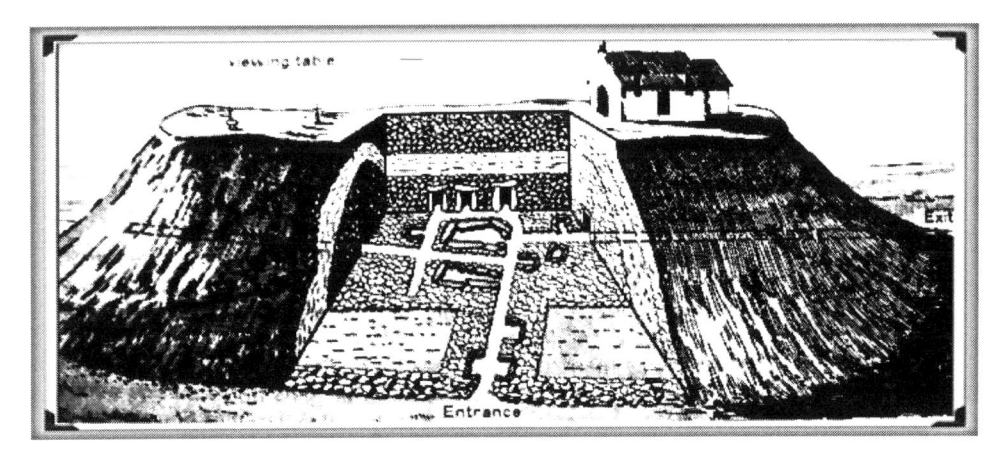

Figure 92- St. Michaels Long Barrow - Carnac

The number and condition of these bones show us that they were disarticulated, with only the larger bones and skulls being brought to the sites after death, probably after the bones had been defleshed. We believe their shape and design are of great importance. Firstly, the monuments are long and thin, with the entrance at the end of the mound. The entire Long Barrow mound originally had a ditch dug completely around its exterior, to represent water and the voyage to the afterlife.

During the prehistoric period, Long Barrows like West Kennet were on a peninsula, surrounded on three sides by water. This groundwater now gives us a clue as to why the ditches that surrounded the monument were dug, for the bottom of the ditches would have been below the groundwater table at this location. Therefore, the ditches of today were moats of yesteryear.

The other noteworthy aspect of Long Barrows is the size and construction of the monument. At West Kennet and other Long Barrows, giant megaliths were used to highlight the entrance to the chambers; these boulders are over 15 tonnes in weight and four to five metres in height. They are an unnecessary addition to the construction, but they are visible even a couple of miles away on a clear day. Long Barrows when first constructed would have been covered not with grass as today, but with the sub-soil that came from the ditches they dug that surrounded the monument, in the case of West Kennet, it would be bright white chalk. The massive size of these monuments must also be taken into consideration as they are over 100m in length - five times longer than the chambers they hide within them, and they are tapered from the helm 4m high to the bow, just 1m high. Making them look like a gigantic direction indicator.

Another remarkable aspect of Long Barrows is their location and position on the landscape. If we look at the extensive river ways after the last ice age, we notice that these monuments are built parallel to major rivers and appear at junctions where rivers converge. Moreover, they don't appear on the top of the hills that surround the rivers, but actually appear just over halfway up - so that they cannot be seen over the top of the hill on the opposite side. Because of their size and construction materials, these 'markers' are visible for miles like white pointers in daylight, but because they are pure white, they can also be seen at night with 'moonshine'.

The Long Barrow represents the boat culture of this ancient society; they lived in boats, and so, when they died, they were sent on their last voyage by boat to the afterlife. Even today, we still have a custom of placing money over a dead person's eyes as their fare to be collected by the ferryman. Consequently, this also gives us a fantastic insight into the design of the boats used in this period. This boat looks more like a barge than a canoe, with the back end (the stern) being where they steered the craft with a rudder, which means they used sails (not paddles) for power.

Page | 191

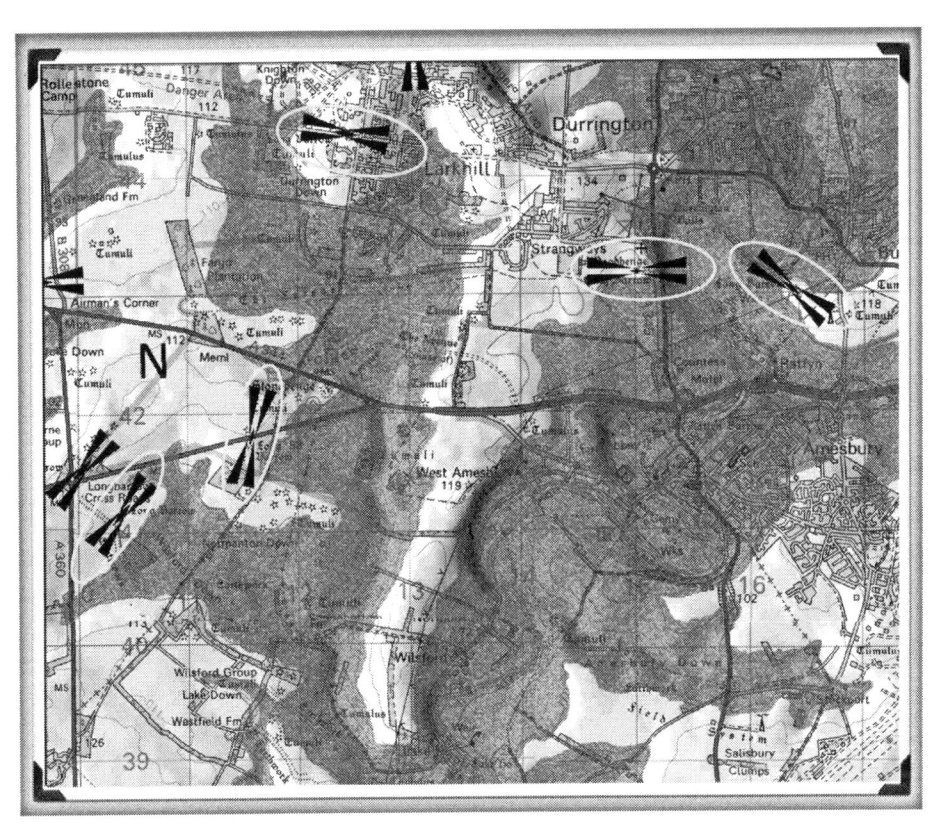

Figure 93- Stonehenge area with eight Long Barrows aligned to the River Avon indicating direction to sail

28. The positioning of Long Barrows high on hillsides overlooking and in full view of ancient waterways - proves that they were used to navigate the higher/larger rivers of Mesolithic Britain and Northern Europe.

Prehistoric Britain – The Stonehenge Enigma

Round Barrows

In our examination of Long Barrows, we have discovered that this civilisation traded heavily with other cultures, tribes, clans and groups within prehistoric Britain and beyond.

Herefordshire businessman Alfred Watkins was sitting in his car one summer afternoon, during a visit to Blackwardine in Herefordshire in 1921, when he happened to consult a local map and noticed that a number of prehistoric and other ancient sites in the area fell into alignments.

Subsequent field and map work convinced him that this pattern was indeed a real one. Watkins came to the conclusion that he saw the vestigial traces of old straight tracks laid down in the Neolithic Period, probably, he surmised, for traders' routes.

He concluded that after modernisation in the later Bronze and Iron Age periods, the tracks had fallen into disuse during the early historic period. The pattern had been accidentally preserved here and there due to the Christianisation of individual pagan sites that were markers along the old straight tracks. He published these theories in two books.

Reaction to Watkins' book 'The Old Straight Track' was sharply divided. Many thought he had uncovered a long-forgotten secret within the landscape, and The Straight Track Club was formed to carry out further "ley hunting", while orthodox archaeologists vehemently dismissed the whole notion. And with a few notable exceptions, this situation still exists today.

There are two kinds of tracks: Firstly, as we have shown, the older Long Barrows were markers based on islands and peninsulas within the river routes to known sites; then, after the groundwater subsided, Round Barrows were used for overland routes.

When the groundwater subsided after the Neolithic Period, our ancestors needed a further navigational aid to allow them to find the location overland rather than by river as in the past. These markers are known today as Round Barrows, and they are consequently, more frequent than Long Barrows because dense foliage makes the line of sight shorter for someone on foot than for someone taking the same route by boat and secondly, there are more routes by foot, than by river to navigate.

The incorrectly conceived aspect of Watkins land markers is that they did not run in perfectly straight lines, but actually to the high ground. This was because the lower ground that had been flooded in the Mesolithic period would still be boggy and wet in some seasons, and therefore impassable. Therefore, these tracks are straight, but not ruler-straight as Watkins first believed. One of the closest sites to Stonehenge is Quarley Hill, to the East, the path between these two sites passes 13 barrows, in a 15 km distance.

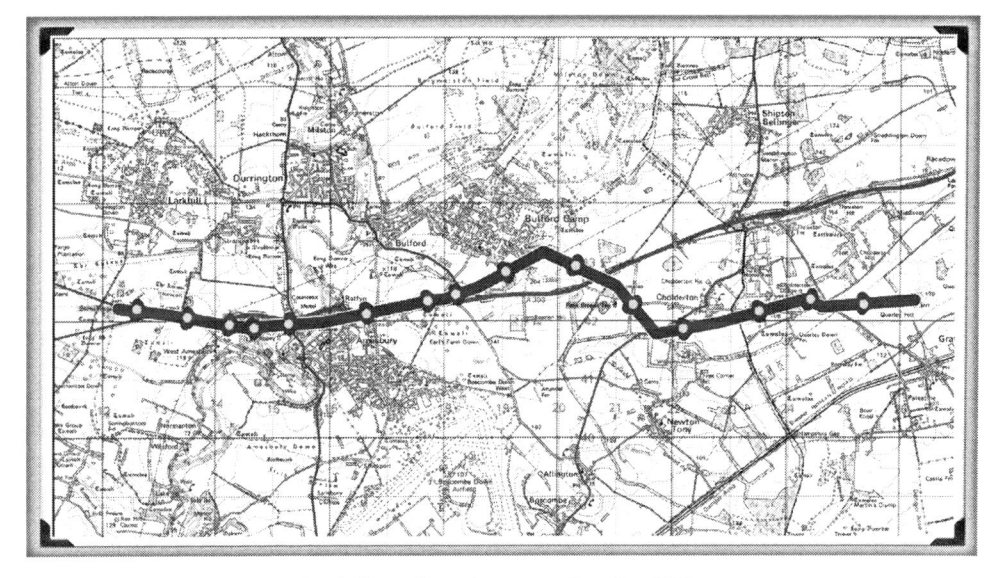

Figure 94- Round Barrow Path from Stonehenge to Quarley Hill

If you stand on top of one of these barrows, you can see the next one in line very clearly. You must also take into consideration, that farmers have ploughed out nearly half the barrows, and that the mounds would have been at least 30% larger, and pure white, at time of construction. Even so, they can still be seen as path markers today in some areas, 5,000 years later.

It is almost impossible to know what information would have greeted a walker in the Neolithic when he reached a Round Barrow, but we still have roman milestones surviving today on our modern roads, and I believe, this is a relic from our ancient past. One can only imagine that somehow the barrow, like a milestone, would give an indication of the distance to be travelled, this was probably on a standing stone, buried upright in the centre of the barrow. It should also be noted that the burials within these Round Barrows, were placed in them at a much later date, which would explain why these barrows do not contain burials at the centre and have been dug into the edges as an afterthought and not the original design.

Pond Barrows
Now we have established the use of the majority of prehistoric barrows by our ancestors. We can look at the 'other' barrows catalogued by archaeologists, to see what function they had in helping our ancestors navigate from town to town in prehistoric days. Pond barrows' shape is just as described: 'pond-like', and as we now understand, the groundwater tables were higher in the past, consequently, creating artificial ponds.

Water, in any civilisation, is critical to survival. Our ancestors were no exception, so when they travelled on foot to other towns or sites, the provision of water was essential. Most pond barrows have the centre dugout, which would have tapped into the groundwater course; this would allow the pond to flood, depending on the tide levels. This tradition continues into modern days by the use of dew ponds, which are of the same size and shape, but relied more on rainwater to fill the pond.

Other Barrows
These barrows are the original path markers that have either eroded over the last five thousand years or the remains have been altered and adapted over time by later descendants. Burials mark a change in use for these round barrows by later civilisations including the mimicking of similar round barrows by Bronze and Iron age people (including the Vikings) as a mark of respect for their ancestors who they wish to be buried amongst and hence the historical confusion and variety.

Case study- Winterbourne Stoke Crossroads

The Winterbourne Stoke Crossroads round barrow cemetery comprises a linear arrangement of 19 late Neolithic / Early Bronze Age circular earthwork monuments, commonly known as round barrows. Winterbourne Stoke 3 (Monument Number 870372) to 10 (870444) are aligned to the north-east of the Neolithic long barrow known as Winterbourne Stoke 1 (Monument Number 219696). They extend south-west / north-east for nearly 600m: this alignment continues after a gap of circa 100m (see Winterbourne Stoke 22: Monument Number 219720). A roughly parallel secondary alignment immediately to the west comprises Winterbourne Stoke 2a (Monument Number 866648) to 12 (Monument Number 870446). A cluster of barrows sits slightly apart, circa 250m north-west of the main alignment (Monument Number 215072). Most of the barrows were excavated by Sir Richard Colt Hoare in the early 19th century.

What is missing from the above explanation by English Heritage, is the earthworks throughout the site which are both unmeasured and unexcavated. This is because the most fundamental understanding of the environment at the time of these barrows' construction is unknown or misunderstood. If they looked under the surface of the soil, they would see that not too far away from this large number of barrows are the remains of a large Palaeochannel river.

If you look at a map of this area, you will see the modern crossroads that now lies in the middle of the barrow complex; this intersection is no accident of history. As we have discussed previously, Round Barrows are markers for Neolithic pathways and therefore, when these prehistoric roads cross, you will get a collection of barrows from separate directions. Modern roads are mainly built on the remains of previous roads which in turn are constructed again on their initial ancient pathways.

> But if we place the Mesolithic water line into the landscape, something incredible happens.

The closest earthworks to the winterbourne crossroads run North West (NW) to South East (SE) for about 500m, it then seems to meet another earthwork running NNW to SSE for about the same distance making the entire earthwork about one kilometre long. If the size is like our Wansdyke earthwork case study, we are looking at a 20,000 cubic m³ excavation taking about 20,000 hours using stone age tools, or 100 men taking about 20 days or one man taking 5 years (non-stop) - so not the small farming feature archaeologists may have you believe.

Sitting at the height of 110m above sea level it is a curious feature, it can't be defensive, as you can walk around the edge, it can't be for animals as it stops nothing - fences would have been much more effective and take less than five years to build.

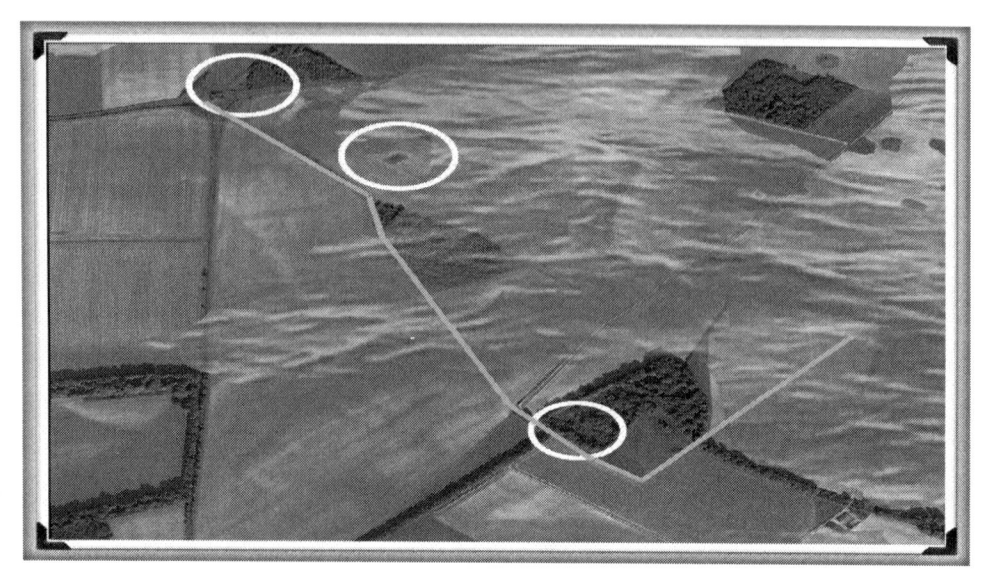

Figure 95- Winterbourne Crossroads - showing the three Long Barrows and the interconnecting Dyke

With the Mesolithic groundwater level (85m – 95m), the Long Barrow – Wilsford 34 is surrounded (like Stonehenge) on three sides making it a peninsula. But as the Mesolithic waters receded, the Long Barrow became isolated, so a dyke (canal) was built to meet the new shoreline. This new dyke would eventually service not just one but three long barrows (Stoke 1, Wilsford 34, and Wilsford 41).

Even more surprising is a second dyke that was in a completely different direction (southwest) cuts into the Neolithic waterway (which is 10m lower at this point) creating a dyke to the 'lake group' of round barrows connecting with the Long Barrow dyke. Although these existing earthworks have not been investigated and sadly mostly destroyed through ploughing – they still are scheduled monuments and appear as part earthworks in two parts on most OS maps. Fortunately, the size and extent of this feature can still be seen on satellite photographs.

The northwest dyke has been cut to lead to not just one, but all three Long Barrows in this area, which is beyond a coincidence. As we have already discussed the Long Barrow is where our prehistoric ancestors buried their dead's bones from the excarnation site. If Stonehenge was the last place of rest, then these are three of the four Long barrows on the river Avon that are nearest the site.

So why bother cutting these dykes, where does it lead too?

Using 'Archaeology of the Landscape' techniques, we can now estimate that initially the Mesolithic shoreline reached Wilsford 34 and turned it into a peninsula, which indicates that it is the oldest of the Long Barrows. Stoke 1, seems to be the second oldest in the late Mesolithic or early Neolithic as the dyke appears to have been extended, northwest to the crossroads. Finally, during the Neolithic, the Last Long Barrow Wilsford 41 was built, and the dyke was again extended South East this time and a second dyke running Northeast (from the Neolithic river level) was finally built to meet the first dyke, which may have started to lose water height and volume..

This just one example of how the prehistoric raised groundwater levels not only giving us the reason for these strange landscape features, but also dates and sequences for these Long Barrows at Winterbourne.

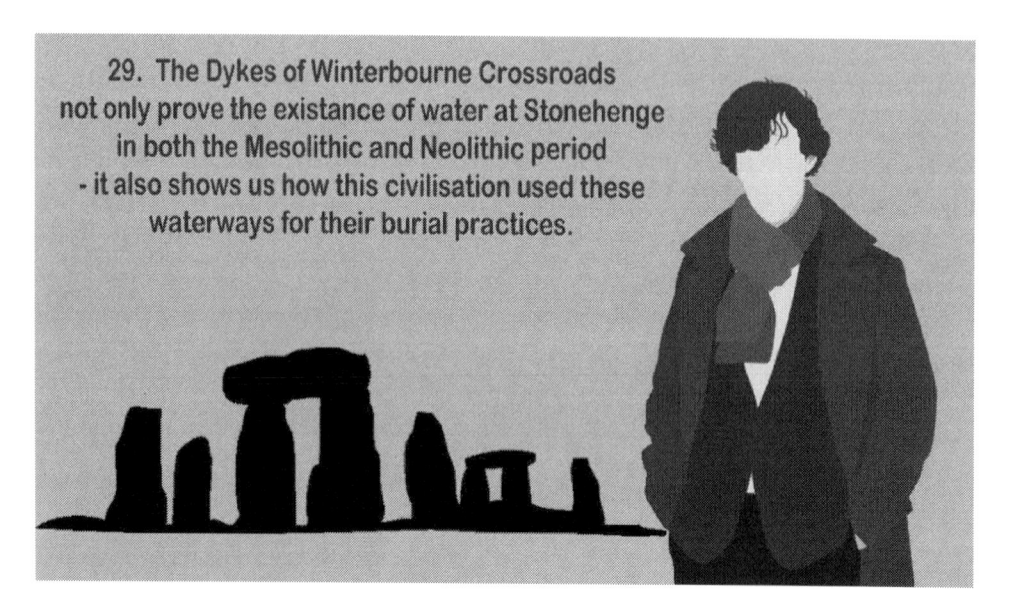

29. The Dykes of Winterbourne Crossroads not only prove the existance of water at Stonehenge in both the Mesolithic and Neolithic period - it also shows us how this civilisation used these waterways for their burial practices.

Case Study- The Cursus

If you draw a line from Stonehenge altar to the Preseli mountain region in South Wales, you will find that your line not only points to the horizon where the midsummer moon sets, but leads over the far Western edge of the Cursus, past a point believed to contain yet another crescent Bluestone circle facing North West, which was first suspected by Atkinson but has yet to be located.

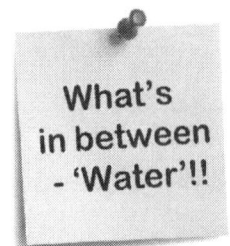

What's in between - 'Water'!!

Now, if you do the same exercise with the direction of the summer solstice sunrise, drawing a line from the centre of Stonehenge through the Heel Stone, you will see on the horizon another long barrow which, though it has now been ploughed out, marks the other end of the Cursus.

So, we have an alignment from the centre of Stonehenge to the Preseli Mountains that cuts over the Western end of the Cursus, and an alignment over the Eastern end of the Cursus to Woodhenge. If you examine the profile of this area, the Cursus cuts across a valley that we have now proved was full of groundwater in the Mesolithic Period. This would have given the monument the appearance of two islands separated by groundwater, and clearly, this is what our ancestors saw.

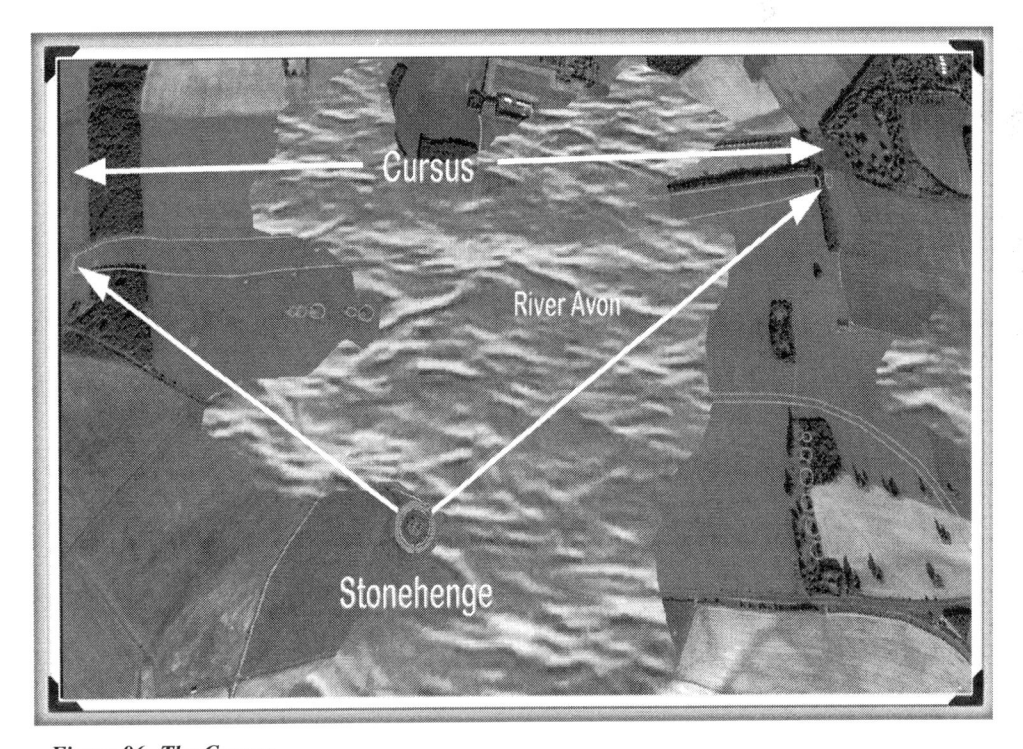

Figure 96- The Cursus

This being the case, it does not take much imagination to see that when the groundwater receded during the Neolithic Period, to maintain the water connection between the two end sites of the Cursus, they dug a ditch that encapsulated the entire region. What we see in the Cursus is a giant model of the world as our ancestors perceived it. On the Eastern side was a long barrow representing death, where the bones were stored. In between lay the water and the final journey to the afterlife. On the western bank of the Cursus was an island, probably marked with a large standing stone, where the ancestors arrived after death, no doubt to be reborn again. What we see at the Cursus is the first sculptural artwork in the history of humankind, and the size and magnitude of this artwork gives us a clear indication of the resourcefulness and dominance of this great civilisation.

30. The Cursus makes no sense in the landscape until we place the waters of the Mesolithic when it becomes a boat crossing between death and the afterlife - this proof is verified when they attempted to continue this water connection in the Neolithic by adding a ditch to create a moat around the site.

Chapter 9 – Dykes, Ditches and Earthworks

The modern word dike or dyke most likely derives from the Dutch word "dijk", with the construction of dikes in the Netherlands well attested as early as the 12th century. The 126 kilometres (78 mi) long Westfriese Omringdijk was completed by 1250 and was formed by connecting existing older dikes. The Roman chronicler Tacitus even mentions that the rebellious Batavi pierced dikes to flood their land and to protect their retreat (AD 70). The word dijk originally indicated both the trench and the bank.

If you study archaeology at university or even on an ordinance survey map at length, you will notice strange earthworks on the sides of hills of Britain, with no rational explanation to why they are there and for what reason. At university, these features are mostly ignored, or an excuse is made for their construction. The reality is that these features do not make any sense unless there are other factors in operation, which have been ignored.

The first thing to notice is that the word 'Dyke' is associated with water. It does seem strange you would call an earthwork on top of a hill a Dyke, unless there was some history passed down through the years to its real use. If we look at the most famous Dyke in Britain 'Offa', we notice that it is attributed to a Saxon King and therefore could not be prehistoric. Or is this a clear indication of how archaeologists find excuses for these features rather than true empirical evidence?

"Offa's Dyke (Welsh: Clawdd Offa) is a massive linear earthwork, roughly followed by some of the current border between England and Wales. In places, it is up to 65 feet (19.8 m) wide (including its flanking ditch) and 8 feet (2.4 m) in height. In the 8th century it formed some kind of delineation between the Anglian kingdom of Mercia and the Welsh kingdom of Powys."

At face value, this explanation seems to answer all the questions about this dyke - except the water connection. But if you delve further down to look at the evidence such as findings from the dyke and any written history you get a different version, for the Roman historian Eutropius in his book, Historiae Romanae Breviarium, written around 369 AD, mentions the Wall of Severus, a structure built by Septimius Severus who was Roman Emperor between 193 AD and 211 AD:

"He had his most recent war in Britain, and to fortify the conquered provinces with all security, he built a wall for 133 miles from sea to sea. He died at York, a reasonably old man, in the sixteenth year and third month of his reign."

So, the Romans built the dyke 700 years before Offa, or did they? For they are now finding Neolithic flints inside the ditches of dykes - so how did they get there?

As we have shown on our case study on Old Sarum, the Roman are famous for taking existing features, such as ditches and adding a defensive bank for their own use as did the Normans who followed them so time later in history. Offa's Dyke has nothing to do with Offa, but this archaeological reality or misinterpretation is the key to why our history is not as we perceive.

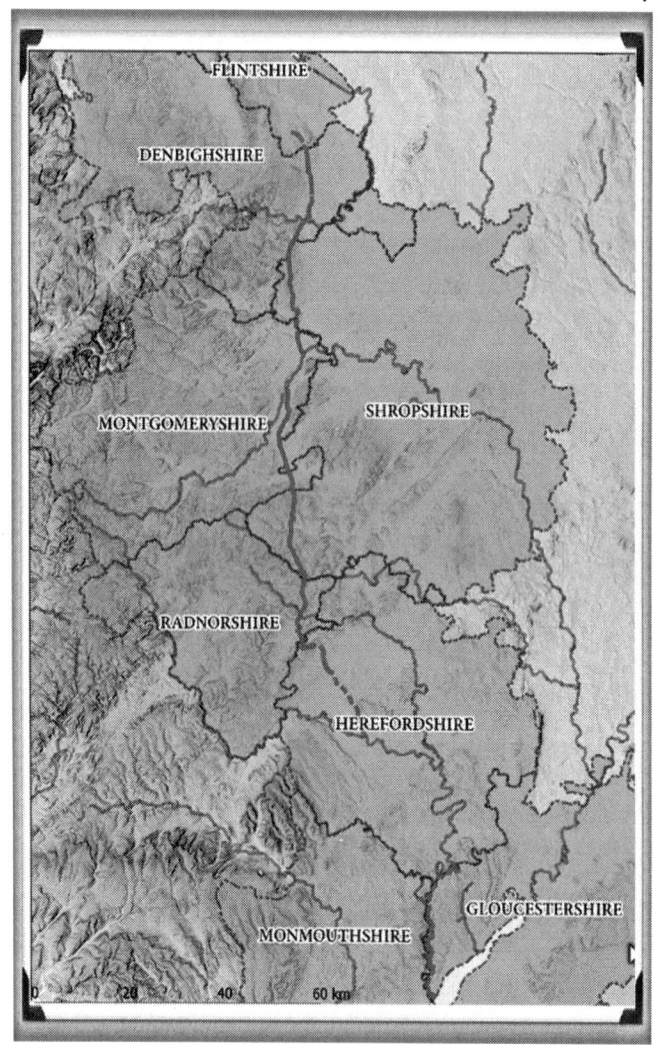

Figure 97- Off's Dyke (Red) - note that it is only complete if you connect the existing rivers to the ditches

But that is not enough to prove the higher groundwater levels in prehistory contributed to these strange earthworks, so let's look at some in our study area where we have constructed detailed inflated river maps of Wiltshire in both the Mesolithic and Neolithic periods of history.

CASE STUDY- Wansdyke

According to Wikipedia Wansdyke consists of two sections of 14 and 19 kilometres (9 and 12 mi) long with some gaps in between. East Wansdyke is an impressive linear earthwork, consisting of a ditch and bank running approximately east-west, between Savernake Forest and Morgan's Hill. West Wansdyke is also a linear earthwork, running from Monkton Combe south of Bath to Maes Knoll south of Bristol, but less impressive than its eastern counterpart. The middle section, 22 kilometres (14 mi) long, is sometimes referred to as 'Mid Wansdyke', but is formed by the remains of the London to Bath Roman road. It used to be thought that these sections were all part of one continuous undertaking, especially during the Middle Ages when the pagan name Wansdyke was applied to all three parts.

East Wansdyke in Wiltshire, on the south of the Marlborough Downs, has been less disturbed by later agriculture and building and remains more clearly traceable on the ground than the western part. Here the bank is up to 4 m (13 ft) high with a ditch up to 2.5 m (8.2 ft) deep. Wansdyke's origins are unclear, but archaeological data shows that the eastern part was probably built during the 5th or 6th century. That is after the withdrawal of the Romans and before the takeover by Anglo-Saxons. The ditch is on the north side, so presumably it was used by the British as a defence against West Saxons encroaching from the upper Thames Valley westward into what is now the West Country.

West Wansdyke, although the antiquarians like John Collinson considered West Wansdyke to stretch from south east of Bath to the west of Maes Knoll, a review in 1960 considered that there was no evidence of its existence to the west of Maes Knoll. Keith Gardner refuted this with newly discovered documentary evidence. In 2007 a series of sections were dug across the earthwork which showed that it had existed where there are no longer visible surface remains.

It was shown that the earthwork had a consistent design, with stone or timber revetment. There was little dating evidence, but it was consistent with either a late Roman or post-Roman date. A paper in "The Last of the Britons" conference in 2007 suggests that the West Wansdyke continues from Maes Knoll to the hill forts above the Avon Gorge and controls the crossings of the river at Saltford and Bristol as well as at Bath.

As there is little archaeological evidence to date the western Wansdyke, it may have marked a division between British Celtic kingdoms or have been a boundary with the Saxons. The evidence for its western extension is earthworks along the north side of Dundry Hill, its mention in a charter and

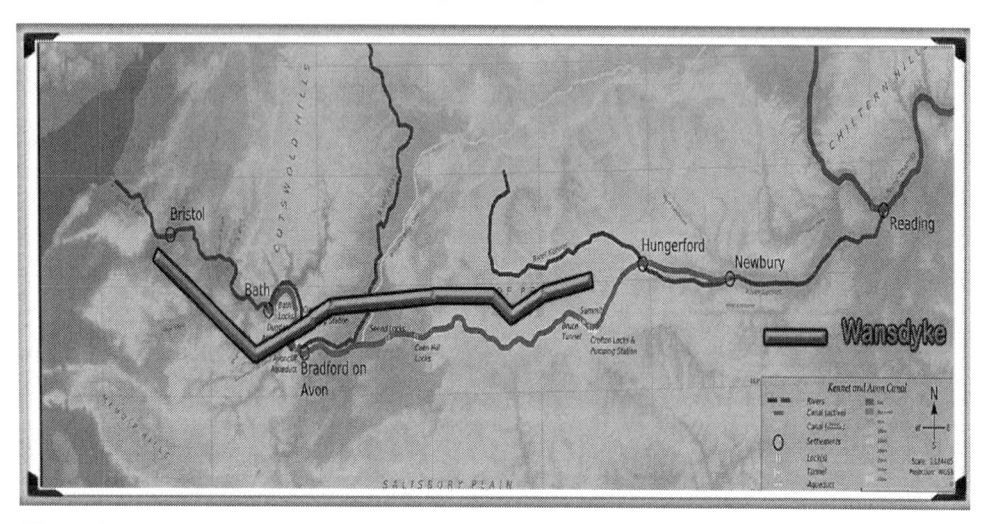

Figure 98- Map comparing Wansdyke (green) to the Kennet and Avon canal

a road name.

The area of the western Wansdyke became the border between the Romano-British Celts and the West Saxons following the Battle of Deorham in 577 AD. According to the Anglo-Saxon Chronicle, the 'Saxon' Cenwalh achieved a breakthrough against the British Celtic tribes, with victories at Bradford on

Avon (in the Avon Gap in the Wansdyke) in 652 AD, and further south at the Battle of Peonnum (at Penselwood) in 658 AD, followed by an advance west through the Polden Hills to the River Parrett. It is however significant to note that the names of the early Wessex kings appear to have a Brythonic (British) rather than Germanic (Saxon) etymology.

I thought I should give you all the 'considered' opinions of this dyke, just to show how confused and inaccurate our history books are today.

There have sadly been very few excavations, or thorough investigations of these dykes (remembering there are over 1000 dykes in Britain), one of the earliest excavations was overseen by Lieutenant – General Pitt Rivers, who excavated Wansdyke at Shepherd's Shore, Devizes.

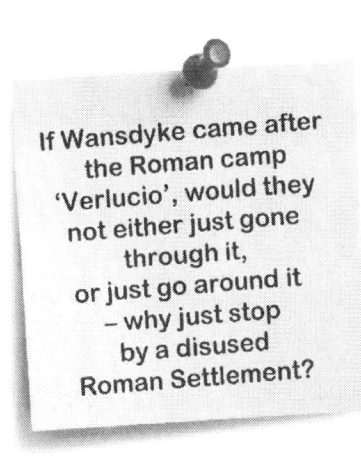

> If Wansdyke came after the Roman camp 'Verlucio', would they not either just gone through it, or just go around it – why just stop by a disused Roman Settlement?

Although most of the findings and accounts lack scientific accuracy, we find some aspects that support the dating of dykes earlier than current 'expert' theories of Saxon Britain. In one of his cuttings through the ditch and bank he noted that "At Wand's house, there is a break in the line of the Dyke, which is occupied by the site of the Roman station of Verlucio, where quantities of Roman pottery are scattered on the soil".

Pitt-Rivers also found vast amounts of pottery and iron nails in the bank of Wansdyke further down the earthwork. Isn't it more likely, that the Romans placed their settlement actually on the Dyke as it may have still held water two thousand years ago and looking at the positions of the findings, actually cleaned it out, which would allow them to take and receive supplies by boat to and from the river Kennet? Moreover, he noticed that in Section 5 Stockley to Heddington and by the Roman settlement in Spye Park – **the river was still running inside the Dyke**!

In fact within his excavation of the dyke we noted that: "Very little 'silting' had accumulated on the escarp, but in the ditch, it had collected to a depth of about 3 feet in the centre" - showing that the main purpose for the dyke was to take water like a canal.

The final proof of the fact that the Dykes predate the Roman invasion can be found strangely with empirical evidence from a drawing produced by the first British archaeologist William Stukeley in 1724. Where the Roman road is clearly made on and above the Wansdyke ditch and then cutting through the dyke's bank – this is impossible to do if the bank and ditch was built AFTER the road (archaeologist and historians, please take note!!).

Figure 99- Stukeley's Map of 1724 showing the Roman road 'sitting on top' of the Wansdyke ditch

If we look at Wansdyke on an OS map, to the East, the ditch ends in the middle of nowhere, just before the forest of Savernlake. The question that archaeologists fail to answer is 'why stop there'?

If you continued another 6km, you would have reached water - a natural boundary (remembering you have already cut 19km), or just turn south and that's a mere 3km. To the west it's even worse, you could go south again and connect to the river, using that as a natural defensive boundary, but no – it just stops dead.

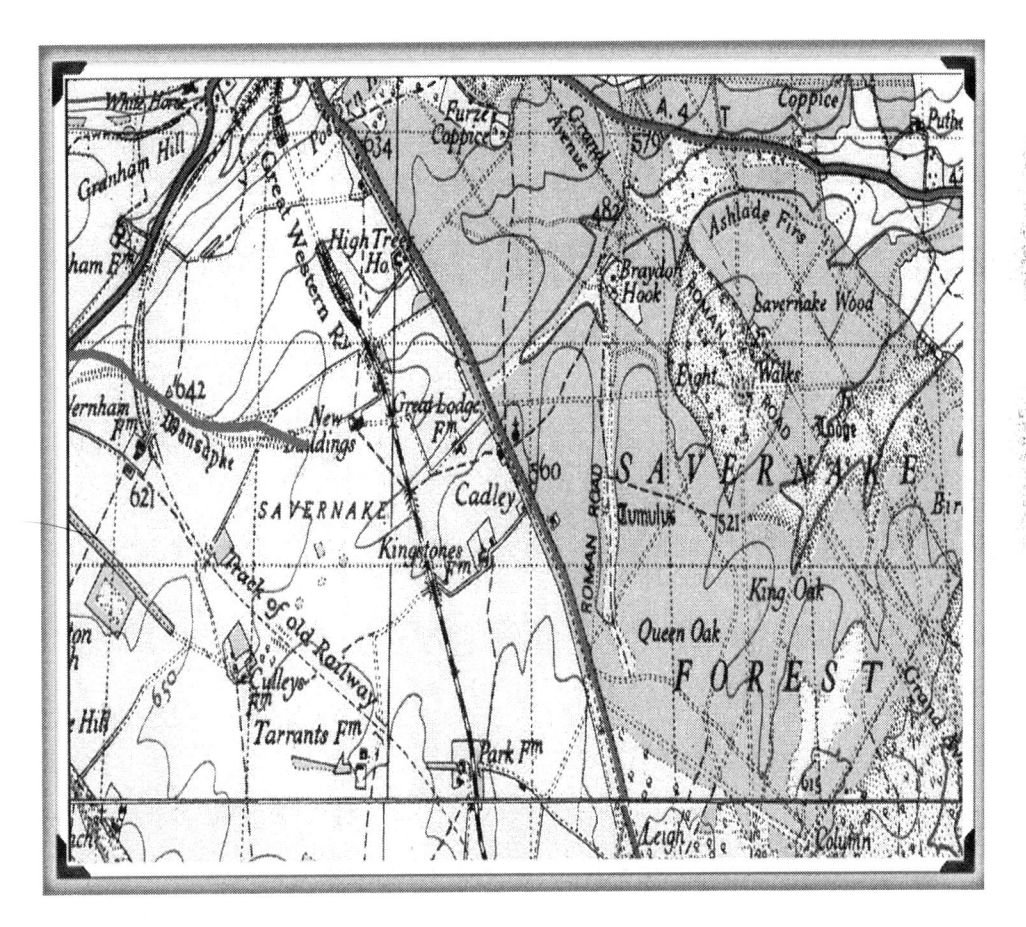

Figure 100 - Wansdyke East section just stops - the forest would not have been there during Roman times and hence the roman road going through the centre

Prehistoric Britain – The Stonehenge Enigma

If you were to attack the ditch you would be mad - as you just walk around it as the German's did on the Siegfried line at the outbreak of World War II.

The final proof of that the ditch is not defensive can be found in its method of construction. Going back to the work of Pitt-Rivers, he produced a series of detailed cross-sectional drawings to support his investigation. These drawings showed two significant findings: firstly, the ditches fill was spread over both sides of the ditch (one side slightly more than the other) – you

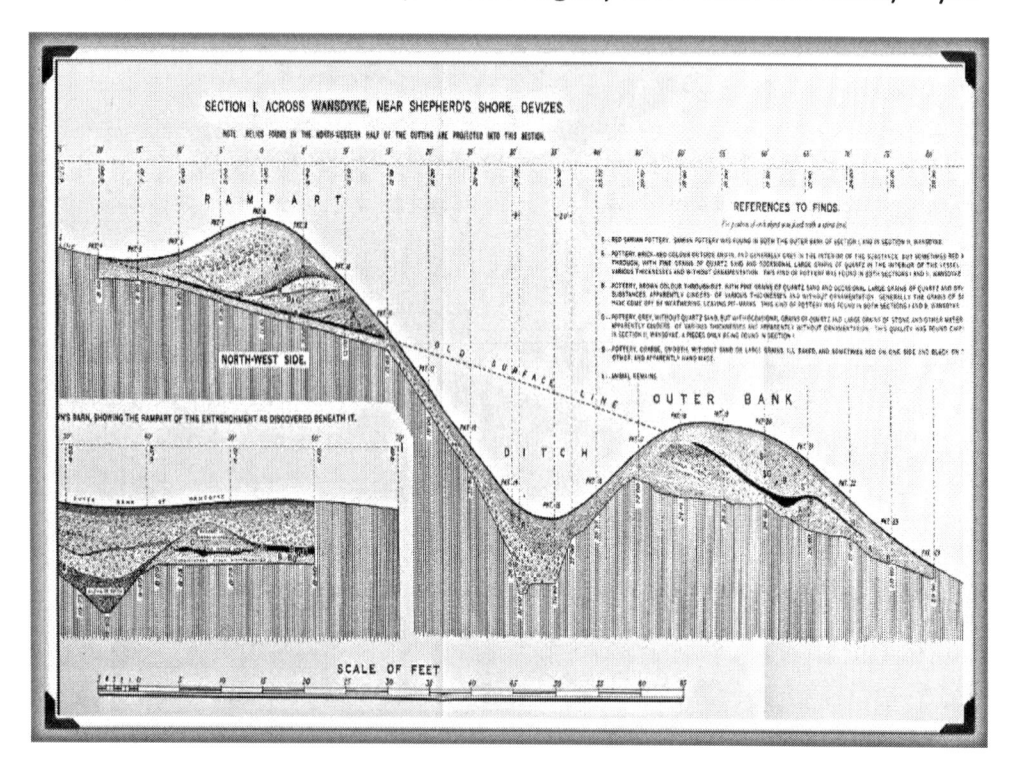

Figure 101- Pitt-Rivers cross section shows ditch fill spread on BOTH sides - so not defensive

would not do this if it's a defensive feature as you would want all the 'high ground' on your side to help defend. This kind of slightly even distribution we see on Iron Hill ditches and other featured sites such as Durrington, Stonehenge, and particularly Old Sarum. In fact, the only site we don't see this happen is at Avebury.

Prehistoric Britain – The Stonehenge Enigma

Secondly, and most importantly, the bottom of the ditch is flat, again just like Stonehenge, Avebury and Durrington – it could also be Old Sarum, but sadly nobody has done an excavation of the ditches to date.

If it's not a defensive feature – then what is it?

You do not make the bottom of a ditch flat if used as a defensive ditch or a land marker (you're doubling the time it takes to make a ditch). On Pitt-River's excavation plan the flat bottom is a third of the width of the ditch.

The Kennet and Avon Canal (Fig. 93) is a waterway in southern England with an overall length of 87 miles (140 km), made up of two lengths of navigable river linked by a canal. The name is commonly used to refer to the entire length of the navigation rather than solely to the central canal section. From Bristol to Bath, the waterway follows the natural course of the River Avon before the canal links it to the River Kennet at Newbury, and from there to Reading on the River Thames. Quite remarkably Wansdyke was constructed just 3 km north of the Kennet and Avon canal. If it was a prehistoric waterway, it would have achieved the same purpose of joining the River Thames to the Bristol Channel but some 6-8K years before the Victorian's great canal system.

Now let us consider the human resources it needed to create such a structure. At 33 km in length (33,000m), its volume can be calculated as about 618,750 cubic metres of Chalk (if it is 2.5m deep and 7.5m wide as an average) this is the approximate volume of material removed from the ditch. This is five times more than what was excavated at Avebury and two and a half times larger than Silbury hill. So, according to Atkinson's calculations at Silbury Hill, we are looking at 45 million working hours, which equates to 100 people working for 12-hours every day 365 days a year for 102 years.

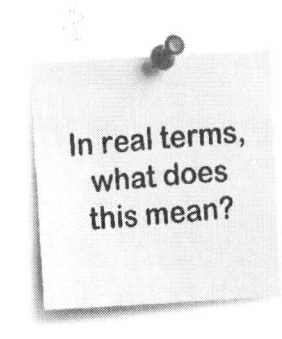

In real terms, what does this mean?

Prehistoric Britain – The Stonehenge Enigma

It took the Victorians one hundred years to build the Avon & Kennet Canal using metal tools and steam engines. Moreover, the Victorian canal was only 1.3m deep and 6m wide - the ancient canal ditch is in places twice as big as the Victorian counterparts. So, whoever built it must have spent many years in completing this task - which suggested it was essential at the time of construction.

Figure 102- Wansdyke showing it rolls with the contours of the landscape and not a boundary marker

If you study a geological map of this area, you will be struck by the endless twisting rivers that once flowed on and around the Wansdyke earthwork. These are called 'superficial deposits' and consist of sand, silt and pebbles. This is evidence that 'once upon a time' rivers formerly flowed in these what we call today 'dry valleys' (Palaeochannels) and the clue just like the name for these earthworks (Dykes) is in the title.

If we add the known prehistoric groundwater rivers (based on our hypothesis) to the map of this great ditch, we find that springs would feed the ditch naturally, flooding it - and there you have yourself a canal. This 21-mile canal links (just like the Avon & Kennet) the river Thames to the Bristol Channel. And there can be only one reason for this massive undertaking (boat travel for the purpose of trade) just like the Victorian ancestors would achieve some six to eight thousand years later.

However, the most miraculous revelation about these Dykes is the fact that the builders had a greater knowledge of hydrology than even today's engineers and geologists, for the weakness and final demise of the canal system in Britain was the fact they were very slow (the Victorians had to build at least one lock per mile of the canal to keep in the water high) the Kennet and Avon have over 100 locks. The original prehistoric channel had none as it relied on the natural groundwater table levels to fill the canal. Therefore, it was straighter and shorter in length, than the Avon & Kennet, which would have allowed them to travel from the Thames to the Bristol Channel almost a hundred times faster than the Victorian barges.

Moreover, if you find this difficult to believe, you should bear in mind that there are over 1,000 dykes in Britain; a majority, 90% are straight and less than 1km in length. To date, every single dyke we have investigated has underground links to these prehistoric rivers created from the 'post-glacial flooding' after the last ice age.

Furthermore, some of these Dykes are linked to ancient sites directly, as shown in this case study confirming the age of these earthworks. For if we add the known prehistoric groundwater rivers (as we have done with previous Case Studies like Old Sarum, Durrington Walls and even

Stonehenge), we find out why this remarkable canal has two dead ends. For West side of the dyke is in the middle of a prehistoric island, which perfectly cuts the island into two, and would allow boats to sail from one end of the island to the other in the Mesolithic. At a later date an extension was added (as the water table levels dropped) to keep it connected to the Bristol Channel in the Central and West Section.

This explains why the Central section is different and straighter than the Eastern section of Wansdyke and is often referred to as a 'Roman Road' on OS maps. Moreover, it proves beyond doubt that it was not built as a boundary marker of a defensive ditch as it would have had a 6-mile gap in the middle of the earthwork.

This Dyke was built over hundreds if not thousands of years, which reflects not only the engineering and organisational skills of this advanced civilisation, but moreover, the sophistication and complexity of this trading society.

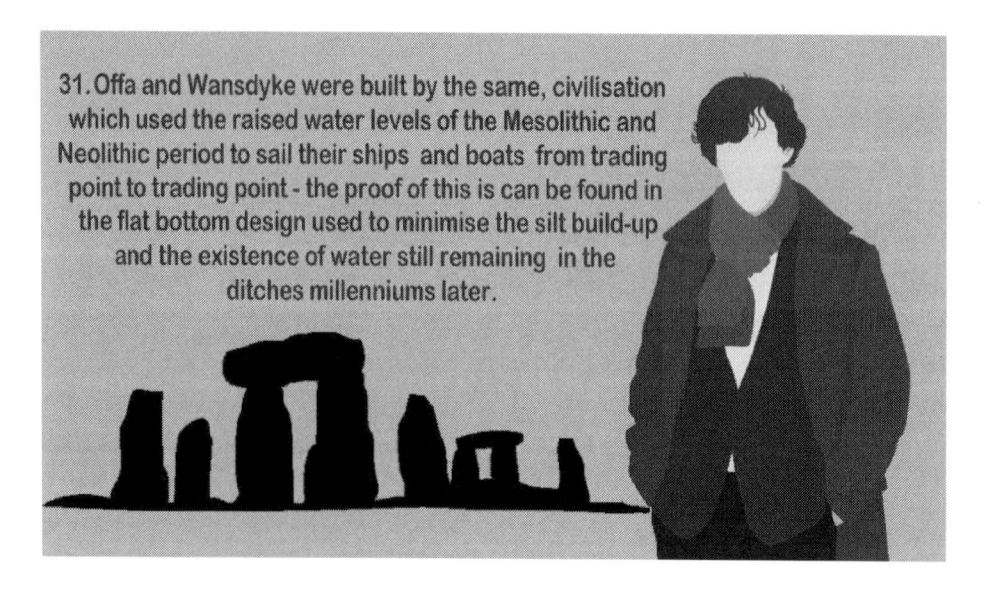

31. Offa and Wansdyke were built by the same, civilisation which used the raised water levels of the Mesolithic and Neolithic period to sail their ships and boats from trading point to trading point - the proof of this is can be found in the flat bottom design used to minimise the silt build-up and the existence of water still remaining in the ditches millenniums later.

Epilogue

In this second book of the trilogy, we have looked at the archaeology of the ancient sites around Stonehenge and on the river Avon, to see if we can find any archaeological evidence for higher water levels and flooding, to support our 'The Post-Glacial Hypothesis' - which suggests that the landscape was flooded in the Holocene period directly after the last ice age.

We have found over thirty 'proofs of concept' and scientific evidence to support this hypothesis, which suggests that the traditional history of our ancestors and their monuments is incomplete and, in some respects, fundamentally flawed in its concept.

The empirical evidence that we observe within the landscape, in the form of rounded hills and valleys, are clearly created by water and not just rainfall, but by massive volumes of water cutting gorges, canyons and the gigantic concave hollows within chalkland bedrock. This can no longer be ignored by geologists and archaeologists and simply written down to times before humanity occupied these lands.

The scientific evidence put forward in this book proves, beyond any reasonable doubt, that water has not only affected the landscape much more recently than has been estimated in the past. As a consequence, it has had a profound effect on the inhabitants of Britain in prehistory and has shaped its evolutionary progress and interaction to become the society we know today.

This distorted history, we will attempt to correct, in the last book of the trilogy 'Dawn of the Lost Civilisation' - were we will look at this newfound archaeological evidence and piece together, not only how this civilisation communicated and used the raised waterways of the Mesolithic and Neolithic to trade and develop their engineering and social knowledge. But, moreover, by using DNA analysis and historical writings, we will trace theses ancestors back to their emergence from Asia some 30,000 years ago and understand the nature of their society.

Appendices

References

All images and quotations that have been added to the original text are of sole responsibility of ABC Publishing Group and not the author. Any copyrighted material, the use of which may not always be authorised by the copyright owner, as they have been obtained under the 'public domain' classification. Such materials are used under the 'fair use' legislation, as this additional material is used to support the books scientific hypotheses, which allows publishing such content under the copyright act.

All efforts have been made to find the authors of such copyright material not designated as 'Public Domain' contained within this book. However, if individuals or companies object to the inclusion to such material, then the publisher will be happy to withdraw said material without question instantly. As this book is either electronic or 'print on demand' this will immediately stop the circulation of said article.

All objections to copyright material contained in this book should be emailed to: copyright@abc-publishing-group.co.uk or in writing to the publisher's office address on the inside of the book

Endnotes

1. JNCC. 2011. Towards an assessment of the state of UK peatlands, JNCC Report No. 445, JNCC, Peterborough, ISSN 0963-8091.
2. Current Archaeology Magazine issue 219, https://www.archaeology.co.uk/issues/ca219.htm
3. Wiltshire Archaeological & Natural History Society, 68, (1 Jan. 1973)

Bibliography

A.G. Brown, L.S. Basell, P.S. Toms, R.C. Scrivener, Towards a budget approach to Pleistocene terraces: preliminary studies using the River Exe in South West England, UK Proceedings of the Geologists' Association, 120 (2009), pp. 275-281, 10.1016/j.pgeola.2009.08.012

Blum M.D.,Törnqvist T.E., Fluvial responses to climate and sea-level change: a review and look forward Sedimentology, 47 (2000), pp. 2-48, 10.1046/j.1365-3091.2000.00008.x

Brown A.G., L.S. Basell, P.S. Toms, J.A. Bennett, R.T. Hosfield, R.C. Scrivener, Later Pleistocene evolution of the Exe valley: a chronstratigraphic model of terrace formation and its implications for Palaeolithic archaeology, Quaternary Science Reviews, 29 (2010), pp. 897-912, 10.1016/j.quascirev.2009.12.007

C.P. Green, D.H. Keen, D.F.M. McGregor, J.E. Robinson, R.B.G. Williams, Stratigraphy and environmental significance of Pleistocene deposits at Fisherton, near Salisbury, Wiltshire, Proceedings of the Geologists' Association 94 (1983), pp. 17-22

Castleden R.. The Making of Stonehenge. New York: Routledge. 1993. Pp. xiv, 305. $35.00. ISBN 0-415-08513-6. Albion, 27(1), 87-88. doi:10.1017/S0095139000018548

CG, Bain & Bonn, Aletta & Stoneman, Rob & Chapman, Stephen & Coupar, A. & Evans, M. & Geary, B. & Howat, M. & Joosten, Hans & Keenleyside, Clunie & Lindsay, Richard & Labadz, Jillian & Littlewood, N. & Lunt, Paul & CJ, Miller & Moxey, Andrew & Orr, H. & Reed, Mark & Smith, P. & Worrall, F. (2011). IUCN UK Commission of inquiry on peatlands.

CLEAL, R.M.J., K.E. WALKER & R. MONTAGUE. 1995 Stonehenge in its Landscape: twentieth-century excavations. London: English Heritage.

D.R. Bridgland, River terrace systems in north-west Europe: an archive of environmental change, uplift and early human occupation, Quaternary Science Reviews, 19 (2000), pp. 1293-1303, 10.1016/S0277-3791(99)00095-5

Donn, W.L., 1962, The Journal of Geography, Vol 70. No.2, pp206 -214, University of Chicago Press.

E. Egberts, L.S. Basell, P.S. Toms, Quaternary Landscape Change and Evidence of Hominin Presence in the Avon Valley. The Quaternary Fluvial Archives of the Major English Rivers. INQUA 2019 Field Guide Ed

Gaigalas, A.L.G.I.R.D.A.S., 2000. Correlation of 14C and OSL dating of Late Pleistocene deposits in Lithuania. Geochronometria, 19(5), pp.7-12.

Gallego-Sala, A. V., Charman, D. J., Harrison, S. P., Li, G., and Prentice, I. C.: Climate-driven expansion of blanket bogs in Britain during the Holocene, Clim. Past, 12, 129–136, https://doi.org/10.5194/cp-12-129-2016, 2016.

Gallois, R W. (2009). The lithostratigraphy of the Penarth Group (Late Triassic) of the Severn Estuary area. Geoscience in South-West England. 12.

Hopson, P.M., Farrant, A.R., Newell, A.J., Marks, R.J., Booth, K.A., Bateson, L.B., Woods, M.A., Wilkinson, I. P., Brayson, J. and Evans D.J. 2007. Geology of the Salisbury district – a brief explanation of the geological map. Sheet Explanation of the British Geological Survey. 1:50 000 Sheet 298 Salisbury (England and Wales)

K.E. Barber, A.G. Brown, Ibsley organic deposits, K.E. Barber (Ed.), Wessex and the Isle of Wight. Field Guide, Quaternary Research Association, Cambridge (1987), pp. 65-74

L.G. Allen, P.L. Gibbard, M.E. Pettit, R.C. Preece, J.E. Robinson, Late pleistocene interglacial deposits at pennington marshes, Lymington, Hampshire, southern England, Proceedings of the Geologists' Association, 107 (1996), pp. 39-50, 10.1016/S0016-7878(96)80066-6

Lewin, J., Macklin, M.G., 2003. Preservation potential for Late Quaternary river alluvium. Journal of Quaternary Science 18, pp. 107–120.

M.R. Clarke, C.P. Green, The Pleistocene terraces of the Bournemouth - Fordingbridge area K.E. Barber (Ed.), Wessex and the Isle of Wight, Field Guide (1987), pp. 58-64

Maddy, D, Bridgland, C.P. Green, Crustal uplift in southern England: evidence from the river terrace records, Geomorphology, 33 (2000), pp. 167-181, 10.1016/S0169-555X(99)00120-8M. 1985. Flood-plain sedimentation in the upper Axe valley, Mendip, England. Transactions of the Institute of British Geographers, 10, 235–44.

Mike Parker Pearson et al. Craig Rhos-y-Felin: a Welsh bluestone megalith quarry for Stonehenge. Antiquity, 89, pp 1331-1352. doi:10.15184/aqy.2015.177.

Pettijohn F.J.. Sedimentary Rocks, .Second Edition, 1957, 718 pp., 119 tables, 173 figs., 40 plates. Harper and Brothers, New York. Price $12.00. Geological Magazine, 94(6), 516-516. doi:10.1017/S0016756800070254

Singaraja, Chelladurai & Sabarathinam, Chidambaram & Noble, Jacob. (2018). A study on the influence of tides on the water table conditions of the shallow coastal aquifers. Applied Water Science. 8. 10.1007/s13201-018-0654-5.

Proofs of Hypothesis

1. The steady rise in sea levels over the last ten thousand years, proves that water was still sitting on the land, in the form of enlarged rivers, which would have kept the landscape flooded for thousands of years after the ice caps had melted. (Page 26)

2. Lewis & Macklin's 2003 scientific paper proved that the rivers in Britain have flooded over 100 times in the last ten thousand years, with some of these events lasting over hundreds of years. (Page 28)

3. Peat is a product of wet marshy ground and plant growth – this proves not only the extent of the Post-Glacial Flooding, but moreover, the dates of these episodes. (Page 31)

4. The Avon terraces between T7 and T10 consist of river silt, and OSL dates indicate that they are 'out of sequence' to the traditional observational model. (page 36)

5. The location of Stonehenge at the edge of a Palaeochannel (dry river valley) – proves that the environment was flooded at the time of initial construction. (page 42)

6. Hawley found evidence of a 'water sealant' at the bottom of the Stonehenge ditch, which he described as 'foot-trampled mud' in association with a 'flint layer' – proving that water was planned to be in the ditch. (Page 48)

7. Hawley found evidence of a 'dark layer' in most of his ditch excavations, proving the presence of a moat with water decayed organic matter and sediment. (Page 49)

8. The Stonehenge Ditch was constructed of individual pits with seats and internal walls - the only reason you would build such a structure is if it was a moat of water. (Page 52)

9. The extensive number of 'Bluestone' fragments, in proportion to the Sarsen Stone chippings- Proves that the Bluestones were deliberately broken up to be used for bathing within the moat. (Page 57)

10. The 58 Aubrey Holes show that Stonehenge was initially closely connected with the moon and its direct effect on both the tides and associated water table levels- this proves that the ditch was a moat fed by this same water table. (Page 60)

11. The Palisade has confused archaeologists ever since its discovery- the fact that it connects two active Mesolithic Palaeochannels and was extended later to meet the lower Neolithic water level (like the Avenue) proves that the river Avon as present at Stonehenge Bottom during both construction phases. (Page 69)

12. The Mesolithic post holes can not only date Phase I of Stonehenge - they also prove that a river existed at Stonehenge Bottom at that time and was used to move the Bluestones from the Craig Rhos-Y-Felin quarry. (Page 82)

13. The Avenue ditch on the northern side is 10% deeper than the southern side- this variation also happens where the Avenue ditch meets the main Stonehenge ditch. This is proof that the ditches were dug to find the water table at the time of construction. (Page 84)

14. The Avenue initially terminated at Stonehenge Bottom where the water table level had dropped during the Neolithic period – this is proven by the existence of post holes and two loading platforms in different locations down the Avenue, indicating river shore variations. (Page 88)

15. The Station Stones (including the Heel Stone) were constructed to point towards Stonehenge's neighbouring sites on the River Avon. Ditches were dug around the stones to turn them into moats- proof that this was a boat society with their sites on the Mesolithic shorelines. (Page 96)

16. The Slaughter Stone was deliberately buried into the chalk bedrock and hole WA1165 was dug two metres deep to tap into the ground water and flood the ditch surrounding the stone to create a feature of an island surrounded by water - this proves that groundwater remained even during the Neolithic period around Stonehenge (Page 101)

17. The lack of Mollusca (snails) and the finding of calcium carbonate at certain levels in the Coneybury Henge ditch - proves that a moat surrounded the monument was full of water in the Mesolithic period like Stonehenge, due to a higher water table. (Page 107)

18. The moats that surround the Northern, Southern and Heel Station stones have been found to contain silt and marl within these ditches - proving the presence of water due to higher water table levels at their time of construction. (Page 119)

19. The relocation of the Bluestones to the edge of the Avon after the closure of the Stonehenge moat - proves that water was a key requirement for the healing properties of this stone, which therefore must have been present in the Stonehenge Ditch. (Page 122)

20. The Mesolithic Avon River height (98m) found in the post holes in the Old Car Park at Stonehenge, if duplicated at Durrington Walls, creates a natural harbour as shown on the magnetometer surveys
- proving that water was present at the time of construction and the eastern ditches were added at a later date Page 128)

21. Durrington Walls has post holes (mooring points) at the exact same Neolithic Water Level height, as we found at the end of Stonehenge Avenue - this proves that water as present at higher levels (on both sites) throughout this period in history. (Page 131)

22. Woodhenge is a wooden tower next to a harbour which suggests that it was a fire beacon (Lighthouse) - proving that the River Avon was much larger (and higher) in the past than today which was utilised by this civilisation. (Page 141)

23. The two dykes (canals) within Old Sarum that connect the inner and outer ditches - proves that these features are moats and therefore a higher water table was present during the Mesolithic and Neolithic periods. (Page 145)

24. The raised platform and pathway cut through the outer bank of Old Sarum – proves that ships and boats serviced the site on the higher water table of the Neolithic period. (Page 148)

25. The Norman well in Old Sarum has run dry today – is a proof of the changes in ground water levels over time. (Page 148)

26. THE SMOKING GUN!! The excavation in 1914 by St. George Grey had to be halted as the ground water had been reached and the Ditch started to flood becoming a moat once more - this proves beyond all doubt that the higher river levels (as indicated in the BGS superficial deposit map) would have flooded the Avebury ditch with water. (Page 154)

27. The remarkable discovery of Silbury Avenue based on a just a few crop marks and the Post-Glacial Hypothesis - proves that not only is the theory correct and rivers were much higher in the past than today, but moreover, this technique can be used to find and date the lost monuments of Britain. (Page 175)

28. The positioning of Long Barrows high on hillsides overlooking and in full view of ancient waterways - proves that they were used to navigate the higher/larger rivers of Mesolithic Britain and Northern Europe. (Page 191)

29. The Dykes of Winterbourne Crossroads not only prove the existence of water at Stonehenge in both the Mesolithic and Neolithic period - it also shows us how this civilisation used these waterways for their burial practices. (Page 198)

30. The Cursus makes no sense in the landscape until we place the waters of the Mesolithic when it becomes a boat crossing between death and

the afterlife- this proof is verified when they attempted to continue this water connection in the Neolithic by adding a ditch to create a moat around the site. (Page 200)

31. Offa and Wansdyke were built by the same, civilisation which used the raised water levels of the Mesolithic and Neolithic period to sail their ships and boats from trading point to trading point- the proof of this is can be found in the flat bottom design used to minimise the silt build-up and the existence of water still remaining in the ditches millenniums later. (Page 212)

Author Biography

Robert John Langdon

Robert John Langdon is a writer, historian and social philosopher who worked as an analyst for the government and some of the largest corporations and educational institutes in Britain, including British Telecommunications, Cable and Wireless, British Gas and University of London.

Since his retirement ten years ago, Robert has studied Politics, Archaeology, Philosophy and Quantum Mechanics at the Museum of London, University College London, Birkbeck College, The City Literature Institute and Chichester University

He has three children and two grandchildren and lives in West Wales – in a deserted cottage overlooking the Sea – hiding from the HMRC.

Printed in Poland
by Amazon Fulfillment
Poland Sp. z o.o., Wrocław
30 October 2021

a728b27d-fdea-41ca-b4e5-a6e39539f813R02